WHAT THE BIBLE SAYS ABOUT
THE HOLY SPIRIT

WHAT THE BIBLE SAYS ABOUT ABOUT THE HOLY SPIRIT

David Pawson

ANCHOR RECORDINGS

First published in Great Britain in 2014 by
Anchor Recordings Ltd
72 The Street
Kennington, Ashford TN24 9HS

**For more of David Pawson's teaching,
including MP3s, DVDs and CDs, go to
www.davidpawson.com
For further information, email: info@davidpawsonministry.com**

ISBN 978 1 9098865 4 4

Printed by Lightning Source

Contents

This book is based on a series of talks. Originating as it does from the spoken word, its style will be found by many readers to be somewhat different from my usual written style. It is hoped that this will not detract from the substance of the biblical teaching found here.

As always, I ask the reader to compare everything I say or write with what is written in the Bible and, if at any point a conflict is found, always to rely upon the clear teaching of scripture.

David Pawson

Chapter One

WHY DO PEOPLE SEEK THE HOLY SPIRIT?

'If you love me, keep my commands. And I will ask the Father, and he will give you another advocate to help you and be with you for ever – the Spirit of truth. The world cannot accept him, because it neither sees him nor knows him. But you know him, for he lives with you and will be in you. I will not leave you as orphans; I will come to you. Before long, the world will not see me any more, but you will see me. Because I live, you also will live. On that day you will realise that I am in my Father, and you are in me, and I am in you.'

John 14:15–20, NIV

'All this I have spoken while still with you. But the Advocate, the Holy Spirit, whom the Father will send in my name, will teach you all things and will remind you of everything I have said to you.'

John 14:25–26, NIV

'I have much more to say to you, more than you can now bear. But when he, the Spirit of truth, comes, he will guide you into all the truth. He will not speak on his own; he will speak only what he hears, and he will tell you what is yet to come. He will glorify me because it is from me that he will receive what he will make known to you. All that belongs to the Father is mine. That is why I said the Spirit will receive from me what he will make known to you.'

John 16:12–15, NIV

We need to study what the *whole* Bible says about the Holy Spirit. Then you can judge and discern, and hold fast what is good. Until you have a real grasp of what scripture has revealed about the Spirit it is possible to be deceived and go into wrong paths which bring neither blessing to you and others nor glory to God's name.

A little girl was taken to a Church of England parish church for the very first time. Seeing the vicar come sailing in, wearing a long white surplice, she said in a whisper that could be heard all around the church, "Is that the Holy Ghost?"

Her mother immediately corrected her and said, "Of course not."

The little girl, persisting with her question as little children are prone to do, went on to say, "Then if that isn't, who is?"

At this point the mother was getting well out of her depth theologically and in every other way, and she simply did what parents do when they are unsure how to answer, telling the child to sit still and be quiet. But that child was perfectly right in expecting to see the Holy Ghost in church, and she was perfectly right to ask such a question.

There was a day when Paul on his missionary journeys came to a place called Ephesus where he found a group of people worshipping God (see Acts 19). At first sight they seemed to be just like other Christian believers but there was something missing. He realised there was no evidence of the Holy Spirit's activity in that group of people, so he asked them a leading question, which should be asked of every person professing to believe: "Did you receive the Holy Spirit when you believed?" Their reply is translated slightly differently in various versions but they all amount to much the same thing: "We have never even heard that there is a Holy Spirit." It was as much as to say, "This is news to us." They believed in Jesus, but they had not heard anything about the Holy Spirit.

In the first half of the twentieth century you would not have heard the Holy Spirit mentioned much in the mainline Protestant churches of this country. You would hardly hear the Holy Spirit mentioned by the members. Some have even said that you would hardly hear about the Holy Spirit from the preacher except on Whit Sunday (Pentecost) when he felt bound to try and tackle this subject. Now I think there is an element of truth in this. In those days the Holy Spirit was scarcely mentioned by ordinary churchgoers.

But there came a change so that the Holy Spirit began to be talked about, thought about and preached about to a far greater degree than before. Prior to this great change, somebody said that they had come to the conclusion that the Roman Catholics believed in a trinity of Father, Son, and blessed virgin, and that the Protestants believed in a trinity of Father, Son, and Holy Scripture, but that from their language neither believed in Father, Son, and Holy Spirit.

That situation changed, and I am going to mention six of the reasons for this. Three are good and three not so good. I mention both kinds of reason because we must have discernment. We must be able to think clearly about these things, otherwise we might swallow everything or reject everything, either of which would be an extreme and wrong attitude. The Bible tells us that we must test and find out what is not so good and let that go, and hold fast to what we find that is good.

First, the three reasons which are not so good for the growing interest in the Holy Spirit. One: intellectual curiosity—there are those who ask about the Holy Spirit for no other reason than that here is an area of knowledge they know little about and they would like to. Some of those who profess this kind of curiosity would be just as interested in the

Society for Psychical Research and I mention that because it has often gone together. There is curiosity in the occult and the supernatural which tends to ask about the Holy Spirit also. When Paul got to Athens he found a bunch of people who were always ready to listen to some new thing. The trouble with mere curiosity is that as soon as it is satisfied, it will jump away on to something else.

Therefore when somebody comes to me, and people have often done so, and say, "I'm interested in the Holy Spirit, can you tell me more about this subject?" – my first question is: "*Why* are you interested?" If it is just curiosity then I doubt whether telling them anything would be of any lasting value. Sometimes it is true that curiosity leads on to something else. Moses saw a burning bush. Then he looked twice at it because the leaves were still there. He went a bit closer out of mere curiosity and said, "I will turn aside and see this strange sight," but he found himself getting involved with God. Sometimes intellectual curiosity has led to a real dealing with God that is healthy. But most times intellectual curiosity, as soon as it has found out a bit more, jumps off on to some new subject.

The second reason which is not so good, for the interest in the Holy Spirit today, is emotional dissatisfaction. The philosophy of existentialism which was first propounded towards the end of the nineteenth century, started in Germany, spread to France, and hit Britain later. It is a way of thinking about life that says something like this: "real meaning in life is not found with the mind but with the heart; it is found in emotions, in meaningful experiences here and now; it is found in anything that gives you feelings about life." That kind of thinking spread very rapidly and produced by the 1960s and 1970s a searching, particularly among young people, for meaningful emotional experiences. They tried sex, they tried noise, they tried drugs, and they tried Eastern mysticism. The popular culture of the 1960s and thereafter represented a very significant movement which embraced the new search for emotional meaningful experiences. People were ready to try anything that would give them emotional thrills. One danger when that kind of thinking is common is that there will be an interest in the Holy Spirit purely for emotional experience. That does not lead to anything satisfactory because it has only touched the emotions and not the mind and the will, and it is a passing phase. It is very interesting that young people who have been on drugs are often very interested in the Holy Spirit for this reason.

Now the third not so good reason for the growing interest in the Holy Spirit was this: psychological inadequacy. Now we are living in a period of strain, of emotional tension, and there is a rapid growth in psychological disorders. It has been suggested that as many as half our hospital beds are occupied by people with psychological rather than physical disorders. This is the world in which we live, in which there are strains, stresses and tensions. Psychiatry may be of some help for emotional disorders but, by and large, a Christian or a churchgoer with psychological needs tends to look for a spiritual experience that will suddenly meet that disorder, instead of seeking the treatment that over a period of therapy might help them to overcome the inadequacy. So among Christians under strain today (and a lot are) there is a searching for a spiritual experience that will solve all their shyness, their sense of inferiority, their difficulties in relationships and so on. When such people hear of the Holy Spirit and seek an *experience* of the Holy Spirit as an answer to their psychological problem, they are going to be disappointed, and sooner or later they will discover that even though an experience of the Holy Spirit is an immense help, it is not necessarily an answer to psychological inadequacy.

What is wrong with these three reasons: intellectual curiosity, emotional dissatisfaction, and psychological inadequacy? You can see it at a glance. *All these three groups of people are seeking the Holy Spirit for themselves, not for others.* They are saying, "Lord, I want my intellect satisfied, I want my emotional needs met, I want my psychological inadequacies fulfilled." Therefore these three motives invariably lead to a disappointing experience of the Holy Spirit and I have had to counsel many people who have had a disappointing experience because this was one of the motives in their hearts.

When we were offered the Holy Spirit, the Lord offered us the power of the Spirit for other people, and that is the only adequate motive for seeking to be filled with the Holy Spirit. Not to meet my needs, not to sort out my disorders, not to fill my emotions, but that I may be able to serve other people in their need. Of every gift of the Holy Spirit mentioned in the New Testament, there is only one given for yourself. Every other one is given to pass something on to somebody else. *With that one exception, the gifts of the Spirit are not gifts from the Spirit to me, they are gifts from the Spirit helping someone else through me.* A gift of healing is not for me; it is to pass healing on to someone who is sick. A gift of knowledge is not for me, it is to help someone who does not know. A gift of miracles is to help someone who is in need. Therefore if I am seeking something for myself, I have already blocked the channel. I have already twisted the experience. Jesus said, "Wait in Jerusalem until you receive power." Then the disciples could go out and help the whole world, witnessing everywhere. That was their motive. What they were praying was not, "Lord, I've got psychological problems, fill me with the Spirit" or, "Lord, I've got emotional dissatisfaction, give me nice feelings." They were saying, "Lord, we want to go to the ends of the earth and be witnesses to others and we can't do that without your power," and so their motives were right.

Simon Magus (described in Acts 8) was a professional magician. Some of us go through a stage when we want to dazzle people, to be able to do things others cannot do, to impress them quickly and easily. So we understand the motive which may be about being superior to others in some way. Simon the magician came to Peter and offered money in exchange for the power the apostles had. Peter said to Simon, "Your money perish with you," which meant: to hell with you and your money. Peter knew at once that Simon was seeking something for himself.

What are the other three reasons why people are getting interested in this subject? One is *the weakness of the church*. We have to face the fact as Christians that the church is a declining influence in our society and has been for many decades. Whatever is happening to the numbers (and every major denomination reported a decline in membership over the past half century, even as the population has grown), at issue is not so much the quantity as the *quality* of the life of churches, so that society goes on like a mighty juggernaut unaffected by Christians within that society. Decisions are made in Parliament that seem unaffected by Christian opinion. The nation moves on, the churches are there often as a kind of museum piece, but life as many people live it seems quite unaffected by Christian believing.

There was a period in the twentieth century when it was thought by many people that if you could just get all the churches into one big power bloc, one organisation, we would have the power to move society, and this was one of the biggest motives in the ecumenical movement. One commentator described that movement as reminding him of a group of drunken men outside a park, each of them unable to stand by themselves but managing to hold each other up.

This is not strength and it is not power.

Then it began to be realised that merely uniting would not bring any more power, and that it is not so much reunion as renewal that the churches need. That was a healthy development. We can see that if you put together two lukewarm glasses of water you don't finish with a glass of hot water, just a bigger glass of lukewarm water. If you put two half-dead churches together that doesn't make them one live church, just a bigger half dead one. So there is a growing realisation among all churches, partly fostered by the coming together in closer relationships, that what we need is power from God, and that simply putting together mergers of denominations does not enable us to turn the world upside down.

A sense of the weakness of the church has made many people ask: "Did Jesus intend such a weak church? Did he plan this? Did he not make any more provision for the church than to tell us to get on with it in our weakness?" This has made people go back to the Bible, and here we have the second factor – *the study of scripture*. There arose, in the 1970s and subsequent decades, a much greater interest in Bible study by people in the pews. Members in small groups began to go back to the scriptures asking: "What does God say about the church?" Then they discover that in the early days there was a church that turned the world upside down, a church originally composed of a tiny handful of people, that won the Roman empire in less than three hundred years. They find an astonishing contrast to the picture of the church today. By the way, the early church didn't turn the world upside down, it was actually turning it right way up. But everybody else was upside down so they didn't see it the proper way. But the Christians were turning the world upside down in the eyes of the world, right way up in the sight of God.

The early Christians were a powerful church. How did they make such an impact? How did they lead people to Christ in such huge numbers? How were they able to spread and move all over the globe? This was a movement, not an institution. It was a dynamic fellowship. The answer, when you study the New Testament, is very simple: the Holy Spirit. If you read the book of Acts you discover that the Holy Spirit is mentioned forty times in the first twelve chapters—it is the account of *his* acts. He is the one who brought the power to them, and who enabled them to do such things. So that the weakness of the church, realised increasingly in the twentieth century, brought people to look at the Bible again and that has led them to see the secret of the early church, which was not just "believe in Jesus" but the power of the Holy Spirit – which led them to ask the question: are such things for today? Could they happen now, or has there been some radical change in the church and in God's purpose since those days? Putting it bluntly, is Pentecost Sunday simply a commemoration of something that took place in the past, or is it the possibility and promise of something in the present? That is the question that Bible study led people to ask. They read of miracles taking place. They read of the healing of disease. They read of the spreading church with power and they say, "Are these things over?"

That brings me to the third thing which has promoted interest in the Holy Spirit: *the spread of Pentecostalism in the twentieth century.* Pentecostalism has for quite some time been the fastest growing Protestant stream in the world, and it is probably now the largest. It has all happened since 1907. It is the most remarkable development in Christianity in modern times, causing other Christians to sit up and take notice and ask whether they haven't got a point.

It was only some time after World War 2 that Pentecostals ceased to be regarded as a cult or a sect, and began to be accepted by other Christians as thoroughly orthodox in their beliefs in the gospel and in Christ. So there arose relationships between Pentecostals and other denominations which did not exist before then, and that was bound to raise the issue. The other factor in the 1960s and 1970s was that the things that had hitherto happened within Pentecostal circles started happening in other denominations, primarily the Anglicans (Episcopalians in America), later in America among the Presbyterians and Lutherans; in England, second to the Anglicans, mostly the Baptists, but also some Methodists.

The old Pentecostalism which had begun with a Methodist minister from Oslo and an Anglican vicar from Sunderland in northern England in 1907 grew and spread throughout the world. Strictly speaking, it had already begun in Los Angeles, but in Britain the year 1907 saw it as one of the by-products of the Welsh Revival, spreading to other regions after that.

As well as that older stream of Pentecostalism, there arose what came to be called the new Pentecostalism, which has sprung up within many denominations, including Roman Catholicism, in the form of the Charismatic Movement.

Of course, every Christian who is really concerned about being dynamically effective for the Lord Jesus is interested in the Holy Spirit because there would seem to be no other way to be effective.

Well now, what do we do about this? Do we all rush off around the corner to join the Elim church? Or do we start becoming spiritual tramps as many have, and start running around from one little group to another, looking for something in this, getting dissatisfied with that, moving on to another group? Alas, there has been as much division as blessing caused over this subject because of unwise and hasty action on the part of those who were seeking, as well as on the part of those who didn't want them to seek. There is need for wisdom, love and patience. We are going to look at what the Bible actually does say until we are quite clear in our minds what God would have for us and what God wants to do with us.

Then I hope that, having thought clearly, we will not stop there, but will pray and seek what God has for us. When he blesses, there comes, finally, an act of submission to the Lord when we need to let go, and let him have control. To lose self-control *without* the Holy Spirit's presence leads to chaos, division, disorder, and disaster, because then no one is in control and hysteria can take over. But if the Holy Spirit is ever to control, there will come a point where we relinquish self-control and let him take over. It is that step which many are quite unwilling to take.

Many believers want to be the best that they can be, provided they are still in control of themselves. For three years our Lord made the disciples *think*: he taught them, he opened the truth to them, and particularly the night before he died he taught them step-by-step about the Holy Spirit. Between his ascension and Pentecost they *prayed*. But on the day of Pentecost they *did* extraordinary things and they found that God saved three thousand people that day.

When we talk of the Holy Spirit, what do we mean? We think of five things: vitality, purity, personality, deity and trinity.

First of all, *vitality*. The very word "spirit" means this. In most ancient languages the three words "breath", "wind" and "spirit" are the same word. Even in English we understand the connections between those three words. For example, we say "Wait till I get my wind", or, "I've got my second wind." What do we mean? We mean that breath is coming more easily. Or, if you are "winded", you have lost your breath. So you can understand why breath and wind are the same word. Both are air in motion, so when I breathe, that is a little wind, literally. Wind and breath – we understand that connection, but why do "spirit" and "breath" cover the same meaning in scripture? The answer is very simple. I don't know if you have ever been present when a person has died. If you have, you notice that they invariably breathe out and wind stops, breath ceases. At the moment when they "give up the ghost", that is what occurs. You can understand why in ancient language, not knowing all that we now know about medical and biological facts, when a person breathed their last the phrase used was "Give up the spirit", "gave up the ghost", to "give out the wind" – to give out the spirit, the breath, the wind. You see how it was tied up together.

It is very interesting that when Jesus actually died on the cross, one version says, "He gave up the ghost", another says, "He yielded up his spirit", and one modern English version says, "He breathed his last." All these are valid translations because the word used can mean breath, wind, or spirit. So I am linking this collection of three words in the one word "spirit". Whenever the Bible uses the word "spirit" it means wind, breath, spirit, in other words: life, energy.

You have a lovely picture in the beginning of the Bible of God giving the kiss of life to a corpse. It was a corpse that had never lived, a corpse that he had created. But God breathed into it and his breath entered the corpse and the corpse began to breathe, and the life and the energy was now in that body, and Adam became a living soul. Life came in from breath, and if the kiss of life helps you to think of breath as bringing life then by all means use that picture.

We can go a little further than this. There is one complication about this word in the Hebrew language, in which there are two words for breath. One is the quiet imperceptible breathing that you hardly notice. The other is the heavy breathing of an asthmatic or of a person who has been running a mile and is breathing so loudly that the breath is coming hard, fierce, noisily. The word for the quiet breathing, *neshama*, is a very soft word, the word for the hard breathing, *ruach*, is a hard, noisy word. The interesting thing is that whenever the breath of God is mentioned it is always this hard, noisy, strong, powerful word. In other words, if it had been the soft word it would simply have meant life as existence. But because it is the hard word, it means life as energy. Some people exist but they seem to have no energy. Maybe you feel like that sometimes on a Monday morning! You know you have got existence but you don't have energy. You are alive but only just, and you wouldn't say "How alive that person is" when they are without energy.

The word *ruach* means existence and energy rolled into one – real life, vital life, abundant life that enables you to do things. Therefore the breath of God doesn't just make a person barely live, it fills them with energy, moves them with power and vitality, so that they are not a half-alive Christian, but they are a vital, dynamic, alive Christian and they have got spiritual energy. So when we pray for the "breath of God" to breathe on us we are praying for energy, not just existence.

The Spirit of God makes a tremendous difference to the worship in a church – from barely alive, merely routine singing to vital, dynamic worship, making a joyful noise to the Lord.

The breath of God did extraordinary things in the Old Testament days, dividing the Red Sea, for one thing, and when that wind blew, those waters were pushed back. It has happened since, and it does require a very strong wind to do it. When the wind pushed back the waters of the Red Sea it was a howling gale. Moses called it, "The blast of thy nostrils." That is a most wonderful phrase. God was breathing hard to divide the Red Sea, and that gives you the picture of what they thought of the breath of God.

Likewise, when Pentecost came, that really was a gale, a rushing, mighty wind. This was what they heard. It was force ten and more.

So God's breath brings vitality, energy, life that moves things, and when a gale blows, things are moved. Recall my earlier observation: if someone is really just seeking an emotional experience, a kind of thrill from the Holy Spirit— that person may be moved but won't be moved anywhere. They will not be moved to where they ought to be, they will not be pushed by the Holy Spirit, they will not be urged to do something about it, but where the Spirit of God breathes on us, things will happen.

When I study the Acts of the Apostles I see a church on the move, being blown along, its sails set, and before Pentecost the sails were up and the disciples were praying. They needed the breath of God. They needed life. They had the "machinery", the church was waiting and ready for the wind of Spirit.

The next thing the words "Holy Spirit" mean to me is *purity*. This is one of the reasons I find people afraid of the Holy Spirit, (and I do find people afraid, though they have no need to be). The Bible tells us that we are not given a spirit of bondage to fear but a spirit of love, of a sound mind, of power. Why then are some people afraid of the Holy Spirit? Because they know perfectly well there are spirits which can give similar experiences and delude and mislead the people of God.

Here are some examples. Intoxication with alcohol or drugs. Intoxication produces remarkably similar symptoms to being filled with the Spirit, which is why on the day of Pentecost the disciples were accused of being drunk, and why Paul in Ephesians 5 says don't get drunk with wine but be filled with the Spirit and sing. Singing is a characteristic of both experiences, at least at a certain stage. Secondly, there is mass hysteria, which is a thing that doesn't come down from heaven but is usually worked up from earth. There is a technique for working up mass hysteria, which works better and better, the bigger the crowd. Such effects have been observed at some pop concerts.

Thirdly, there are those who are afraid of religious mania and there is such a thing. We are not always right in saying who has got it. Festus said to the great missionary Paul: Paul you're mad; you're beside yourself; you're a schizophrenic; you have been reading too many books; you've got religious mania. Paul hadn't, but some people do get it.

Then there is possession by demons and evil spirits and that can happen, and evil spirits can reproduce and counterfeit spiritual gifts to the delusion of God's people.

All these are false and wrong. People are afraid of the Holy Spirit because they know there are other spirits that can get hold of them.

What is the answer to this? The answer is that there is only *one* Holy Spirit. I hope you won't think this irreverent but I think it will fix what I want to say in your mind: God does not suffer from bad breath. When *he* blows, it is clean and pure and the results of it can be nothing else. When the Holy Spirit comes upon someone this will produce holy fruit—it is bound to. One of the ways you can test the spirits is by their fruit. See what the results are. Is this person claiming to be filled with the Spirit more alive to God, more full of love for Jesus, more full of love for other people, more eager to worship God in spirit and in truth? Then it is the Holy Spirit who has done that. No other spirit can. So when I say the "Holy Spirit" I mean the only one who can produce holy things, holy people, holy love, holy attitudes. No other spirits can produce that. Other spirits produce proud people, argumentative people, divisive people who destroy rather than build up, people who break down fellowship by their

pride and by their criticism, people who break down the
work of God. The Holy Spirit builds up the work of God and
the whole church is edified and grows and is strengthened.

holy things
holy people
holy Love
holy attitude
Build up the Work of God

Chapter Two

THE HOLY SPIRIT IN THE OLD TESTAMENT

Hebrew thinking is about the living God who speaks and acts in time and space. As long as I am operating in time and space I am living. When I am dead, I may still be somewhere else and still be conscious, but I am dead as far as time and space goes. It is in that sense that the philosopher Nietzsche said, "God is dead." He did not mean that God had ceased to exist, but that as far as he could see, God was no longer saying or doing anything within the world of time and space. A student in a German university wrote up on the wall, "God is dead, signed Nietzsche," but somebody else wrote underneath, "Nietzsche is dead, signed God," which I thought was quite a neat rejoinder. The God of the Bible, a living God, is not timeless. He is not outside time, but time is inside God, and everything God says and does within time and space he does by his Spirit.

I want to begin with the name for his Spirit, which is *ruach*, and that is a very significant word. We are talking about the *ruach Adonai*, the Spirit. That word is what we call onomatopoeic—a word that sounds like its meaning. That "ch" at the end, you have to breathe very hard to say. You can actually hear the breath. That is important because *ruach* essentially means moving air, so it can be used for wind or breath or spirit, but it's not for any kind of wind or any kind of breath, it's for the kind of wind and breath that you can hear. You can say "spirit" without anybody hearing you breathe, but you can't say *ruach* without the breath, and that is what *ruach* means. Hebrew has another word for normal breathing that you are not aware of. *Ruach* is breath or wind that you are aware of, not a gentle breeze. The air is constantly moving around the earth because the earth is revolving and the air does not move at the same revolutions per minute and most of the time you are not aware. When there is a gale blowing, you are very much aware of it. That is *ruach*. It is not normal, moving air. Likewise breath – most of the time we are not aware of people breathing, we don't hear it, but when people are breathing heavily, after they have been jogging, that is *ruach*. Therefore, you are aware through your senses of *ruach*, where you are not aware of *neshamah*, the normal breathing.

Therefore we get a clue straightaway. It is God's moving air, his breath, but it is abnormal, not the normal. It is so abnormal that you become aware of the effect through your senses in this world of time and space. The word carries a lot of associations. First of all, the association of *life*, because breath and blood are the two essentials of life. The people of the Bible never knew the connection between breath and blood, but they knew very well that life ceased when either you lost your breath or lost your blood. Always *ruach* meant life as opposed to death.

It also has a lot of associations with might and with power, because a gale has power. The normal moving air that we live in doesn't have much power, but a gale, a hurricane, has power in it. According to a psalm it can fell the cedars of Lebanon. It can drive a windmill, and we have had hurricanes in this country that have introduced us to the destructive power of the wind. *Ruach* has a destructive side, sometimes called in the Old Testament "the blast of God's nostrils." When God snorts and you hear the blast of his nostrils, that usually heralds a destructive act of judgment.

You will find the *ruach* or *Spirit* of God synonymous with

26

the *hand* of God and even the *finger* of God, which are very powerful. In Matthew, Jesus is recorded as saying, "If I, by the Spirit of God, cast out demons then the kingdom of God has come upon you," and Luke's version has, "If I by the finger of God...." God with his finger can do things that are beyond the might of man.

There is also an association of movement—*ruach* is mobile, and the *ruach* of God moves people. I remember a lady telling me after one sermon I preached, "I was really moved by your sermon." Since I'm not sanctified yet, as I'm sure you know, I said, "Where to?" She was quite cross, and she walked off from me and I could see her stamping her feet down the church path. I thought, "I must apologise to her tonight at the service." She came back in the evening, surprisingly, and I said, "I'm sorry I spoke like that to you." She said, "I'm glad you did. All the way home I kept hearing the Lord say, 'Where to, where to, where to?'" She said, "I had to sort it out with him when I got home. I had been moved, but not moved to anywhere!"

Now the *ruach* of God moves you *to*—it doesn't just move you emotionally; the *ruach* of God moves you to a different position. We worship a mobile God. He's a God who is on the move, a God who walks. It is why he didn't want a stone temple. He was content with a tabernacle, because you could pull the pegs up and move a tabernacle. You read Nathan the prophet's words to David when he wanted to build a temple. Those who are men of God are those who walk with God. They keep on moving. Old Enoch went for such a long walk with God that we are told he disappeared because God took him. That's how Enoch went to heaven. All the way through, God walks and his Spirit is on the move. So we have been shown that God is powerful and, as when air is really moving in a *ruach* way, you can *hear* the effect – invisible, yes, but not inaudible.

That is another clue that opens up the whole Old Testament to us. Above all, *ruach* is associated with speech. When I talk to someone, in order to speak I have to move air. Even if my voice box was vibrating, unless there was moving air, you would not hear a word. Communication depends on moving air, and all that loudspeakers do is to amplify sound and move the air more effectively so that you hear what a speaker is saying. God's speech and his acts in the world of time and space are all due to his *ruach* operating.

The very first mention of the *ruach* is in the first three verses of your Bible. I used to wonder who God was talking to when I heard that he said "Let there be light". Was he just thinking aloud or shouting into space, or was he talking to someone? Then I noticed that God didn't begin to speak at creation until there was someone on planet Earth to hear what he said. Have you ever noticed that? Genesis 1:1 says, "He created the heaven and the earth," but doesn't say what he said. When planet Earth was simply a globule of fluid matter floating through space, there was someone hovering just above it. As soon as the *ruach* was hovering just above the flood, then God spoke, because now he had someone on earth to hear and to obey. That one insight opens up the whole of the Bible to you. The will of God in heaven, expressed from his throne in the form of commandments, and expressing his rule, is executed on earth wherever his *ruach* is.

That is why there is such a close link between the kingdom of God and the Spirit of God. They are almost interchangeable in the New Testament. Where the Gospels talk about the kingdom, the epistles tend to refer to the Spirit and there is a very close link. Wherever the Spirit moves, one of the things that happens always is new music and new songs. Invariably, where the Spirit is moving in a new way, the songs are about the King, his majesty, the kingdom. Have you noticed that? We are first of all presented with God as

King. That is the fundamental understanding of God through the Old Testament. You have to read a long way before you find out that God is Father. You have to read almost to the end of the Bible before you find the statement, "God is love", but all the way through the Old Testament God is King. He is the King of the universe. Some of the Psalms are about nothing else but his dominion. The kingdom of God – the rule of God – is expressed in Genesis 1. You get the impression God is commanding things to happen. The first ten commandments are in Genesis 1, and every one of them was totally, immediately and fully fulfilled.

When we read Genesis 1 to our little daughter, she looked very thoughtful when we had finished, and then she said, "No sooner said than done!" which is a perfect theology of creation. Why was it no sooner said than done? Because the *ruach* of God was here to see that it got done, and he is the executive member of the godhead. So right away, on the first page, we have got a feel of the *ruach* of God, expressing his rule on planet Earth – and wherever the Spirit is, there the kingdom of God will be manifest.

Here we have a *ruach* of God who brings order out of chaos, light out of darkness and life out of death, which he is still doing. Whenever you preach the gospel, that is the same *ruach* of God doing those things in the lives of those to whom you preach.

So the Holy Spirit is mentioned right from the beginning. Do you realise that God the Father, God the Son, and God the Holy Spirit worked together to make the world in which we live? All three persons were involved and they are all there in chapter 1 of Genesis, working together to create this wonderful universe which science is exploring. The Spirit of God was brooding over the waters. Why does it tell us this? Because we are to know from the very beginning that when the Holy Spirit operates, order comes out of chaos, and anything that goes in the reverse direction is not of the Holy Spirit. God is a God of order, not of confusion, and when the Holy Spirit comes on chaos he produces order out of it. He doesn't produce more chaos, and so, over the formless and chaotic, the Spirit was brooding – the literal Hebrew word is "hovering".

The creation of man is neither the word nor the work of *ruach*. It is very interesting that we often misinterpret, and God breathed the breath of life into Adam and he became a living soul. How misunderstood that is. First of all, a living soul simply means a breathing body, and it is applied to animals in Genesis 1, it does not mean a spiritual being. The breath of life here is *neshamah*. It is the normal breathing that brings life. God was not putting his *ruach* into man.

Nevertheless, because man is made in the image of God, he has spirit. There is a *ruach* of man, as well as the *ruach* of God. It is essential that the *ruach* of man be overcome by the *ruach* of God. It can also be overcome by other *ruachs*— lying spirits, unclean spirits; but the normal life of man is that *neshamah* life, that normal breathing, the normal activities of man. *Ruach* is also contrasted with flesh and in a very real sense we are going to see something now—that *ruach* will enable men and women to do what is totally beyond the capacity of the flesh to do. *Ruach* is always associated with abnormal activity, what the Greeks unfortunately call "supernatural", and we will come back to that. The amazing thing is that God's *ruach* can take over man's *ruach*. We are the only religion in the world that teaches a God who will reside within his worshippers.

The next mention I just want to look at in passing is that very sordid story in Genesis 6 where over two hundred angels seduced women and impregnated them. That is as disgusting to God as intercourse between human beings and animals. It is totally against God's order, and it led to a world that was filled with occultism, which began then with kinky sex and with violence. Violence filled the earth and it is a very sordid incident, and we still suffer from that.

In the middle of that sordid story you find the statement: God says, "My Spirit will not always strive with man." It is in association with the saddest verse in the whole Bible. I can't read it without being moved. God says, "I regret that I made men and women," like a parent saying, "I wish we'd never had our children." God regretted making us. He didn't regret anything else, the rest was good, but he regretted making us. That was when he wanted to wash the world out—the whole account of Noah.

That little verse, "My Spirit won't always strive" tells us a number of things. It tells us first the Spirit of God strives with people but never forces them. That is an essential insight, as we will see in the New Testament. Spirit never makes people do things. Evil spirits do, there is a compulsion there, but self-control is part of the fruit of the Holy Spirit. If someone claims to be totally forced by the Holy Spirit to do something, I question that. We can grieve him precisely because he doesn't make us do anything.

We shall see when we look at the Spirit in church history that the Spirit's ministry right through the ages has been entirely channelled by what people expect him to do. He does not operate outside people's expectancy. That is why for many centuries, the church did not know on a wide scale gifts like tongues, healing and prophecy, precisely because they didn't expect it, didn't look for it, didn't want it, and it wasn't forced on them because the Holy Spirit strives with us. But it also tells us that the Holy Spirit can get to a point, or God can get to the point where his patience runs out, and he says, "I'm not going to go on striving," and that's a serious side of the Spirit.

I have indicated already that the Spirit of God acting on

the spirit of man enables people to do that which is totally beyond their capacity to do, and to be what is beyond their capacity to be, and to say what is beyond their capacity to say. Those are the three areas in which the *ruach Adonai* throughout the Old Testament operates—enabling men to do, to be, and to say what is totally beyond the reach of their flesh and is therefore abnormal. It is always *sensible* in that people can hear and be aware of his activity. He is mobile, living, able to turn us into different men and women.

A key passage tells of the moment when Saul actually found himself among the prophets and God told him, "The Spirit of the Lord will come upon you and you will be turned into another man" – not the man as he was born, not his natural capacities. You will find yourself doing things that you would never otherwise have done—that is the key to the Spirit in the Old Testament.

Let us look at the dimensions I have already referred to. The first mention of the Holy Spirit coming on people is amazingly his coming on someone to *do* something with their hands. There are Bezalel, Oholiab, and a team of men on whom the Spirit of the Lord came to construct a building— the tabernacle — but before the Spirit gave them an ability with their hands, he gave them an ability with their heads. Now a hobby of mine has been designing church buildings. But I find there are many people who can't read plans. They can't look at drawings of a building and, as it were, in their minds construct a three-dimensional picture. They can't get the feel of a building from just one-plane plans, so for them I make models. Some people can see a model better, but Bezalel and Oholiab didn't even get plans. They had no drawings whatever, so the first thing they needed was mental ability to visualise the building from a specification without plans. That is quite a difficult business, but it says that God gave these men first the ability to see it in their minds. Isn't that interesting? From a written specification to see the thing whole, and to see what it was all going to be like and how it would all fit together.

Then he gave them ability. They were going to have to use silver and gold. They were going to have to carve, they were going to have to do intricate embroidery—all sorts of things, and it says the Spirit of the Lord came on them to give them wisdom and knowledge to understand what he wanted, and then to give them the ability with their hands to do things they had never done before.

I think of a man in our church in Guildford who had been a prisoner of war in Germany during World War II, and so virtually had to work in the open air, and he was a gardener. He had a simple camera and loved taking photographs of fungi. Somehow the Lord developed this in him and he began to show his slides to others, and they loved them, so his son bought him a state of the art camera with gadgets and many buttons. The dear old gardener looked at it. He could hardly tell which way to point it, so he simply went out with the Lord and prayed, "Lord, tell me how to operate this camera," and from then on he knew perfectly how to do so and how to take the most perfect pictures of fungi. He went on to give lectures two or three times a week all over the country, and he brings God into his talks. He doesn't like Attenborough's talk about "Mother Nature", He talks about Father God who made all this, but the Lord taught him to use a most complicated camera with no human help whatever.

The Lord can do this—it's practical. "The work of my hands, establish it, Lord." So, you see, all this is within time and space. Not very "spiritual", is it? But it is Greek thinking that limits the Spirit's activity to what he does with your soul but won't let him touch your body. We are whole men and women, and the Spirit can touch the whole person, but that is where it starts, that is one of the first occasions God gave a detailed specification, the wisdom to understand it, the knowledge to see it together, and then the skill of the hands to produce one of the most beautiful buildings that is a copy of the one in heaven. The tabernacle was a place where God could live, his special tent in the middle of all their tents, yet it had to be portable. Wouldn't it be great to have portable church buildings for which you could just pull the pegs up and move again? That is what God wanted.

Later, of course, physical ability came to Samson. He got supernatural strength. Every Sunday school take-home paper I ever saw showed an Arnold Schwarzenegger kind of physique. But Samson never looked like that. If he did, do you think Delilah would have said, "What's the secret of your great strength?" I thank God that Samson had a physique like mine. His strength was not in his muscles in his biceps, it was physical supernatural strength. The New Testament backs that up. "If the Spirit of him who raised Jesus from the dead dwells in you, he will quicken also your mortal body." That's great isn't it?

Of course it leads us right into miracles of the Holy Spirit. A miracle is something a man cannot do unless the *ruach Adonai* makes it possible. Incidentally, looking at the ministries of Elijah and Elisha, in asking for a double portion of Elijah's spirit, Elisha was not saying, "I want to be twice the man you've been." That is a gross misunderstanding. When any Jew died, if he had four sons, his money or property was divided into five portions, and the son and heir who took over the family business got a double portion because he had the heavier responsibility. To pray for a double portion of your spirit is to say, "May I be your son and heir? May I carry on the ministry?" But all their miracles were done by the *ruach Adonai*. The Spirit would rush upon them and they would do it.

A unique aspect of the *ruach Adonai* in scripture is the

connection with music. Again, it is a physical skill, and yet it was given by the Spirit of God. King David was wise, he never chose a choirmaster who was not also a seer. You won't have so much trouble with your choirs if you have prophetic choirmasters or worship leaders or music group leaders. It is important that you really have musicians in your church who are prophetic and who have the *ruach Adonai* guiding them, otherwise letting them loose on your congregation is the most dangerous thing to do, but David was uniquely gifted in music by the *ruach Adonai* and he composed many psalms. Elijah would call for a minstrel to minister to him in music, that he might prophesy. So did Ezekiel. You find there is a very close connection between musical skill and the Spirit's moving on people and speaking on people. The power to interpret dreams; the power to be transported from one place to another – that comes in Old and New Testaments and it is the *ruach Adonai* that can literally pick a person up and plant them down somewhere else. That is what they thought had happened to Elijah until they found out that God had picked him up and planted him in heaven.

All this is "abnormal" stuff, and the trouble is that the church has got to the point where we regard the *ruach* of God as "normal". We have such silly hymns as "Soft as a gentle breeze, soft as the breath of evening." Have you heard that? The *ruach Adonai* doesn't come soft as the breath of evening, he comes like a rushing mighty wind.

We so often "spiritualise" the work of the Spirit. Take one example from Zechariah: "'Not by might, nor by power, but by my Spirit,' says the Lord." We apply that in all kinds of spiritual ways. It is about a building and getting it finished and getting the top stone on the roof, and Zechariah was told, "You won't get that building finished by human effort or by your own fleshly strength. You will get it finished by my Spirit." We wear "Greek" spectacles and forget that the physical and the spiritual are not separated in Hebrew thinking, and the *ruach Adonai* affects both. We are whole persons, not a body with a soul inside. In Hebrew thinking, the soul is a breathing body—it has life in it.

We have looked at the "doing", now we turn to "being". The interesting thing is that the main emphasis in the Old Testament is on the ability to lead. Most of those on whom the *ruach Adonai* fell in the Old Testament were leaders of his people. Isaiah 28:6 would be typical: that he will be a spirit of justice to those who sit in judgment. The ability to lead and to judge, the ability to rule, the ability to govern – this comes right the way through.

There were three kinds of leaders in the Old Testament. You can divide it into three chapters of history: chapter one, when they were led by prophets from Moses to Samuel; chapter two, when they were led by kings from Saul to Zedekiah; and chapter three, when they were led by priests, which is from Zerubbabel and following on through to Annas and Caiaphas. Those are the three major phases of leadership in the Old Testament—and in fact the period of the kings was comparatively short, though we often forget that.

All three kinds of leadership eventually failed, but they had been the results of *ruach Adonai* coming upon men. He came upon Moses, to bring them out of Egypt. He acknowledged that it was the Spirit of God who enabled him to do that. He came on Joshua to get them into Canaan. He came on the judges supremely—Judges is a very charismatic book in the Bible, and you find the Spirit of the Lord comes upon Othniel, then Gideon, then Jephthah, and above all, Samson. It was a period of charismatic leadership.

The interesting thing is that they tried to institutionalise the charismatic. When Gideon, by the power of the Spirit, delivered them from the Midianites, do you know what they said to Gideon? "Gideon, we'd like your son to become king

after you, and your grandson to be king after you. Start a dynasty, we want a king and you've proved yourself ideal...."
I have noticed that God rarely if ever operates through physical heredity, and that it is fatal for sons to try and copy fathers. Sons are people in themselves.

The judges had a twofold task: not only to govern within the people of God, but to defend them from external enemies. Just a little point of interest there—Deborah did the former but not the latter; for the latter, Barak had to do it. They were raised up by God, charismatic leadership, but people wanted to try to repeat it or encapsulate it or crystallise it. When you do that, it becomes fossilised and Gideon, thank God, said to them, "You already have a king, and that's the Lord." What we need is not human succession but divine anointing for leadership.

Moving on—in the period of the kings, the Spirit of the Lord came mightily on Saul, but there came a day when it says that the Spirit of the Lord was withdrawn from Saul, transferred to David on the same day, and an evil spirit was put within Saul replacing the Holy Spirit—that's one of the most awesome statements.

From Solomon onwards, there isn't a single anointed king in the Old Testament. Thrones were either seized by military coups or inherited by sons, and Solomon was a mixed bag. He did ask for wisdom for leadership and God honoured that and gave him wisdom. Into his palace came two mothers, both claiming the same baby. One baby had died. Wisdom was greatly needed by a man trying to cope with two women who were angry with each other. Solomon gave the wisest answer that could have been given. He said, "Cut the baby in half and give half to her, half to her." Immediately, the one who was not the real mother said, "That's fine by me," but the real mother would rather have her baby alive in someone else's hands and said, "All right. Let her have the baby," and

Solomon knew. Now he had got the answer, and he realised that, even though the prayer for wisdom had been in a dream, he had asked and the Holy Spirit gave him wisdom. While the Holy Spirit was on him, he could produce the book of Proverbs, he could take the wisest decisions; but like Samson before him, when Solomon stopped trusting the wisdom of the Spirit and was without the Spirit, chaos resulted.

I was once inspired in a very practical way by the biblical account of Solomon. I was preaching in Islington and a young couple came up to me afterwards. They just said, "David, if you don't help us we're going to get divorced," which is quite a challenge.

I said, "Look, I've got to leave in five minutes."

Again they said, "You've got to help us or we're going to get divorced."

"How long have you been married?" I asked

"Three months!"

"You're getting divorced after three months?"

"Yes."

"Do you love each other?" I asked.

"We thought we did."

"Do you love the Lord?"

"Yes, we both do."

"Well, how on earth did you meet?" Then it all came out—she was made a prison visitor and she went to a men's prison. Now that was folly. She led this boy to the Lord, she really did, and she discipled him and he grew and matured, and after some time he came out of prison and he had no family, nowhere to go. She was a single girl living on her own; and she was thirty and wondering if she would ever be married. He said, "You know, as well as being grateful to you for all the spiritual help you've given me, I've got very fond of you. Are you fond of me?"

"Yes," she replied.

He said, "Would you consider us getting together, and marrying and setting up home together?"

"Oh," she said, "Yes, love to."

Then they moved into her flat and she found out he was a rough lad and he ate with his fingers, not knife and fork, and when he undressed at night he would jump out of his clothes and drop them on the floor. She had been brought up in a home with lace curtains and flowers and everything neat and put away in drawers. They were totally incompatible in everything except their faith, and they said, "We can't—after three months we cannot stand each other. We've made the most terrible mistake." I remember saying, "Lord, I've got three or four minutes left. Please, you gave Solomon wisdom—give me some," and he did.

I said, "Now you two listen very carefully. This is what you've got to do. You've got to take 'week on, week off'. The first week you're both to do everything his way, and you—the bride, you're to throw your clothes on the floor and you're to eat with your fingers, but the next week it's his turn and he's got to learn to put his clothes in the drawer, and he's got to learn to use a knife and fork. You're to do that week on, week off." She looked at me, and she said, "That's so weird it's got to be of the Lord." Anyway, they said, "Is there anything else?" I said, "That's all I can hear. Goodbye, God bless you."

I have never seen them again, but six months later I got a letter from them. I could weep over that letter. "Dear David, we never thought marriage could be so wonderful," and they just went on and on about how happy they were, but they never told me the most important thing I wanted to know: were they still doing "week on, week off"? I can now write a book on marriage guidance! I've found the answer! Seriously, I have never told any other couple that since. It was a word of wisdom, and you must be very careful not to try and repeat what the *ruach Adonai* tells you to say.

Solomon got wisdom for everybody but himself. I was told in Sunday school he was the wisest man who ever lived in the Old Testament. Seven hundred wives and three hundred concubines — would you call that wise? Seven hundred mothers-in-law! In fact, it doesn't actually say that the *ruach Adonai* was on Solomon, and of course when he died, the whole thing broke up. You never find such an anointed king again.

Later, after the Jews got back from exile, the Spirit comes on priests. They were led by priests and didn't get a king again, except very briefly in the period of the Maccabees, but they had anointed priests, and the Spirit came on Zerubbabel. So they tried every form of leadership. What they really needed was someone who was going to be prophet, priest and king.

The Spirit of God enabled people to do extraordinary things, particularly to have an ability to lead his people, but the other area was the ability to *say*. This is the most prominent and perhaps the most significant and important ability in the Old Testament. Remember that moving air is linked with the mouth, and *ruach* is directly linked with speech. It enables people to prophesy.

Moses was a prophet primarily. Many regard him as the greatest prophet in the Old Testament. It is interesting that of the seventy elders whom he appointed, the Spirit of the Lord came upon them and they prophesied, but they did not do it again – just that once.

Prophesying is always something from the mouth. The Spirit of God takes over a person's mouth. The Spirit of God can even take over a donkey and cause the donkey to speak the words of God. I often say to Christian wives with unconverted husbands: "You should go to your husband with this problem, not me." They say, "But he is not a Christian,

THE HOLY SPIRIT IN THE OLD TESTAMENT

he's not converted." I say, "It doesn't matter, you only need a little faith that God will speak to you through your husband." They can't believe that, because their husband's not a Christian. Then I say, "But God once spoke to a man through his donkey," and then they believe it! Isn't that interesting? Which tells me exactly what they think of their husband at that stage; but when the *ruach Adonai* gets hold of someone he can speak because he can hear, and God will put words in his mouth.

When Saul was turned into another man, and the proverb says, "Is Saul also among the prophets?"– it says they were prophesying. That is very interesting – they were playing music when he met this band of prophets. Whatever they were doing, it wasn't anything they were doing for people; they were doing it for God, and it was certainly abnormal behaviour, and I don't rule out that it could have been tongues. There certainly was the gift of tongues at Babel, so it was in the Old Testament. They were doing things that normally you would never do, and that again is something that is characteristic of the *ruach Adonai*. He overcomes your inhibitions. You do things you would normally never dare to do. David dancing before the ark is just one example. His wife didn't think much of it, but God didn't think much of his wife. It says that Saul stripped and prophesied—crazy, but people whom *ruach Adonai* touches do crazy things.

The one important thing I would underline is this: never try to copy any of those crazy things. Poor Isaiah had to run naked through the streets of Jerusalem! We are so quick to copy what the *ruach Adonai* does with someone else! One of the weaknesses of charismatic fellowships is looking around for the latest thing, the big answer that will solve everything, and they hear that the *ruach Adonai* did this – "Ah, that's the answer! We must all do this here." He deals with us differently. Let him tell us what we are to be and to do and

41

it will be unique, because we are each unique.

Later, however, prophesying had more intelligible content, and it became very sharp messages from God. We begin to get prophets who speak out boldly in the name of the Lord. Moses had done that already, but you get a whole group of prophets who come at a particular crisis in Israel's history. They have a message from God that is related to past, present and future. Prophesying does all three, and we mustn't limit it to predictions about the future, though that is a vital part of it.

Their message was an appeal to the past—the covenant that God made with them in Sinai; a very astute diagnosis of their problems in the present; and an accurate prognosis of the future that is bound to follow from that unless there is a change. They had this overall understanding of the God of time. He is past, present, and future and these men it says, were all prophets by the *ruach Adonai* coming upon them— the Spirit of God enabling them to be prophets.

One of the outstanding qualities of both what we call the major prophets because their books are bigger, and the minor prophets because their books are smaller (and what a silly title that is) they spoke out the word that God gave them regardless of cost or consequence—that is boldness. In the New Testament, the Greek word is *paresia*, and that is more frequently used than tongues as a proof of being filled with the Spirit. Boldness of speech: courage to say the truth, whatever your reputation, whatever happens. Some of those men really paid the price for being bold in their utterance. I think of Isaiah—do you know what King Manasseh did to him? First he forbade him to speak, so Isaiah wrote it down in a book. Thank God he did – we've got it now – but then Manasseh took him and put him in a hollow tree log and ordered carpenters to saw him in two. He is the one referred to in Hebrews 11: "some were sawn asunder." I'm tempted to say biblical scholars are still trying to do it with his book—cut it into Proto-Isaiah and Deutero-Isaiah and all the rest. Poor Isaiah paid the price. Jeremiah was thrown into a pit. They had to live their message, which again took courage. "Jeremiah, you're not to marry." "Hosea, you're to marry a prostitute." "What?" "Go and find a prostitute and have three kids by her. The first one she will love; the second one she won't love, and the third one will not even be yours, Hosea." "What then, Lord?" "Well then she's going to go back on the streets." "What do I do then with three kids?" "Go and buy her back from the pimp who's controlling her and bring her back home and love her again." "And what do I do then, Lord?" "Then go and tell my people Israel that's how I feel," says the Lord. Ezekiel had to lose his wife and not even cry.

Those men had an incredible courage. That was the *ruach Adonai* coming on them, a mark of all those on whom the *ruach* comes. I have sometimes been asked, "What's the proof that you've been filled with the Spirit?" I reply, "I'll tell you in one word – trouble." If you haven't been in trouble since you were filled with the Spirit, I wonder if you are walking in the Spirit. Telling the truth as it is gets you into trouble. I'm always upset by testimonies that say, "I came to Jesus and all my troubles were over." My testimony is simple. I came to Jesus when I was seventeen and my troubles began. Years later I got baptised in the Spirit and my troubles got worse. It fits Jesus' promises because he said, "In the world you're going to have big trouble," but he also said, "Cheer up. I'm on top of it."

Prophets paid the price. You find specifically that Micaiah, Jahasiel, Zechariah, Micah, Isaiah, Ezekiel, Zechariah, they all attributed to the *ruach Adonai* the words they were speaking and the courage they showed – power to *say*.

In summary: the Holy Spirit came on very few people in the Old Testament. If you add them all together you probably come to not more than a hundred and fifty. When you consider that two and a half million Hebrew slaves came out of Egypt, and add that to all the subsequent generations, actually very few people experienced the *ruach Adonai*. It was mostly some of their leaders, their prophets, priests and kings, but not many of the ordinary folk. So there were a lot of heroes, big names, but we live in a new covenant, a very different one. It doesn't depend on just the few big people. I am glad I don't live in the old covenant because I could have been one of the millions of the people of God whom the *ruach Adonai* didn't touch. The Holy Spirit came on the few who served the many, and never was so much owed by so many to so few. There is no emphasis at all on the ordinary, average, common, everyday Israelite experiencing the *ruach Adonai*. I find it helpful to notice what the Bible doesn't say as well as what it does say—looking at the things that are missing you see so much.

Even the few on whom the *ruach Adonai* came, he did not stay. This was not a permanent situation or state, he came and went. Now having said that, there are hints that in some of them the Holy Spirit was more or less continuously operating. The only ones I could find were: Joseph, Moses, Joshua, Daniel, Samuel, Elijah and Elisha. The hint is that they are described as men in whom the Spirit of God is.

There is in the whole Old Testament one man alone of whom it is specifically said that the Spirit remained with him from the day the Spirit came on him, and that is King David. He is the only one on whom the Spirit came and rested and remained, and it specifically says, "From that day forward, the Spirit mightily came on David." How interesting—the one type of the Son of David was the king who was also a prophet but not a priest. Interesting that in the Old Testament you have got some, a few, who were priests and prophets, like Ezekiel; and some who were prophets and kings, like David.

There is not one who was ever prophet, priest, and king.

But there came the dreadful day when David broke five out of ten commandments in that one day. He coveted his neighbour's wife, bore false witness against the husband, stole the wife, committed adultery with her and murdered the husband. That was pretty bad for a man after God's own heart. When he was faced with it, and Nathan the prophet said, "You're the man," do you know what his major anxiety was? "Lord, take not your Holy Spirit from me!" Psalm 51 — there is a man who was conscious of the continuing presence of the Spirit. The one thing he feared most was that he would lose the Holy Spirit through that incident, and he didn't lose the Holy Spirit. That was his prayer, "God don't take the Spirit away from me."

The other thing to mention is that in the Old Testament there is an emphasis on ability rather than character. It is power, primarily, rather than purity that is the work of the Holy Spirit in the Old Testament.

The Old Testament hopes for the future divide into two, one of which is a far narrower experience of the *ruach Adonai* than before, and the other of which is a far broader experience, so that in one sense the zoom lens goes right in and then right out again. You get this concentration first on the hope of a Spirit-filled sovereign who would receive the Holy Spirit without any limits; who would have all the abilities and all the character that the Holy Spirit can bring: a perfect king—the Messiah in Hebrew, *Christos* in Greek, King in English. That hope was fulfilled when Jesus was born.

The other side of the hope was Spirit-filled subjects for that king. The combination of a Spirit-filled sovereign ruling over a people, each one of whom was Spirit-filled, is what the Jews understand by the term "kingdom of God". Jesus never defined or explained the phrase "the kingdom of God" because every Jew knew what it meant. The kingdom of God is not just of a Spirit-filled sovereign, but of every subject being Spirit-filled as well. That is the concept of the kingdom of God for which many longed and prayed.

Let us just take the two halves of it – first the Spirit-filled sovereign. We find this particularly coming out in Isaiah a thousand years before it happened. Here we have this picture of a man who is so filled with the Holy Spirit that he combines the functions of prophet, priest and king—that he is everything we need in a leader, and that he will have the character, the gifts and abilities; that he will have on him the Spirit of wisdom and understanding, counsel and might, knowledge and fear of the Lord—that is all there in Isaiah 11, and he would come from the stump of Jesse, the tree that had been cut down, and as a new shoot comes from the stump, this Spirit-filled king would come from that stump. That is why he was born in Bethlehem of the stump of Jesse.

We recall again that Isaiah 42 includes what would be the text for Jesus' first sermon at Nazareth, "The Spirit of the Lord is upon me", listing the things he was going to do: bring good news to the poor, release the captives, those that are bruised, and so on. Do you know what that is? That's the Jubilee year. Every fifty years they had a Jubilee in Israel. It was good news to the poor because all property went back to the original owner, and everybody started level again—a radical economic measure, but I think a wonderful one, so that you are constantly preventing the rich from getting too rich and the poor from getting too poor—that's God's answer. It is not good news for the rich!

Also in the Jubilee years, slaves were set free. It is the acceptable year of the Lord. What is acceptable to the Lord about it? Everybody's going to be equal again and the slaves are going to be free again, that's what makes it acceptable. Jesus announced, "The Spirit of the Lord is upon me to proclaim the acceptable year of the Lord." The Jubilee had begun.

Isaiah never realised that the king in the earlier prophecies he gave, and the suffering servant who would die for his people and rise from the dead in the second half of his prophecy, were the same person – and to this day most Jews don't realise it. Even though God gave them the scroll of Isaiah from the Dead Sea Scrolls in the year that they founded Israel, they still don't see the significance of it. It was the only book that was complete in the Dead Sea Scrolls, and they have got it alone in the Shrine of the Book near the Knesset and they don't see it – they are blinded.

They can only look for a coming king; they couldn't handle a suffering servant. We know that these two are together because the Spirit of the Lord, the same Spirit who is on the King who was to be filled with wisdom and counsel and might, is also on the servant to die for his people, and by his stripes we are healed. That is the narrow hope for the future; the broad hope for the future is that he will have a kingdom in which every subject is Spirit-filled.

The Holy Spirit is not called the "Holy Spirit" in the Old Testament except when David says, "Take not your Holy Spirit from me." "Holy Spirit" is his name in the new covenant, and it is a very important addition. He is not called the Holy Spirit because he is never called God in the Old Testament and he is never actually treated there as a person. He was thought of as the power of God, but I think to the Jews he was more of an "it" than a "him". There were one or two exceptions. Isaiah got very near it when he said, "Don't grieve the Holy Spirit." Note that it was Isaiah who said that first, not Paul. You can't grieve an "it". Nevertheless we have to say that if we only had the Old Testament you could be excused for not thinking of the Holy Spirit as a person. That is why they never had to wrestle with the problem of the Trinity. They only knew that there is one God, yet right at the very beginning we have an extraordinary statement in Genesis 1 that God is called *Elohim*, which means that he is three or more. *El* is one, *eloha* is two, but *elohim* is three or more, and yet, even though God is *Elohim* all the way through Genesis 1, all the verbs are singular.

"In the beginning Gods" [plural] "created" [singular]…. Now of course, the Jews don't know what to make of that. They say it's the "we" of royalty when God says, "Let us make man in our own image." We now see the *Spirit* as God and as a person, but he is not really fully treated as a person in the Old Testament. It is more the breath of God, the force, the invisible force of God coming, so there are limitations. In the earlier part of the Old Testament he is usually called the Spirit of God, either *ruach Adonai* or *ruach Elohim*. Later, as people became more familiar with the moving of the Spirit, they simply called him the Spirit, but as soon as we move into the New Testament he is the Holy Spirit, the third person of the blessed Trinity, and we know so much more.

Thank God for the foundation laid in the Old Testament, but thank God we are living in a brand new covenant which Ezekiel says was a covenant in which God's Holy Spirit would be poured out upon us; a covenant in which Jeremiah said the Spirit would keep us obedient to God from the inside instead of the law on the outside; and in which, as Joel said, we will all be prophets – the "prophethood" of all believers is now a possibility in the new covenant.

In the incident mentioned earlier, from 1 Samuel 9:27 through into chapter ten, we read of Saul encountering Samuel the prophet, who gave him an extraordinary message—that he is to be the first king of Israel. Prophetic words are spoken over Saul, and he was to meet a band of prophets coming down from the high place with harp, tambourine, flute and lyre before them, prophesying. Then the Spirit of the Lord would come mightily upon Saul, and he would prophesy with them and be turned into another man. People would ask, "Is Saul also among the prophets?" *Here is the theme of the whole of the Old Testament in relation to the Holy Spirit: that the power of the Holy Spirit coming upon a man turns him into another man, another kind of character, another person able to do things that he was never able to do before.*

One of the lies of the devil, which I am constantly coming up against is that you cannot change human nature. Humanly speaking, that is true. There is only one power in the whole universe that can take a man and turn him into another man and make him more of a man than he was before and not less – making him more of a human being, more of a personality – and that is the power of the Holy Spirit.

I am impressed with the fact in the New Testament that when the people of Pentecost were filled with the Holy Spirit, they didn't become mechanical robots. They became more intensely themselves than they ever were before. They became more attractive characters; they became greater personalities in their own right. In the rest of the New Testament the personalities of John and Peter and Paul are still so different from each other, even more different. Yet somehow they are new people; somehow each has been turned into another man.

All the way through the Old Testament we learn that the Holy Spirit "came on" or was "poured out upon" someone, or "filled", and the immediate result was they became another person.

In all that the Spirit does, there is order and there is purity. Let us return to that picture we are given in Genesis of the Spirit "hovering". You may have seen a hawk hovering in the sky, almost motionless, watching the things that are happening far below. From the very beginning we are almost told to think of the Holy Spirit as a bird hovering above, watching what is happening. That picture comes again in John's Gospel where, when Jesus was baptised, as he stood up in the water afterwards, praying, the Holy Spirit hovered over him – and the order of our Lord's life was due to the Holy Spirit bringing God's order. You get the impression from our Lord's life that he was never hurried; he never had too much to do even though he was always busy. He had an ordered life that was able to do all that the Father wanted him to do. The Holy Spirit hovered over Jesus at his baptism as at the first day of creation the Holy Spirit hovered over the waters. *An ordered Life*

Now let me apply that even more directly. If the Holy Spirit comes in power on a church, the result will be order, not chaos. The result will not be the kind of noise that is purposeless, the kind of activity that is disturbing and chaotic. The result of the Holy Spirit's coming will be to bring God's order into that church. Now it may disturb the order that is already there because that order may be a human order that is not of God, but it will not be chaos. It will build up, not destroy, and when the Holy Spirit really operates, there is an order and a decency that is of God. It is one of the tests of the power of the Holy Spirit: does this bring order or chaos? The Holy Spirit is brooding.

Then in Genesis 2, you have God *breathing* and now we recall that the word *spirit* and *breath* are the same—God spiriting a corpse; God breathing into a corpse; God giving the kiss of life to Adam. So, again we remember, vitality, life, power, is there; but *purity* is also allied to the vitality. Order is allied to the life, and where the Holy Spirit comes he gives life and order. I remember as a biology student I had to learn all the Latin names of the families of insects. I can think of few things more boring than trying to learn the Latin names of the various species of flies and spiders

Vitality Life, *order, Purity*

and beetles and things, but it was part of our course and we had to go through it, and what struck me immensely was the order of it all. I know that man has produced the Latin words, but it was God who put the order there in the first place, or man could never label it like that. Man can only analyse what God has ordered, and it strikes me now that as I learned those Latin names I was learning the order of the Spirit of God, brooding over the chaos and producing after their kinds those creatures which God had ordained.

It is the Holy Spirit who brings true *greatness*. If I were to suggest that you write down the names of all the great people of the Old Testament, as many as you can remember, I think you would probably get up to about thirty or forty if you tried hard and you know your Bible at all well. You could write down Abraham, Moses, Joshua, Gideon, Samson, Saul, David, Solomon and the rest. If you checked up, you would find that there is a statement about every single name that you have written that connects that person with the Holy Spirit. It is one of the most astonishing discoveries, and I didn't make it until I went through and looked at each of these men, that every great man in the Old Testament owed it to the Holy Spirit, not to anything or anyone else. Having made a list of "heroes", I then divided them into three groups—those who were great because of something they *did*, those who were great because of something they *said*, and those who were great because of something they *were*. Here are the three forms of human greatness. If anybody ever says about you, "You're great," except in the modern colloquial sense, but if anybody says of you, "You're a great person," then they will mean one of these three things—that you did something great, that you said something great, or that you were something great.

Consider first of all those who were great because of something they *did*, some great achievement, which put them in the front rank of leadership, and the names I have mentioned would cover people who did great things. How did they get that greatness? When I look at my bunch of heroes, I find they were desperately ordinary people with neither a great classical breeding in their family tree, nor an educational system that could produce them. How then were they able to do the amazing things? The answer is: the Holy Spirit turned them into other men at some point in their history.

We need to look more closely at the word "prophecy", which is not preaching but is quite a different gift. Preaching is essentially the fruit of a man's mind meditating on God's Word and explaining it and expounding it to people, but prophecy is not that at all. In prophecy the prophet's mind is not thinking, but God's mind is using his mouth for an immediate, direct, inspired utterance from God for his people. Isaiah, for example, didn't sit down and have a good think about the political situation and then preach a sermon about it. Isaiah opened his mouth, and the mind of God used it. This is something that is written right through Scripture. There is one phrase of four words that occurs 3,808 times in the Old Testament alone: "Thus says the Lord," and that phrase comes again and again. Wherever it comes, it is not a man preaching, it is a man prophesying. It is a man who has the supernatural power to open his mouth and speak directly from the mind of God and it happens all the way through the Old Testament.

Now if I start making a list of the prophets – Amos, Hosea, Micah, Isaiah and then through to Jeremiah and Ezekiel and Habakkuk and Zephaniah and Haggai and Zechariah – if you look at these men, there is a statement about each of them that they said what they did because the Holy Spirit gave them the power to do so. Without the Holy Spirit they could never have said it; they wouldn't have known what to say. There is even a statement in the New Testament from Peter that they said things about the future which they didn't understand, and they talked with each other about what they had said. This is prophecy.

It starts way back in the Old Testament. Abraham is said to be a prophet. Moses is described as a prophet. He was a great leader, but he was also a prophet. How do you think we got the Ten Commandments and the law of God from Moses? Did he sit down and think up a new ethical system? Did he consult the professor of advanced legal studies in the court of Hammurabi, or what did he do? No, he prophesied and the words came from the mind of God. You go right through the Bible and you find that every prophet had this gift of his vocal cords being completely available to God's mind.

One of the most extraordinary stories in the Old Testament about the Spirit of God is how God enabled a donkey to speak rational, intelligible words. Now a donkey has vocal cords. If you've ever had an ass in a field behind your back garden then you will know that. God can control a donkey's or an ass's vocal cords just as easily as he can control the vocal cords of a man to produce intelligible speech. Unless we see that the Spirit of God has this power of control, the story of Balaam's ass will be a complete mystery to you, but it is there. The same Spirit who is able to make an Isaiah, a Jeremiah, an Ezekiel speak the words of God can make Balaam's ass speak words too.

The Holy Spirit, brooding over nature, can give a completely accurate diagnosis of the present, and secondly, make a completely accurate forecast of the future. These are two things that are completely beyond the mind of man. We can make some kind of diagnosis of the present. We can make some kind of guess about the future, but only the mind of God can tell us exactly what is going wrong in the present and exactly what will happen in the future. The prophets were men who could do both. Let the prophet Micah speak for them all. "I truly am full of power by the Spirit of the Lord, and I declare to Israel his sin." Incidentally, it is interesting that the Holy Spirit usually sent a prophet when things were going wrong. That is why they are always prophets of doom, and though they have hope for the future they were always critical of the present and this made them very unpopular and it was why people stoned the prophets.

I remember a dear old preacher who was a very simple man, a man who had no education to speak of, a man who had spent his days working with his hands, but he was a great preacher. I once asked him about his preaching. I said, "How did you start preaching?" I remember him saying, "Well, you know, if God could use Balaam's ass to speak intelligibly, he could use me." So he said, "I just let him." There is a very interesting little word, and this is what I am saying. Every single person in your church could do something great for God and say something great for God, by the power of the Holy Spirit; even if you have no natural gifts, even if your heredity is all awry, even if your environment hasn't given you a chance, everybody could do this, for the Holy Spirit is no respecter of persons and can use anybody who is willing.

Now I come to my third group of "heroes"—those who were great because of what they were. I think that this is the greatest greatness of all. We may be remembered for great things we've done, for great things we've said, but oh to be remembered for great things we were. In a little chapel in Cumberland that I once visited, the wall is plastered with marble slabs. You can read the history of the church on them. Each had a long essay all about the person. I walked around this church and these great big tributes on the walls of bygone worthies, and I came to a tiny one right at the end – of the village schoolmaster. Instead of a long essay about his achievements and contributions there were just three words— "kind and good". In a sense, looking at all the others, they were about what people did. This was about what he *was*, and I felt I had come to the greatest stone there.

Now this is how we remember real greatness—people for what they were, not just what they said and did. Who were the greatest people in the Old Testament? I will tell you one of them straightaway: King David was surely a man after God's own heart. He is described as that, and the thing that strikes me most about David is not what he did, though he enlarged the borders of Israel more than any other king; not so much what he said, though he said some very wonderful things, and we have got the book of Psalms. But from his life, I get the impression that the greatest thing about David was what he was. Think of David's magnanimous attitude to Saul when Saul tried to kill him; how he forgave his enemies—a great man.

What was David's secret? You discover the secret when David went wrong and got into trouble. Again, you will remember the incident: he saw Bathsheba bathing, he broke four of the Ten Commandments in one fell swoop— he coveted his neighbour's wife; he arranged to murder Bathsheba's husband in battle, so he killed, he stole his wife, and he committed adultery. And the prophet of God came to David and said, "You've done wrong."

David prayed a prayer for forgiveness, He said, "Lord, take not your Holy Spirit from me." He knew he didn't deserve to have the Holy Spirit living in his life. He didn't deserve to have this power to be a saint. He pleaded: take not your Holy Spirit from me; restore to me the joy of your salvation; forgive me, put me back; I have sinned very deeply. David realised that God could now take his Spirit from him. It is a wonderful prayer.

There are many other great people mentioned in the Old Testament. Did you know that Joseph is the only man in the whole Old Testament of whom not a single fault is ever recorded for us – unless you count his telling his dreams to his brothers. Was that a bit of pride? I don't think it was. I think he was quite surprised by their reaction to it. Do you want to know Joseph's secret of how in a foreign land when enticed by Potiphar's wife he could resist even though no one would know about it? Do you want to know how he could be thrown into prison unjustly and still be kind to the prisoners? Do you want to know what was the secret of a man who could be so cruelly dealt with by his own brothers and then forgive them and give them food? Here is the secret, in Genesis 41: "Joseph was a man in whom the Spirit of God was."

Now do you see where all this is heading? I think this is lovely. All the great people of the Bible are ordinary people like us without great advantages and they are doing extraordinary things. They are doing the work of God by the Spirit of God. They are being turned into other people and therefore they are no longer limited to natural gifts, they have supernatural gifts as well. I pray that every believer will realise that every one of us could do anything by the Spirit of God and stop saying, "I could never do this. This is beyond me." Humanly speaking, it may be; divinely speaking it is within your capacity because it is within the power of the Holy Spirit.

The Old Testament closes by looking forward to what was revealed by the prophets: the hopes for the future concerning the Holy Spirit: that one day there will come a king like David, a "Son of David", who will be perfectly filled with the Holy Spirit and be able to do anything, and to say anything and to be anything. The hope is called the hope of the Messiah, and the word Messiah means anointed one. Throughout the Old Testament, oil is used as a symbol of the Holy Spirit, and every king was anointed with oil as a visible prayer that God would pour out the Holy Spirit upon them. In the Greek language, the word Christ also means anointed one.

The Old Testament looks forward to a day when there will come a king who is anointed with the Holy Spirit in power, and is able to be perfect and to perform any miracle and to speak anything of the mind of God. They had never had someone quite so full as that, and so they looked forward to the coming king, the Messiah, the Christ, the anointed king, full of the Holy Spirit. They waited a thousand years and that dream was fulfilled when Jesus was born at Bethlehem.

Powerful

Chapter Three

THE HOLY SPIRIT IN THE NEW TESTAMENT: AN OVERVIEW

When we turn to the New Testament we have vastly more material on the Holy Spirit than we had in the Old. But there is a huge difference when you enter the New Testament: we meet the Holy Spirit – not Spirit of God, *ruach Adonai*, but the Holy Spirit. This is now not just a description or title but the name of the third person of the Holy Trinity. He has many other names in the New Testament which he never had in the Old: the Spirit of truth, the spirit of prophecy, promise, holiness, life, gladness; the Spirit of grace, of glory. God has one first name and many second names; so has the Spirit. I was translating a part of Genesis some time ago and I said, "Lord, I don't like to use this word "Yahweh" – that is your name but it comes awkwardly from my lips and it doesn't thrill me, it doesn't excite me." I said, "Please would you give me an English word that would be equivalent to Yahweh [which is a participle of the verb "to be", as you know] and straight into my mind came: "always".

I thought: that is a good name for God, but that is only his first name. He is always my helper, always my provider, always my banner – *always*. Out of the 250 names and titles that his Son has – more than anybody in history has ever had – one of my favourites is "Yes". He is the "yes" to every promise of God. With a Father called "Always" and the Son called "Yes" you cannot have a more positive trait than that.

But the Holy Spirit has many second names and I have just given you a few of them, and the big changes are these: first, in the New Testament the Holy Spirit is shown to be fully

Holy Spirit

personal. He is a person, he has the attributes of a person, he has a heart that feels, he has a mind that thinks, he has a will that acts, he has all the attributes of a personality. He also has all the activities of a personality in the New Testament. He speaks, he searches, he cries out, he prays, he testifies, he teaches, he guides, he leads, he forbids, he calls, he appoints; only a person can do all these things. So we are now dealing not with just the power of God but with a person who has all the attributes and activities of a person.

There are things you can do to him that you can only do to a person. You can make him unhappy, you can grieve him, you can lie to him, and you can insult him. So we have the fully personal Spirit of God revealed in the New Testament. We also have the fully *divine* Spirit here. He is described as the eternal Spirit. He is said to be omnipresent — everywhere; omniscient — knowing everything; and omnipotent — able to do anything. These are all divine attributes and so here we have a person who is fully God, but he is distinct from the Father and Son and often listed alongside them: Father, Son, and Holy Spirit. He is sent by the Father and the Son, named after the Father and Son, and he is the Spirit of God and the Spirit of Christ. He speaks from the Father and the Son, and he glorifies Christ as Christ glorifies the Father. There is a clear subordination there, though he is fully personal, fully divine, he takes his place to serve the Son, and the Son takes his place to serve the Father. He is one with them, and you cannot have the Spirit without having the Father and Son as well. You cannot have one person of the Trinity without the other two. They are so much one that when Jesus promised that the Spirit would come and dwell in us, at the same time he says the Father and I will come and make our home.

So when we receive the Spirit we are receiving Father and Son as well, and yet there is a clear distinction between them. The Spirit is fully personal and the definite article indicates *the* Holy Spirit, there is no other. Though he is fully personal, he is also still the impersonal force of the Old Testament, and unfortunately most English translations don't carefully observe the presence or the absence of the definite article. He is sometimes simply referred to as Holy Spirit and in that case the absence of the definite article indicates the power rather than the person, and it is no coincidence that such phrases as "baptised in Holy Spirit" and "filled with Holy Spirit" and "anointed with Holy Spirit" and "sealed with Holy Spirit" lack the definite article. For these are essential experiences of the power rather than experiences of the person.

Being baptised in Holy Spirit is essential to experience his power and to be filled with Holy Spirit. Unfortunately our English translations constantly put in the extra word "the", which is naughty. We are baptised in Holy Spirit.

I want to divide the work of the Holy Spirit into three phases: the pre-Messianic phase, the Messianic phase, and the post-Messianic phase. I have said a little about his person because you have got to understand that first. In fact, it is far better to approach your thinking about the Spirit through his work than as an abstract person. Again the Hebrews thought of the Holy Spirit as primarily living, active and his work, where Greek thinking wants to think of him as an abstract person, timeless.

Nothing has damaged the Church more than the introduction of Greek philosophy into biblical theology. It was Augustine who introduced Platonic thinking and it was Aquinas who introduced Aristotelian thinking, and I am afraid that we have suffered from that. The Bible is a Hebrew book, and although the New Testament is written in Greek, it was written by Hebrews with one exception. So the thought forms of the Bible are Hebrew, and Hebrew starts with living, active Holy Spirit not theories about the Trinity.

There had been four hundred years with no recorded

activity of the Spirit. Now suddenly there was an outburst of prophecy and miracle centred around the birth of Jesus. John, who never did any miracles, was filled with the Spirit from before he was born and right through his life, and he was a strange mixture of external boldness and internal depth.

The pre-Messianic outburst of the Spirit around Jesus' birth has all the characteristics of the Old Testament work of the Spirit – the Spirit coming on people to do something extraordinary – but it is not yet the pattern that we see later. Jesus said that even John the Baptist was less than the least in the kingdom.

Then to the Messianic: Jesus was the fulfilment of the Old Testament hope of a Spirit-filled sovereign. He was born of the Spirit, and a new pattern of the Spirit's activity was introduced in Jesus. Jesus' baptism became a model for all later Christian baptisms. The Holy Spirit did not come on him *in* his baptism but *after* – when he came up out of the water and was praying. That is the very best time to pray for someone to receive the Holy Spirit. There are one or two exceptions, but the norm for the rest of the New Testament is baptism in water followed by baptism in Spirit, and Jesus had that. The Spirit came in the form of a dove, reminding us that this was the beginning of the new creation. The Spirit gives an assurance to Jesus that he really is who he thought he was: "You are my beloved Son and I am pleased with you."

The only earlier glimpse we had of Jesus was at the age of twelve. In those days the women walked first with the children under that age, they reached a campsite after fifteen miles, they put up the tents and cooked the evening meal, so by the time it was ready the men arrived. So then Mary might have said, "Joseph, where's Jesus?" "Well, I thought he was with you." But he was twelve now. They found out that first night that he was with neither. You see how it happened. I used to think they were careless. They weren't, each of them was sure he would be with the other, and so they went back to search. At that age a Jewish boy becomes a man. We suffer in our culture from not having a recognised step like that. This is why men stay boys nowadays, and the only difference between men and boys is the price of their toys! At the age of twelve a Jewish boy put away childish things, and he became a partner in his father's trade or business – and they found Jesus where? In the temple. Isn't it interesting that Mary said, "Your father and I have been looking everywhere for you," because she was frustrated, and it shows that she had never told him who he was: "Your father and I." Jesus said "My Father..." He was twelve now, a partner in his father's business. Perfectly normal for a Jewish boy. But at his baptism, when the Spirit came, the Father said: "You are my beloved Son," and there was no doubt about it whatever.

In evangelism, when a person is baptised in the Spirit, that is the moment of assurance, God's confirmation, the seal, the proof, the earnest, the guarantee that the relationship has been established. An evangelist should not be content until someone has received the Holy Spirit and power. You are not really evangelising if you just get them to "decide for Jesus". The heart of conversion is the reception of the Holy Spirit. The other part of it is the forgiveness of sins. These are the two things that we must include in evangelism at the very beginning or we are not doing it the New Testament way. It's not "Come to Jesus"; it's not "Let Jesus into your heart"; it's not "Give your life to Jesus". It is: "Get your sins forgiven and receive the Holy Spirit." That is New Testament evangelism. For Jesus, who of course was without sin: after his water baptism the Spirit came and the assurance came. When someone receives the Spirit, not only do they know it but others present know it as well. Immediately, Jesus is led by the Spirit.

Jesus didn't start his mission until then because Jesus was the Son of Man and he was going to preach and do miracles *by the power of the Holy Spirit*. He did miracles as the Son of Man filled with the Holy Spirit of God. It is on that basis that he could say, "The works that I do, you will do too." Because he did them as the Son of Man who, after his water baptism received the anointing with power, we can do what he did. His first big battle was that he had to settle scores with Satan – he had to bind the strong man or he would never be able to plunder his goods. Every temptation started with, "If you are the Son of God..." "*If...*" are you sure? Oh you have received the Spirit and you heard the voice, try and turn these stones into bread. Actually his first miracle was water into wine so what's the difference between turning stones into bread and water into wine? The difference is that stones into bread would have been for himself, and the water into wine was for other people. He had not come to prove things to himself or to get a kingdom for himself.

Satan offered Jesus the post of Antichrist, and one day a man will accept the offer. "I'll give you all the kingdoms of the world if you bow down to me." Jesus refused. Because of that initial private battle in which he overcame Satan, Jesus could now plunder his goods. He came full of the Spirit and in the power of the Spirit to Galilee, and then he began to do, to say, and to be things – the three divisions we saw in the Old Testament – but he did them superlatively because the Spirit was given to him without measure or limit.

All his miracles were done by the power of the Spirit, whether they were miracles with people, casting out demons, healing disease, raising the dead; or his miracles with things—cursing a tree so that it died, telling the winds and the waves to shut up. He didn't say "Peace be still," that's the polite English version. He said, "Get muzzled," that's the translation. That's the way you talk to a Rottweiler, and he said stop jumping up at my disciples – and the wind and the waves got muzzled. Now all that was done by the power of the Spirit.

Furthermore, everything he ever said was a prophecy. Did you ever notice that? He said "I don't say anything but what I'm given to say." He was the prophet and he never opened his mouth without prophesying because he only said what he was given to say.

The Spirit was on him, the spirit of counsel and wisdom and understanding. All the gifts of the Spirit are superlatively seen in Jesus except one. As far as the record goes, he never used the gift of tongues. Now we don't know he didn't, it just doesn't say he did so we don't know, but if he didn't, I can understand that. If there is one person who didn't need help with his prayer life it was Jesus, and that is what the gift is given for anyway. He had such perfect communion I can understand why he didn't use it, but every other gift – the word of knowledge, the word of wisdom, miracles, healing are all there. In a sense as all the gifts were in his physical body then, he now wants all his gifts to be in his body so he can continue his ministry. He is the church packed into one person. He is the whole body, and the fullness of the godhead dwelt in him bodily, as God wants to dwell in us bodily.

It was through the Holy Spirit, says the letter to the Hebrews, that he offered himself up as a sacrifice. What carried him through with the cross? You know Jesus went through hell for three hours on the cross. From noon till three Jesus was in hell. How do I know? Hell is a place where there is no natural light, a place of utter darkness, and hell is a place of great thirst; that was when he said, "I thirst." Hell is a place where God is not. That's when he cried out "Eli, Eli, lama sabachthani?" "My God, my God why have you left me?" That's hell, and Jesus went through hell for three hours so that we need not.

How on earth did he manage it? The first time he had ever been separated from his Father in the whole of eternity, it was through the Holy Spirit that he offered himself up.

His resurrection was also the work of the Spirit. Most Christians don't see what the significance of the resurrection was. It had to happen on the first day of the week because it was the first new thing that God his Father had created since he made the universe. God made the universe in six days, whether they were short or long I do not know. The seventh day was very long, it lasted all through the Old Testament. God did nothing new all through the Old Testament period. The word "new" hardly ever occurs in the Old Testament. The only verse I can think of is: "Behold, there is nothing new under the sun." The Creator, having finished his work of creation, rested from it all the way through the Old Testament. But that first Sunday morning – it had to be the first day of the week because that's God's first working day – God went back to work and he made a new body for his Son because it was a new body that Jesus got into. It was an act of creation, it was the beginning of the new creation.

So we are living in the second week of creation; the eighth day of creation. That is where we are in God's calendar. The only difference is in the first creation he made the heaven and earth first, and men and women last. This time around he is making new men and women first, and the new heaven and the earth last. He is doing it in reverse order so that he can get people out of the old and into the new. There are people being made new. The first act of creation since God made the universe was to raise his Son from the dead and give him an immortal body, a body that could eat fish and walk through doors. I am getting on to the resurrection, but it was all through the power of the Spirit, and if the Spirit of him who raised up Jesus from the dead dwells in you, your mortal body will be quickened. I look forward to getting my new body. Do you know how old I am going to be when I get it? Thirty-three, and I can't wait to be thirty-three again because it says I am going to get a glorious body just like his. When you are an old age pensioner it is good news that you are going to be thirty-three again and be in your prime and have a body just like Jesus.

In a sense, Jesus is the climax of prophets, priests, and those kings who were anointed by the Spirit in the Old Testament – all narrowed down to one person in whom the Spirit is superlatively. What happens then? The whole thing broadens out wider than ever, and the Spirit-filled subjects begin to fill the picture. This is the beginning of all flesh prophesying. Jesus didn't come to monopolise ministry but to multiply it, and came to set free his Spirit in a new body composed of millions of people. So the work of the Spirit now broadens out.

In Acts, as soon as Paul comes on the scene everybody else disappears, because Luke-Acts was written to defend Paul, but God had a bigger purpose for both those volumes and got them into our Bible. John's Gospel has been put between those two volumes – why? Because in Matthew, Mark and Luke the emphasis is on Spirit and Jesus, but in John we have – carefully picked out of Jesus' ministry – all the promises that the Spirit would be passed on to others. In Acts we find the Spirit passed onto others. I believe that is profound because the New Testament is shaped, as we shall see, by an understanding of the Holy Spirit.

When you go through what John's Gospel teaches concerning the Spirit, it is all about those Spirit-filled subjects who are going to receive the Spirit. The very first statement about the Spirit in John's Gospel tells us something that had never been said before: that the Spirit-filled sovereign will be the means of filling his subjects with the Spirit. It was God who said to John the Baptist: "The one on whom you see the Spirit come, he will baptise others in that same Holy Spirit." That is a new revelation, and it means that the phrase "baptised in Holy Spirit" was coined by God. So don't be embarrassed to use it. Preach it! I believe there is a key here, because I find charismatic preachers toning down the fact that Jesus is the baptiser in the Spirit. It was God who said that first, and let us hold that. There is a big burden in my heart here because plenty of people will accept the gifts of the Spirit now – it is being *baptised* in the Spirit that is now the "offence".

I must tell you a personal story. One of the founders of the FIEC (Fellowship of Independent Evangelical Churches) was dying in hospital, had a few hours to live and was exhausted and in pain. A friend visited him one Sunday morning and asked ,"Is there anything I can do to help you?"

He replied, "Well, I can't go to church today, and I miss being in church on Sunday. Would you read the Bible to me?"

The friend answered, "I'll do something better than that. I'll go home and get a tape recorder and I'll bring a tape and you can listen to some preaching."

The friend went home and got a tape of mine on John 1, in which I said this, "John the Baptist said the Messiah will do two things for you: he'll take away the sins of the world and he'll baptise you in his Holy Spirit." My whole theme was that we must preach both the negative and the positive side of the gospel. Getting sins out of people's lives will leave them empty, miserable, and vulnerable. If all our gospel is "Behold the Lamb of God who takes away the sins of the world," that is only half a gospel because it leaves them empty, and there is nobody so miserable as somebody in the wilderness between Egypt and Canaan. The whole emphasis was on getting people filled up with the Spirit as well as emptied of their sins.

This dear man listened to this tape and he began to

weep, and he said, "Lord, I've tried to preach the gospel faithfully for years and years but I've only been preaching half a gospel," and he asked the Lord to baptise him in the Spirit – and he did! When his family came in, thinking to say goodbye to him, he said to his son-in-law who is the pastor of a church: "I'm going to preach in your church next Sunday morning."

His son-in-law said, "Yes, well if you're well enough dad, you know."

He said, "No, I've asked the Lord to give me one chance to preach the whole gospel."

The next Sunday he was still alive and they carried him in his pyjamas, in an ambulance, to the church and they sat him in a seat in the pulpit. He said, "I've been preaching half a gospel all my life, but God's given me the chance to preach the whole gospel to you...."

He died the following Tuesday and some who heard of it said, "Oh he must have gone senile at the end, isn't it tragic?"

He preached the whole gospel: the Lamb of God who takes away the sins of the world and the one who baptises in the Holy Spirit. John said you need both, and I can't do them for you, but he can and he will — that is the beginning of John's Gospel.

In John 3, Jesus teaches that being born again is being born "out of water and Spirit". You can't be born out of something until you are in it. In my book *The Normal Christian Birth*, I have argued that when Jesus spoke of being born again "out of water and Spirit" he is referring to water baptism and Spirit baptism and the two are essential to the new birth. Don't spiritualise that away.

We will look at John 7 and the significance of what Jesus said on the last day of the Feast of Tabernacles: "If any of you is thirsty, come to me, I'll give you a drink. I'll fill your belly with living water, like springs."

Chapters 14–16, as we will see, come to a climax. In John's Gospel, almost every mention of the Spirit is about the Spirit being passed on to others through Jesus, whereas the synoptic Gospels are about the Spirit being poured into Jesus. But John says he looks forward to the day: "This he said about the Spirit who was to be given to those who had believed on his name...." In John 14–16, on the last night before he died, extraordinary: they should have been comforting Jesus but he had to comfort them, "Let not your hearts be troubled." They somehow knew they were going to lose him, and he was telling them that they wouldn't lose him; he was going to send the Spirit to take his place, and they would be better off with the Spirit. That is amazing. We shall see why it is the case.

Then we will look at John 20. I don't believe the disciples received the Holy Spirit on Easter Sunday in the Upper Room. I believe that was typical of Jesus, the good teacher, to give them a rehearsal. Just as, for example, in that same Upper Room he had taken bread and wine even before his body was broken and that blood shed, but he prepared them for later. I believe Easter Sunday evening was a dummy run for Pentecost, and I have given many reasons for that interpretation. There is no record of anything happening. It says he blew on them (*ruach*) and then *after* doing that he told them to receive the Holy Spirit so he would have done it the other way around if it was actually happening – but poor Thomas wasn't even there. Whenever later they talked about receiving the Spirit they never talked about Easter Sunday evening, they talked about Pentecost. What he did then was to give them a sign and a command. The sign: he blew on them. The command: "You receive." It is in the imperative: "Receive the Holy Spirit." So just a few weeks later when they are in the temple and they hear, "He's blowing on us, let's receive." I believe that's what that is, and I think we must avoid this "dual reception of the Spirit" doctrine which is usually built on this verse. In the New Testament people only receive the Spirit once: for salvation, for service, for everything else. There are not two receptions: one for salvation, one for service. There is one reception of the Spirit, in fullness, for every believer – this is their heritage.

As far as the Spirit is concerned, John provides the link between the Synoptics and Acts. The Synoptics show that the Spirit is in Jesus. In John we are shown this: the Spirit is going to be in *you* too. In Acts: he is *in us*. Do you see the progress? How could Jesus, in the time of his resurrection appearances, promise to be with them always when he was sending them to the ends of the earth? At first that looks like a complete contradiction. Jesus in his risen body could only be in one place at a time. A body ties you to one place. He could be in Jerusalem, Emmaus or Galilee, but he couldn't be in all three at once, and here he is, promising to send them to the ends of the earth, and promising to be with them always. He could be with them while he was still in the upper room. Now, no sooner did they know he was there and he was gone again. They must have begun to ask, "Where does he go when we can't see him?"

The disciples began to realise that he never really does leave us. All this was preparation for his Spirit coming to be with them always. Weaning them off relying on their senses for his presence until they had learned the lesson, and he would go back to his Father, and the last time he didn't disappear, he just travelled. He went, and now they went back to Jerusalem with joy. Why were they so happy? Because he had told them: just a few days, and you'll have me closer than I've ever been to you before.

So we come to Pentecost and we come to the book of Acts now, and the very centre of controversy about the Holy Spirit. The question is: how far is the book of Acts a model for us, or a unique period of history which we must not expect to happen again? There are many who dismiss Acts as narrative and so not belonging to what they call the didactic part of Scripture, therefore telling us that we must not build doctrine on Acts.

Actually, I know of no-one who makes the whole of Acts a model for today. For example, is there anyone who would say that a person hasn't been baptised in the Spirit if a tongue of fire did not sit on their head? Is there anybody who would say that a prayer meeting is not successful unless there has been an earthquake that shook the building? All of us draw a line somewhere, and the question is where – and we must draw it biblically and accurately.

It is particularly the case with the day of Pentecost. First, do note that Acts is thoroughly Trinitarian. The three subjects of the book of Acts are the kingdom of God, the name of Jesus, and the power of the Spirit, and they are in amazing balance. In the first thirteen chapters alone, how often do you think the Spirit is mentioned? The answer is about forty times. How often is the name of Jesus mentioned? About forty times. How often is God the Father mentioned? One hundred times. I call this book "The Acts of God through Jesus Christ by the Holy Spirit in the apostles and the church." It is a tragedy that we have overlooked the fact that God himself is at the heart of what happens in it. His word appears so often we take it for granted.

Imagine a New Testament without the book of Acts (as some would like us to treat it). We would be lost. Who is this fellow Paul who writes all these letters? We wouldn't know. Above all, you wouldn't know what baptism in the Spirit is. It is mentioned in the epistles and the Gospels – what is it? Which leads us then to this question: is Pentecost unique, unusual or universal? I am afraid that divides the church right down into three parts all over the world. I think it is very important that we face this difficulty and come up with an honest biblical answer.

On the whole, catholics and liberals ("catholic" covering more than Roman Catholic here) say that Pentecost was unique, a one-off, meaning Whitsunday is simply an anniversary, a remembrance of something that happened years ago, and in much the same way as the Jews remember the crossing of the Red Sea – that's all. A majority of the churches in the world do just that. Pentecost is something that happened long enough ago to be safe.

The next position is the evangelical position that Pentecost did happen again, but that it was unusual. I want to deal very carefully and firmly with this view. It is that there were in fact three repetitions of Pentecost, namely in Samaria, the household of Cornelius, and at Ephesus. Traditionally, evangelical teaching is that there were four occasions when the Spirit came in a manifest way and that they corresponded to the various ethnic groups that God wanted to reach. Acts 2 is seen as the Pentecost of the Jews, Acts 8 as the Pentecost of the Samaritans, Acts 10 the Pentecost of the Gentiles, Acts 19 the Pentecost of John's disciples. That one doesn't quite fit the series, does it? But then it is a temporary thing because John's disciples have died out anyway, so forget that. So we have three "Pentecosts" – Acts 2, 8, and 10 – and these were not to be expected again.

Then there is the view that what happened on those four occasions was not abnormal but normal. The only abnormal feature on the later occasions was the speed with which it happened, not what happened – that in the Samaritan case they got the Spirit slower than anyone else, and in Cornelius's case he got it quicker than anybody else, before he even could be counselled. They were only abnormal situations, not in what happened but in the timing. The heart of all these occasions is that on all four of them the Holy Spirit was received in a definite manifest, audible, visible way, and even Simon the sorcerer saw something happen. Is that normal or is it unusual? I was convinced from scripture, not from experience, that in fact the third position is the biblical one – that to receive the Holy Spirit in a manifest manner is normal for every believer, and not a few special occasions.

First, take the Samaritan occasion when Peter and John came down. Those Samaritans had repented of their sins, believed in the Lord Jesus, had been baptised in water in the name of Jesus, and: "They were full of joy." I don't know an evangelist today who wouldn't say they had received the Spirit, but in those days it was said that they hadn't. Now here is the question which I have never found asked or even answered in any commentary on Acts, and the question is crucial to me: how did anyone know they had not received the Holy Spirit? Try and answer that question in your mind. They repented, believed, had been baptised, and were filled with joy. How did anyone know they hadn't received the Spirit? Yet everyone knew they hadn't! There is only one possible answer: that up to that point everybody else had received the Holy Spirit in a Pentecostal way. Do you follow me in that? It is an extremely important point. It is the only way they could have known these people hadn't received if everybody else had received in an outward manifest manner. The second question is: how does anybody know the Samaritans *did* receive?

Come now to Cornelius, and this to me was the clincher that really settled it. When Peter was preaching, and suddenly the Holy Spirit fell on the household, do you know what Peter said? "How can we forbid water since they have received the Holy Spirit just as we did?" Who is "we"? Who is he talking to? He's not talking to the 120 on the day of Pentecost, he is talking to the brothers from Joppa he brought with him, and he appeals to their *experience*. There is nothing abnormal about Cornelius. "How can we refuse water when they received just as we did?"

Then when Peter got back to Jerusalem and they said, "We hear you've gone into a Gentile house and you have been baptising people." Do you know what he said and he didn't say it to the 120 but to the whole church in Jerusalem, which now numbered thousands: "How could I refuse since they received the Spirit exactly the way we did?"

Now put all this together, and receiving the Spirit in the book of Acts in a manifest audible, visible way is normal for every believer. The Samaritans were only abnormal because they didn't get that straightaway; Cornelius is only abnormal because he got it quickly, but what they got was normal, everyday experience. Again, that is an extremely important point. While I do not expect flames of fire or a rushing, mighty wind, I always expect the Spirit to be received in a manifest way. When the Lord Jesus baptises in the Spirit not only does the person know it but everybody else knows it who is present at the time. I believe we must preach that often. When we preach with confidence, people's faith rises, but if we preach anything hesitantly, saying, "Well some believe this and some believe that, and my opinion is this ... I'm still thinking it through, but never mind", nobody's faith will rise. They might be interested and want to discuss with you after the service, but nobody reaches out. Imagine if you preached forgiveness of sins in the same way – if you said, "You know there's a bit of an argument about forgiveness of sins ... some think you really get it and some are not sure you get it straight away, but anyway try it out and see what happens." No, the kind of preaching that arouses faith is: "Jesus can forgive your sins. He requires that you repent, but repentance means forgiveness; you can be forgiven, just reach out and get it." In the same way, I believe we should be saying: "Jesus baptises in the Holy Spirit. He wants to pour his Spirit in you. He wants you to receive and know you received, because that is the ground of assurance."

We can divide the work of the Spirit in the epistles into two parts: first his work in the individual believer and, secondly, his work in the church. All the epistles are addressed to believers, and that is why none of them tells you how to become a Christian – because they are all addressed to people who have received the Spirit, have been baptised in water, have repented and have believed, so we must not look in the epistles for evangelism.

Acts is the book of evangelism and it is written on location. It is the only book in the New Testament about evangelism. So when we do come to the epistles I find that there are the four fundamentals: repent to God for your sins; believe in the Lord Jesus; be baptised in water, and receive the Holy Spirit. I don't believe someone is born again until we have led them through those four steps and that is my burden in my book *The Normal Christian Birth*. We have cut them right down to one and a half in the average evangelistic technique, and we need to tell them all four and get them started on repentance above all. To take people through those "four spiritual doors" (as I call them) is essential to the new birth.

We are producing a lot of badly birthed Christians. Many Christians have come to me with a problem, and when I talk to them I say: "Don't talk about the problem, talk about your birth, tell me about your conversion." I listen carefully to see if these four things were properly done. You see, an evangelist is a midwife, and a midwife has to do certain things for the baby to make sure it is going to be healthy and strong. You need to bath the baby, you need to cut the umbilical cord and tie it off. That is repentance, incidentally. I asked our local midwife to give me the things you needed to do for a baby, and she wrote about five typewritten sheets. I thought it was simple, I thought they just popped out, but the number of things that have to be done – and every one of them seemed to have a spiritual equivalent so it was very interesting. Most midwives lay on hands to get them to breathe in and cry out. They believe in the laying on of hands, only with a definite end in view of course!

The work of the Spirit in the individual begins when he convicts someone of sin and righteousness and judgment. I find that repentance begins when someone realises that God is a good deal better than they thought he was and they are a good deal worse than they thought they were, because normal unbelievers think God is bad and they are good. "Why did God do that? I wouldn't have done that if I were God." But repentance begins when you realise how good God is and how bad you are. It really begins with a change of mind, and that is the work of the Holy Spirit. Being born again out of water and Spirit – that is the work of the Holy Spirit.

Assurance, in my New Testament, is based not on scripture but on the Spirit. I want to underline that. There is an evangelical doctrine of assurance that is simply a syllogism from – or deduction from – scripture; "The Bible says it, I believe it, that settles it" – that kind of argument. You convince yourself on the basis of scripture that you are a child of God, but in fact in the scripture itself the basis of assurance is: "I have received the Holy Spirit. I know I belong to God because he has given me his Spirit." The doctrine of assurance is Spirit-based in my New Testament, he is the confirmer. If you have led someone through repentance, faith, and water baptism you still cannot be sure that God has accepted them, but when they receive the Holy Spirit you are 100% sure that God has accepted them. It is the proof; it is the most important part of leading someone to Christ – that they receive the Holy Spirit. But what we have done is to talk about "receiving" Jesus. Have you noticed how we have done that? "Receive him as your

Lord; receive him into your heart; receive him as Saviour". But the apostles did not use such language, and they certainly didn't use the modern euphemisms: "Give your heart to Jesus" and "Hand your life over to Jesus." You never find that kind of talk. What do you find? "Repent each one of you, be baptised for the forgiveness of your sins, and you will receive..." Receive who? The Spirit.

The word "receive" is only applied to Jesus in the Gospels when he was on earth in the flesh, but from the day the heavens received him out of sight the verb "receive" is consistently transferred to the third person. Jesus is at the right hand of the Father, but you can receive the Spirit, the one who has taken his place on earth.

That is what we should do, and then our converts will be Trinitarian from the beginning. They will have repented toward God, believed in Jesus, and received the Spirit. When will we get back to that? It was seventeen years before I got through those four simple steps: repent, believe, be baptised, and receive the Spirit. I am not going to let any convert of mine wait seventeen years when they can have the whole "Peter package" (which is what I call Acts 2:39) immediately. From then on, the Spirit begins a work of salvation.

I want to state something now that is a little controversial, but search the scriptures: *salvation is a process and it is not over in one day*. "We had seven people saved last Sunday night." No you didn't, you had seven people who *began* to be saved. Salvation is a process. I don't use the word "salvation" much these days, I prefer the word "recycling". It is a perfect equivalent. When people ask me, "What job are you in?" I say, "I'm in recycling." "Bottles, papers, tin cans?" "No, people!" God's in the recycling business and recycling is to save people from the rubbish dump called Gehenna, and to recycle them until they are useful to God again, and perfectly restored in the original image, and it

Acts 2:39

takes time. Salvation is a process, recycling is a process, and God is recycling men and women now before he recycles the entire planet Earth. A Christian is concerned about ecology, but he doesn't panic, and he certainly doesn't worship this weird lady called "Mother Nature". We believe there is going to be a new earth. We are the only ones who know this but it is great news. God is going to recycle this planet and he is recycling people to inhabit it. Salvation is not being saved but being salvaged. That was the word in World War II – "salvage" – but now we say "recycle". Our business is to get people recycled and it begins when they receive the Spirit, and the Spirit will go on reproducing in them the character of Christ. We call it the fruit of the Spirit, and there is only one such fruit and it has nine flavours. Don't talk about the fruits but the fruit because they are not plural. The proof is this: unbelievers can demonstrate two or three, even four of those nine flavours without the Spirit, but when the fruit of the Spirit appears in a person's life, all nine flavours appear together. You cannot have one without the other eight, and it takes time to grow, and as we walk in the Spirit the fruit grows. There is a fruit of which you take a bite and it tastes like an orange, take another bite and it tastes like a lemon – it has different flavours in the one fruit. The fruit of the Spirit is like that — in a Christian you taste patience, you taste peace and joy. This is the character of Christ, and it only grows in that nine-fold flavour in those who are walking in the Spirit.

Love
joy
Peace
Patience
Kindness
Goodness
Gentleness
Faithfulness
Self Control

There is still a future salvation, which I haven't got yet and I am looking for it. There is a salvation ready to be revealed in the last time. Christ is coming a second time to bring salvation to those who are waiting for it. He is going to bring salvation to the believer one day, and the completion of the recycling process.

That is what salvation is, not just getting someone across the line or getting a decision, it is getting them totally recycled. God does it, and all that is the work of the Spirit.

There is the individual work whereby the Holy Spirit convicts us, converts us, conforms us to Christ, but the major emphasis in the New Testament is on the community of the Spirit, so we should be aware that reception of the Holy Spirit is the *basis of membership* in the early church. We have made professions of faith and all kinds of other things the basis of membership, but the church is the temple of God and the body of Christ and the fellowship of the Spirit, and until a person has a Trinitarian relationship with the godhead I don't believe they qualify for church membership. The crucial thing that qualified a person to be a member of the body of Christ was baptism in the Spirit, reception of the Spirit, filling of the Spirit, which is all the same thing in the New Testament. In other words, when somebody received the Holy Spirit they couldn't refuse to recognise they were part of the church, but until they did they were troubled.

One of the things my wife told me she missed most when I ceased to be a pastor in a local church was the church members' business meetings. Those were the times when the Holy Spirit told us wonderful things, gave us his direction. Unless your members have received the Spirit, your church meeting is a disaster. It turns into a democracy, and if you bring people into membership who have not received the Spirit then you are bound to have a problem. I believe in open government. I think it is wonderful when shepherds and sheep can share together and shepherds can hear the bleating of the sheep – that is important – but if your members have not received the Spirit then you are opening the door to all kinds of abuse.

Not only should the Holy Spirit be the *basis of church membership*, he is the *source of ministry*. You cannot make anybody a minister, only the Spirit can do that. This means that every member will be a minister. We really have got

democracy

80

rid of the concept of "going into the ministry". The whole division between clerical and lay has limited the work of the Spirit and limited the ministry. In the New Testament church Paul could say freely: "You have each received a gift." This does not mean that someone can do everything. That is the old style of ministry in which you hired a man to do everything. Nor does it mean that anyone can do anything but it means that everyone can do something. The Spirit orders the church so that everyone can do something, and the Spirit wants everybody in the ministry.

There are too many who want to set the gifts and the fruit in opposition and say, "I'd rather have a church with fruit than gifts." So would I, frankly, it's much easier. But the fruit without the gifts are ineffective, as the gifts without the fruit are dangerous. Suppose you go to visit a sick person in the hospital and you demonstrate the fruit of the Spirit to them. You show them love by visiting them in the hospital. You show them joy by cheering them up. You show them peace by calming them down. You show them patience by listening to all the details of their surgery. You show them kindness by giving them a bunch of grapes. You show them faithfulness by visiting them every day. You show them meekness by leaving when the nurse says "Visiting hours are over." You show self-control by not eating the grapes. You have demonstrated the fruit of the Spirit and you have left them sick, because healing is a gift. We need both, and the Holy Spirit wants to grow the fruit in every individual believer and to spread the gifts among all the believers.

Let us now return to the communal aspect of the Holy Spirit, which is the primary thrust in the New Testament—the Spirit inhabits the body of Christ. There are four aspects of the work of the Spirit in the church, and we have begun to think about two of them. The Spirit is the basis of church membership from Acts 2:38 onwards; it is the community of those who have received the Spirit and therefore constitute the *koinonia*, the fellowship of the Spirit. Koinonia means to have something totally in common. The Spirit who is in you is not different from the Spirit in me and that is why when a person is lost to the body, the body is dismembered. Even if you are just a little finger in the body, the body is incomplete without you.

Secondly, we saw that the Holy Spirit is the source of ministry, and he gives different gifts precisely because he wants everybody in the ministry within the body. He gives a gift to each and to all. That was true in the early church. He has given to each one a gift for the rest, for the purpose of edification, to build one another up.

Thirdly, the Holy Spirit in the New Testament church is the model of management. Have you ever noticed that the Holy Spirit is quite different from the Father and the Son? The Father and the Son both are Kings, but the Holy Spirit is never called "king". The Father and Son wear crowns; the Holy Spirit never does. The Father and Son are on thrones; the Holy Spirit never sits on a throne. The Father and Son are Lord, and with one possible exception the Holy Spirit is not called "Lord" in the New Testament. What I discovered when I looked at the verbs that correspond to all this, is that the verbs corresponding to Father and Son are verbs of total obedience and absolute submission. But the verbs used in relation to the Spirit are verbs of co-operation rather than submission. What do I take from that? Quite simply that the Spirit never seeks to bring people into submission to himself but he leads them and guides them to come into total submission to Father and Son. Check this from the Bible. The Holy Spirit wants us to obey Father and Son. He woos us.

There is a similar difference in worship. Worship is in the Spirit through the Son to the Father. Father and Son are directly addressed in worship in the New Testament, but never the Spirit. I find that interesting. It doesn't mean it is a sin to worship the Spirit; I am pointing to the New Testament picture.

Father and Son do not delegate their authority to us. The same verbs that are used of the Spirit are used of church leaders. Our task is not to bring people into submission to us but to bring them under the Father and the Son. The more we do that, the more independent of us the people will be, and the more dependent on the Lord.

Fourthly, the Spirit provides the power in mission. We are trying to communicate the gospel in a way the New Testament didn't. In "all that Jesus began to do and to teach" do you notice the order? In the New Testament they *demonstrated* before they *declared*. In fact, they communicated the gospel in three dimensions: word, deed, and sign. Or, if you like alliteration: words, works, and wonders. In Romans 15 Paul says, "You heard my message. You saw how I lived, and you witnessed signs and wonders all by the power of the Holy Spirit. Thus, I have fully communicated the gospel...." Of word, deed, and sign, do you notice that two of those dimensions are for the eye and one is for the ear? It was the method: let them see the gospel then let them hear it. But we have become so word orientated. When we think of evangelism, it is words all the time. Words preached, words printed, words recorded, words sung, words, words, words. We think if we have given them all the words, if we have pushed the words through their letterbox, we have somehow evangelised. However, the world is not waiting to *hear* the gospel they are waiting to *see* it. They have a right to see it and we have a responsibility to let them see it. Nietzsche (a philosopher behind Hitler) once said: "I would want to be saved if Christians looked more saved." He knew churchgoers and he could not see any difference between them and anyone else.

Think of Jesus sending out disciples two by two. I know they went out with no faith. Read between the lines of scripture. They were quite sure they could not do what Jesus had been doing. All they had to do was raise the dead, heal the sick and cast out demons. Then, when they had done all that, to tell people the kingdom is here.

The communication of the gospel is words, deeds, and signs. It does have to be words because without the words people won't understand what is happening, but we have to let them see it first. Whenever there is a contradiction between what we see and what we hear, we always give the benefit of the doubt to our eyes.

It is very important that we communicate the gospel in the New Testament way. 1 Thessalonians 1 also mentions word, deeds, and signs. Deeds are how we live and signs are the wonders God performs. You can pass on the words without the Holy Spirit. I have known unbelievers pass on the gospel words and people get converted, but you cannot do the deeds or the signs without the Holy Spirit.

Many years ago, my wife and I were with 1,500 young people in a camp called Canvas Camp, in New Zealand, over Christmas week. The temperature was eighty-five degrees. We were using a woolshed which was like a large hall and people were sitting on straw and hay bales, and there was a platform made of more hay bales. Of those attending, 500 were unconverted – gang kids from the streets of Auckland, mainly Maoris, covered with horrible tattoos. One had "Outlawed" tattooed on his throat. Another had, "H-a-t-e" on both hands so that when he came for you, you knew what he thought of you. They asked me to speak on the kingdom of God, morning and evening. Now that is my favourite subject (it was Jesus' favourite subject too.) On the Tuesday morning I jumped up on the platform for my talk and the Lord whispered, "David, you have told them but you haven't shown them." I said, "Where do we start, Lord?" He said, "Dandruff." Dandruff?

I said to the gathering: "I told you that Jesus is King of kings and Lord of lords and that every situation is under his control, and you are now going to see this because Jesus is King of dandruff." My wife was way back amongst the people, and we have been married long enough to read each other's faces. Her face said, "He's finally flipped; been expecting it for years and now it's happened!" She looked as if she wanted to get out of the meeting.

I said, "What next Lord?" He said, "Athletes foot." I said, "You're covering them top to bottom, Lord." I spoke out: "He's King of athletes foot." I said, "What next?" "Warts." There was a man sitting next to my wife, about fifty years of age, and his hands were covered with bumps, and it was like shaking hands with a peanut farmer! He was sitting next to a surgeon who had said to him three minutes earlier, "Look, come into my hospital next Thursday, I will give you a local anaesthetic and we'll have all those off."

Two days later I was sailing on the Pacific with the surgeon. He said, "David, why are you trying to humiliate me this week?" I said, "John, I wouldn't dream of it. What do you mean?" He said, "You've robbed me of two of my patients!" One was this guy with warts. They all dropped off and there were just little pink hollows where the new flesh was coming."

In the meeting, I had then thought, "Where is this going to stop?" I said, "Where next, Lord?" He said, "A withered hand." Now I know the level of my faith and I know where it begins to get a little tottery. I said, "There's somebody here: you can't use your right hand." It was a girl of about fifteen. She had always been like that. One hour later she wrote a letter to her parents: "Dear Mum and Dad, I'm writing this letter with my right hand."

It finally reached a climax with a boy called Andrew, who was sixteen. He had been in a car crash when he was two years old and had a paralysed left arm. Two months before the camp he had been trying to cut up a tree with a petrol-driven chainsaw held in one hand. He was kneeling on this tree and he took his knee right off. They rushed him to the hospital and managed to save his life with a blood transfusion. They joined the bones so he came to camp with a short leg, and his left arm on an aluminium crutch. But he was so lovely, full of fun; everybody loved Andrew. On a Thursday afternoon this boy ran from one end of the sports field to the other, with both arms and legs working! He came running back into the woolshed, jumped onto the platform, and danced before us all. I said, "Throw your crutch away." "No," he said, "I had better take it back to the hospital, it belongs to them."

But nobody was healed of dandruff and on the Friday morning I said to them, "Look, if the Lord has done anything for you this week, come and tell us please. It's good to testify, but I need my faith helped. Everything has happened except one thing, but I'm not going to tell you which it was."

Now a girl said, "Was it the dandruff?" I said, "Yes." She said, "Look, I used to have a snow storm on my shoulders." She showed me a lovely shiny head of hair.

As she was talking, an older young man with long red beard and thinning red hair came up. He said, "I don't believe it, I don't believe it." I said, "What don't you believe?" He said, "The dandruff bit." "Well," I said, "You couldn't have come at a better time. Here she is." "No," he said, "me – I have tried every shampoo, every medication. When I combed my hair this morning it was gone. So I went to the first aid tent and got the nurse to comb my hair and beard. She can't find any. I don't believe it!" I said, "Well don't. Just enjoy it, God bless you, go home."

Another night, the demons manifested. There were Maori boys down on their hands and knees barking like dogs and eating the hay like animals. Other youngsters were just gathering around and dealing with it in the name of Jesus. It was quite a week, but on the Friday morning I said, "Now you've heard about the kingdom, you've seen the kingdom, you know that Jesus is King. This afternoon I'm coming back to the woolshed at four o'clock and I'll tell you how to get into the kingdom if you want to get in. I don't care if just ten of you come back, if you mean business."

They came back, but this is how they came back. It was a beautiful hot and sunny day. Two miles away, at the Pacific Beach, they all went swimming, and fifteen lifeguards were along the beach. One lifeguard went to the second and said, "Could you watch my part of the beach? I want to go and hear David in the woolshed." The second one said, "But I want to go too." So they went to the third, he wanted to go. The fourth: he wanted to go. All fifteen lifeguards wanted to find out how to get into the kingdom, but they couldn't leave the beach. They were watching 1,500 young people. So they got together in a bunch and one of them said, "Let's try this prayer thing." He said, "God, if you are there, get us to David's meeting." They looked out to sea and there were three sharks coming into the bay. They shouted, "Sharks!" and I had 1,500 attenders. So I have found the secret. Just get three sharks to do it for you!

The serious side is that in a simple way we were communicating in word, deed, and sign. They heard the words and they saw the deeds because those lads were living in tents with Christians for a week. They saw how they lived and they witnessed signs and wonders. It was just a beautiful week. Actually, when they came I said, "Now there are four steps that you need to take and I'm going to help you to get started on the first step this afternoon. Today I am going to help you to repent." I didn't take them any further, but they repented. All over New Zealand, over the next five weeks as we travelled, we heard of them seeking baptism, repenting and going on.

You can't birth people in five minutes at the end of a meeting, but you can get them started, so that is what I do: tell them all four steps and say, "Let's get you started on the first." I find if you get them properly started on repentance they never look back. They will go for all the other three as soon as they can get them.

Finally, in this overview of what the New Testament tells us about the work of the Holy Spirit, we need to stress that the book of Revelation is very important.

Unfortunately, most Protestants who look back to the Reformation leave the book of Revelation alone. But try and imagine the New Testament without it. That would be rather like recording a play and finding out it was running late, and that you've lost the last five minutes of it – or getting into a detective novel and finding someone had torn out the last three pages. The New Testament without the book of Revelation would be lost because the whole is something akin to a romance. It finishes up with: they get married and live happily ever after. The Spirit and the Bride say, 'Come!' for the Bride has made herself ready for the wedding. The Father looking for a Bride for his Son.

There is a doctrine of the Spirit in the book of Revelation that is extremely important. Why do people say it is complicated? They think it was written for Bible scholars and theological students. It wasn't, it was written for very ordinary people. The people who can get the message of Revelation are ordinary people who take it at face value.

Chapters 1–3 are concerned with the present state of the church. Then you move into the future and you can divide the rest of Revelation into two simple sections: firstly,

① things will get much worse before they get better; secondly, ② things will get much better after they get worse. That is my summary of the book of Revelation, and it is an apocalyptic view of history.

There is a contrasting Greek view of history, the cyclic – that it goes around in circles, history repeating itself, and you finish up where you began. There is also the epic view of history – it just goes on, up and down, and up and down—cycles of history, empires rising and falling. Then there is the optimistic view of history, which was the main view that came in with the twentieth century, that we are on an escalator of progress that would take us into Utopia. Then there is the pessimistic view of history, with which we entered the twenty-first century. The keyword is not "progress" but "survival", and many believe that everything is going down and down.

One view of history is that everything is going down and will suddenly get better and stay that way. But the Spirit has prepared us for things getting worse, so I expect things to get worse before they get better. That saves me from false hopes and utopian dreams – and false hope makes the heart sick. I am afraid that some years ago many hopes were raised that the kingdom was around the corner, and there is a lot of disillusionment because of the false hopes that were raised. I believe things are going to get tougher for Christians. The book of Revelation is full of martyrs precisely because the Spirit saw a choice coming for believers – between life and death.

Finally, in this brief overview, we do need to be aware that there is a difference between being *filled* with the Spirit and *full* of the Spirit. All believers should be filled with the Spirit but some are full. When they looked for leadership in the early church they didn't look for those who had been filled but for those who were full. There is a sharp distinction in the

New Testament between those who have been filled, and may be filled and filled again, and those who are consistently full.

"Full" not only means fruit in the Bible, it means gifts and fruit. Read Acts 6, where they chose Stephen because he was full of the Holy Spirit, and you find he was full of grace and power.

The ideal maturity for the Christian life is not just to be full of grace but to be full of grace and power. You can be filled and then you have power, but to be full means to be full of grace and power—the fruit and the gifts in perfect combination.

Grace and Power

Chapter Four

THE HOLY SPIRIT IN MATTHEW, MARK AND LUKE

Jesus, full of the Holy Spirit, left the Jordan and was led by the Spirit into the wilderness, where for forty days he was tempted by the devil. He ate nothing during those days, and at the end of them he was hungry.

The devil said to him, 'If you are the Son of God, tell this stone to become bread.'

Jesus answered, 'It is written: "Man shall not live on bread alone."'

The devil led him up to a high place and showed him in an instant all the kingdoms of the world. And he said to him, 'I will give you all their authority and splendour; it has been given to me, and I can give it to anyone I want to. If you worship me, it will all be yours.'

Jesus answered, 'It is written: "Worship the Lord your God and serve him only."'

The devil led him to Jerusalem and had him stand on the highest point of the temple. 'If you are the Son of God,' he said, 'throw yourself down from here. For it is written:

"'He will command his angels concerning you
         to guard you carefully;
      they will lift you up in their hands,
   so that you will not strike your foot against a stone."'

Jesus answered, 'It is said: "Do not put the Lord your God to the test."'

When the devil had finished all this tempting, he left him until an opportune time.

Jesus returned to Galilee in the power of the Spirit, and news about him spread through the whole countryside. He was teaching in their synagogues, and everyone praised him.

He went to Nazareth, where he had been brought up, and on the Sabbath day he went into the synagogue, as was his custom. He stood up to read, and the scroll of the prophet Isaiah was handed to him. Unrolling it, he found the place where it is written:

'The Spirit of the Lord is on me,
because he has anointed me
to proclaim good news to the poor.
He has sent me to proclaim freedom for the prisoners
and recovery of sight for the blind,
to set the oppressed free,
to proclaim the year of the Lord's favour.'

Then he rolled up the scroll, gave it back to the attendant and sat down. The eyes of everyone in the synagogue were fastened on him. He began by saying to them, 'Today this scripture is fulfilled in your hearing.'

Luke 4:1–20, NIV

From my experience, one of the reasons why people become unbalanced in one way or another when thinking of the Holy Spirit is precisely because they will not take the whole Bible. They concentrate on certain parts of it and therefore get out of balance. The whole Bible, and nothing but the Bible, must be our basis.

Between the end of the Old Testament and the beginning of the New Testament there is a gap of four hundred years. That is not because there were no records and no writings then. There are books called the Apocrypha. This is still one of the major points of difference between Roman Catholics and Protestants. Protestants say those books should not be in the Bible because they are not God's word, whereas Catholics believe they are. Why are they not in the Bible? The answer is in a phrase that occurs 3,800 times in the Old Testament, but not once in the Apocrypha: "Thus says the Lord...." No word from God came in that period. There was no prophet in that time who could say, "This is what God says." So the Old Testament begins with the books of Moses, who was the first great prophet, and it ends with the book of Malachi who was the last prophet, and the Bible does not begin again until God speaks again. No matter how thrilling the stories of the Maccabees may be, no matter how many exciting things happened in those four hundred years, the fact is that where the Holy Spirit is not operating on human beings, in God's eyes there is nothing worth recording.

Does that mean that nobody thought about the Holy Spirit for four hundred years? No – they did. In the Old Testament there were two great promises: firstly, that one day there would come from God a king who would be filled with the Spirit and who would be able to do and say the things of God; secondly, when he came, all the people could be filled with the Spirit as well, and God's Spirit could be poured out upon all flesh, men and women, young and old. Those two dreams are all that I can tell you about work of the Holy Spirit between the Old and New Testaments. It must have seemed to those people that the dreams got further and further away. Nobody got filled with the Spirit, nobody spoke the word of God, and nobody performed miracles. The Spirit seemed to have gone, yet for four hundred years they waited for the Spirit to come and fill a king, a son of David, and for the Spirit to be poured out on all flesh. They never forgot those dreams. The Jews have remarkable memories. They have remembered their holy land over almost two thousand years of being out of it. They don't give up their hopes easily! The Jewish hopes for a land of their own have been fulfilled, and they didn't forget these two dreams about the Holy Spirit.

What does the Holy Spirit do in Matthew, Mark, and Luke? About the year 5 BC, the Holy Spirit began to touch people after that time of waiting. The Holy Spirit began again to fill some ordinary people and enable them to say and do supernatural things, first of all by touching an elderly couple and a young teenage couple. Now the elderly couple, a godly pair, were Zechariah and Elizabeth. The young people engaged to be married were Joseph and Mary. Both couples were childless—one because they were too old to have children and had had none, and the other because they weren't even married yet, but to both couples the Holy Spirit gave a son. In the one case a boy called John, in the other case a boy called Jesus. Humanly speaking, in neither case ought there to have been a baby at all, but the Holy Spirit was beginning again to work miracles. The younger couple lived in the north of the holy land, the elder couple lived towards the south. But they were related, so that in fact the boys were probably cousins. Let us look at these two couples and see what the Holy Spirit did to them according to the Gospels of Matthew, Mark, and Luke.

Zechariah had two dreams or ambitions, neither of which had hitherto been fulfilled, and it rather looked now as if neither ever would. The two ambitions were these: Zechariah was a priest and he was one of many thousands of priests who took their duties in the temple at Jerusalem. He lived just a few miles away down the valley but he would go up to Jerusalem, he commuted to the town and he worked in the temple as a priest. Once a year it was the great privilege of one priest to go into the holy place, all alone into the darkness, and burn the lamp of incense at the altar. It was quite obvious that, with thousands of priests, most of them would never get a chance to go in, so how did they do it? They used to cast lots. Every priest hoped that one day before he retired the lot would come to him, and that was Zechariah's first ambition.

The second ambition, which was that of every priest, was to have a son, because the priesthood was hereditary, so then he could pass on the privilege. But Zechariah's wife was long past the age of having children. He had given up hope of one of his dreams and he had been a priest for probably forty years and was near retirement and beginning to give up hope for the other ambition. But one day, when the priests gathered together to cast lots as to who should go into the holy place, the name of Zechariah came up. It must have been a most dramatic moment for this old man—alone with God in a place where God lived among his people, and there Zechariah burned the incense.

Now the staggering experience came to him that he had found he was not the only person inside there, even apart from God. As he looked he saw someone standing in the corner and as he looked more closely he realised that it was not a human being and it wasn't God. He realised it was one of God's supernatural spirits, an angel as they are called in the Bible. He must have been terrified. The angel told him that he was going to have a son and Zechariah, very humanly, asked how he could be sure.

He was thinking without the Holy Spirit, which is what someone is doing if they say something promised by God is impossible. Whenever a church meeting called of God to do something great begins to say, "Can't be done, it's impossible; it's beyond us" they are thinking without the Holy Spirit. The word "impossible" is not a word in God's vocabulary. Jeremiah asks: is anything too hard for the Lord? Jesus said, "all things are possible with God". So the angel told Zechariah he would be struck dumb for nine months for not believing. That proved to him and to others that God was doing something in his life.

The poor chap when he got outside couldn't even tell his wife what had happened but they came together physically as old people, and she conceived and told her husband she was going to have a child. She still didn't know it was going to be a boy. That secret was locked up within Zechariah unless he wrote it down for her. Then came the great day when the boy was born, and when it came time to name the baby, Zechariah wrote down the name John, the name that God had chosen, and immediately his tongue was loosed and he began to praise God. Have you noticed how when people are filled with the Spirit then usually words come from the mouth? Zechariah, it says, was filled with the Spirit and began to speak, and he began to speak words that have been said or sung by Christians down the centuries. Blessed be the Lord God of Israel for he has visited and redeemed his people....

Certain things were said about the boy to Zechariah, which we need to notice. There are some strange contrasts between John and Jesus. Jesus was called a winebibber by his enemies. He was not teetotal. But it is said of John that from his birth he would not touch wine or strong drink. We also learn that he would be the first person in the whole of history to be filled with the Holy Spirit from his mother's womb. Samson had been a grown man when the Spirit filled him, Moses was a grown man when the Spirit filled him, and if you go through the Old Testament, people were adults before they were filled with the Spirit throughout that era.

But one of the most remarkable things about John the Baptist is this: from the moment of his conception he could do extraordinary things and say extraordinary things, and so that people would never get the idea that it was other kinds of spirits that were doing it, John had to keep right off alcoholic drink, so it was utterly clear that the strange things he would do would be of God. That boy grew up in a most unusual way. He was different from anybody else. He spent most of his time out in the desert alone. That was his school, where God taught him. I don't even know if he went to any other school, probably not, but he lived alone out there. At about the age of thirty he began to preach, and he wore the same clothes that Elijah, one of the greatest prophets of the Old Testament, had worn. Elijah had been second only to Moses in the lists of the prophets. Everybody said, "Moses was the greatest prophet, Elijah was the next." John also lived on exactly the same food as Elijah had eaten. Jesus was to be the prophet like Moses, but John the Baptist was to be like Elijah and even that was said by the angel to Zechariah. So John began to preach, and word spread that there was a prophet in Israel again. The people had waited for God to speak, and now he was speaking again. They began to flock out to hear the prophet. This generation had never heard a prophet, though they had read about prophets and they had been told about their great, great, great, great grandfathers having heard a prophet. The people now hearing John had only heard scribes expounding the scriptures, not the prophets who just spoke the word of the Lord direct.

John did not perform any miracles for them. The extraordinary thing about John was that his supernatural power was in what he *said* not what he did. The only unusual thing he did was to baptise people by immersing them in water, which got him the nickname, "John the Baptiser" or "John the Plunger" or "John the Dipper" – that is what it means and he was nicknamed John the Baptist. One day, in the crowd that came to hear him, there came the other boy, now himself a grown man, and the Holy Spirit began to do something even more extraordinary.

Let us go back to the other young couple, Joseph and Mary, and see what the Holy Spirit had done with them. Here were a couple of betrothed teenagers. Girls were betrothed at fifteen years of age. A boy became a man at twelve, and assumed full adult responsibility and married around sixteen, so pictures of Joseph and Mary as middle-aged people are wide of the mark. Imagine a sixteen-year-old boy and a fifteen-year-old girl and you are closer. These two teenagers are very happy. They are engaged to be married, which is a very serious thing. Engagement in those days was much more than going out together or dating. It meant that the girl took the man's name, and if he died before they were married she was regarded as a widow. They were betrothed but the marriage had not been consummated. That must wait some months even some years, until the official marriage ceremony. One day this fifteen-year-old girl is pottering around the house, perhaps at her prayers. She saw somebody in the room who was not human and not God. She realised that one of God's messengers was going to say something to her, and it was the most extraordinary thing. She would conceive and have a son. She was still a virgin so she asked how that could be. The reply of the angel was that the Holy Spirit was going to come upon her – the power of the Highest would overshadow her.

Some time ago there was an examination of some claims to virgin births. It was reported that about seven claims of women to have had babies without knowing men had been examined. All but two of the claims were rejected. But doctors and scientists were prepared to say that in these two cases it had probably happened, and that the female ovum or egg within the womb had spontaneously begun to divide and had formed a baby. This is a physical possibility. There are other species in which virgin births happen more frequently—the sea urchin is one of them, where the egg can begin to multiply, divide and form a body. But here is the most critical and important thing: we are dealing with

THE HOLY SPIRIT IN MATTHEW, MARK AND LUKE

something that is physically impossible because the angel said Mary was going to have a boy, and a natural virgin birth, even if it does take place, cannot possibly produce a male. So we are dealing with the miraculous here. Mary was so thrilled because six months previously she had heard about Elizabeth, an elderly relative who was also expecting a baby. They had thought then that something wonderful was beginning to happen, so she made the journey to visit Elizabeth who was already six months through her pregnancy. Mary came into the house and Elizabeth's baby leapt in her womb. Elizabeth was filled with the Spirit and she prophesied. She spoke like this: "Blessed are you among women and blessed is the fruit of your womb. Why is this granted me that the mother of my Lord should come to me? For behold when the voice of your greeting came to my ears the babe in my womb leaped for joy and blessed is she who believed that there would be a fulfilment of what was spoken to her from the Lord."

Prophecy again – here was a woman prophesying and, as soon as she had finished, Mary was filled with the Holy Spirit and she prophesied and said, "My soul magnifies the Lord...."

Ever since then the "Magnificat" has been sung by Christians. Now you can see what is happening. Over these few years around the birth of these two boys, ordinary men and women were prophesying, being filled with the Spirit, opening their mouths and speaking extraordinary words, which are so much the word of God that we have treated them so ever since.

The boy Jesus was born and we know nothing about him for thirty years except for one little glimpse when the curtain is pulled back and we see a boy who knows already that his father was not Joseph but God. For a long time it puzzled me: why did God not tell us anything about Jesus for thirty out of his thirty-three years? Why is there nothing in the

99

Bible about his childhood? Why is there nothing about how he was related to the people of Nazareth as a carpenter in the village? The answer is very simple: for thirty years the Holy Spirit was not operating through him. Four hundred years are omitted from the history of Israel and thirty years from the record concerning Jesus. Now that may be a staggering thought to you when I present it as bluntly as that, but let me tell you what I mean. Jesus developed physically—he grew in stature. He developed mentally—he grew in wisdom. Socially – he was in favour with others. Spiritually – he was in favour with God. He had a very good development physically, mentally, socially, spiritually. It is a parent's desire that their offspring should do the same.

No doubt Jesus was above average, in that the teachers in the temple noticed that his questions were very astute for his age. But the point was this: the people of Nazareth saw nothing in this boy to make them think he was more than an unusual boy. They saw no miracles; they heard no sermons. He neither gave them the Word of God nor the deeds of God. He was a boy developing into a man and working, and that was all they saw during the thirty years. If you had lived at Nazareth during that time you would not have come to the conclusion that the Son of God was living down your street. You would have said, "Have you noticed Joseph's boy? He is a nice lad, well balanced, I like him."

For those thirty years God tells us nothing about his Son because there is nothing to tell except for that one glimpse, which shows that already he knew he was God's Son—that's all. Even that is a private thing between himself and his parents – there is nothing you need to know, and even if you did know all the details it would purely be of human interest. It would not help you in any way to be a better Christian. Unlike his cousin John we are not told that he was filled with the Spirit from his birth.

We come to the point when the curtain is lifted completely and we are asked to look in detail at his life. It occurs when at the age of thirty (notice his age), knowing what he was doing, he left the carpentry shop for the last time in Nazareth, left his brothers, and walked seventy miles to the Jordan river, the lowest point on the earth's surface. There he came to his cousin John and asked to be baptised. John knew that Jesus was not a sinner and did not need to have sins washed away. He wanted to be baptised by Jesus. But Jesus insisted on being baptised. God had told him to do this. So John baptised him. Then something most unusual happened. After he was baptised, Jesus stood up and prayed and, as he did so, John saw something in the sky high up, something white and fluttering, and it came lower and lower and it came right down and landed right on Jesus' head. He thought it was a bird at first but as he looked closely, he realised it was only something like a bird. It was heavenly – no earthly bird is like that.

John knew, because God had told him, that one day he would baptise a man and would then see the Holy Spirit come and anoint that man. That would be the one for whom the people had waited for a thousand years. They had longed for a Spirit-filled prince. John saw this happen, and Jesus was anointed with power that day. It was only because of this that he was able to do miracles afterwards. When Jesus, the Son of God, was born he was as dependent as we are on the power of the Holy Spirit to do anything – to preach the word of God, to perform the deeds of God – and he couldn't have done it before then.

We know that immediately after his baptism he was tempted by the devil. Do you notice that, being full of the Holy Spirit, he was *led by the Spirit* into the desert to be tempted? Do you notice that when he had won the battle he *came in the power of the Spirit* to Galilee? You keep finding

101

this: "Jesus, full of the Holy Spirit..."; "Jesus, led by the Spirit..."; "Jesus, in the power of the Spirit...."

This is language that has not been used of him before his baptism because it was not true of him before his baptism. Here was the issue in the wilderness: was Jesus as a human being to be controlled by the devil (Satan) or the Holy Spirit?

Satan was trying desperately to say try my way: turn these stones into bread; jump off the pinnacle of the temple. The battle was on. Jesus, a real human being, was at a fork in the road and he could either let the devil control him or the Holy Spirit. He was now going to be controlled by one or the other. There comes a point in a person's life when he reaches the fork in the road and he is either going to be controlled by the devil or by the Holy Spirit. Which is he going to be controlled by? Whose way is he going to go? That is the meaning of the temptations.

It was only now that Jesus began to do his miracles. He began to raise the dead. He began to heal the sick. He began to cause the deaf to hear and the blind to see and the dumb to speak. People had never heard a man speak like this or do things like this. Jesus said, "But if I cast out demons by the finger of God, then the kingdom of God has come upon you."

I can think of no more severe test of a man's ministry than to go back and preach to those who had known him before. Jesus came back to Nazareth, to his own people who would have known him as the carpenter, and now they had heard of these extraordinary miracles. Why didn't they believe?

Now he stood up in the synagogue. I don't know whether the Holy Spirit guided someone to pick the right scroll but they gave him Isaiah, he opened it and read out: "The Spirit of the Lord is upon me to preach good news to the poor ... recovery of sight to the blind...." What is he saying? This is showing what is now different, explaining why he didn't perform a single miracle in Nazareth while he lived there, and why he was now able to do what he was doing, including giving sight to the blind. Jesus was letting people know that he had been anointed with the Holy Spirit and power. Before this he had made chairs and tables, now he could touch bodies and mend them. "The Spirit of the Lord is upon me...." What a sermon!

He is claiming, incidentally, from the prophecy of Isaiah to be the Spirit-filled Prince who was to come. No wonder they tried to throw him off a cliff – a carpenter claiming this? They just couldn't take it and so they tried to kill him after his first sermon at home. His preaching revealed the same thing, that he was the fulfilment of prophecy. He taught them as nobody else in their synagogues ever did. They heard him gladly because he taught them not as a scribe but as somebody who had authority. Now what did they mean by this? That was not derogatory to the scribes. A scribe is someone who takes the Word of God that somebody else has spoken and explains it to people. I am a scribe. I am doing what the scribes did. I take the Word of God and explain it to people, but it is not the word that I spoke. It is the word that Isaiah or Matthew or Mark or Luke spoke. That is all the scribes could do, but Jesus taught them as one who spoke direct. He didn't just quote the Bible to them; he gave them new bits of the Bible.

When he preached the Sermon on the Mount he was not only preaching scripture he was giving more scripture. He has the authority of one who has the Word of God direct from God. The reason is that the Holy Spirit filled Jesus, and he can say: the Spirit of the Lord is upon me to preach good news to the poor, to proclaim the acceptable year of the Lord.... telling the people what God was saying *now*.

I must draw two extraordinary conclusions, which you may never have drawn before in your life. They are absolutely revolutionary in your thinking about the Christian life. Here is the first: *the power of Jesus, which he exercised during the three years we know about was not the power of the second person of the Trinity but the power of the third person of the Trinity.*

In simpler language, when the Son of God became a human being he was subject to the limitations of human strength. Therefore he was unable to perform miracles himself or to preach the direct revelation of God himself until he had been anointed by the Holy Spirit in power, and then as Peter said years later, having been anointed with power he went about doing good. "Doing good" here was an understatement. It was not about cutting someone's hedge or papering their room, but raising the lame and the dead, and it was because he had been anointed with power that he did it. He had the power as a human being, not because he was divine. That is the first revolutionary understanding that I come to when I look at the Holy Spirit in Matthew, Mark, and Luke.

The second even more revolutionary understanding is this: *if that is true and that the power Jesus had was not his own but the power of the Spirit, then any other human being could have the same power.* Now that is revolutionary, and one of the things that Jesus said which I find difficult to believe (and I have met hardly anyone yet who really believes it) is: "The works that I do shall you do also, and greater works than these shall you do." If you read where he said that, you find he is talking about the Holy Spirit coming to the disciples.

In other words, the power that Jesus had you could have. If his power was the power of the Spirit, and if his miracles were only performed because he was anointed by the Holy Spirit, and if we can also be anointed with the Holy Spirit, (all of which the Bible teaches us) then this can happen for us.

D L Moody, the great evangelist, realised this for the first time. He thought you would have to talk about the amazing things that Jesus did as something only he could do, but then he saw this and wrote in his diary: "What could God not do with a man if a man would submit himself wholly and entirely to the Spirit of God?" Then he wrote: "Why should I not be that man?" He began to pray and he began to ask that God would anoint him with the same power that Jesus had. One day, walking down a main street in an American town, Moody was anointed with power from on high and his ministry began that day. Moody became a household name on both sides of the Atlantic and indeed throughout the world.

There is another passage about the Holy Spirit in Matthew, Mark and Luke to which I have not yet referred. Jesus was talking about prayer. He gave the Lord's Prayer, then said that if you are really going to get anything in prayer you have got to go on asking until you get it. He told a story of a man knocking at the neighbour's door at midnight and saying, "I've got visitors, give me some bread", the person inside saying, "Too late I'm in bed." No, I'm going to go on knocking until you get up and give me that bread. The neighbour got the bread and Jesus said, "If you go on knocking, God will open. If you go on asking you'll receive." Then Jesus taught: don't be afraid of what God gives to you because earthly fathers don't give nasty, harmful things to their children. If a child asks for a bit of bread the father doesn't give a stone or a scorpion, and if your earthly fathers don't do that, what about your heavenly Father?

Then he said, "If you then, being evil, know how to give good gifts to your children, how much more will your heavenly Father give the Holy Spirit to those who go on asking him?" In that single sentence he was saying to us that you can have the anointing: you can do the things he does; you can go on with the ministry he has begun if you will go on asking until you get the power.

My Father Holy God

Lord
Jesus, I ask you
to fill me with Holy
Spirit, with power from
on High, Anoint me,
use me, give me energy,
I ask for self control
in eating, speaking;
and taking care of
my body — Give me
a love to do this for
my vessel — Your temple
In Jesus Glorious Holy
Name Amen

1-12-2022

Chapter Five

THE HOLY SPIRIT IN THE EARLY CHAPTERS OF JOHN

The further we go through the Bible, and the further you go in the Christian life, the more interested you become in the Holy Spirit. There is a kind of progression—before you are a Christian maybe you believed in God. Most people do, I meet very few real atheists. I meet a few more genuine agnostics, who say they don't know, but the majority of people in England believe in some sort of "god". But that doesn't help them, that doesn't save them, that doesn't make them Christians. Then there comes a day when you realise that God is more than one person, and that Jesus Christ his Son is also God as well as a great human being. You believe in him, and you become a Christian. Usually it takes some time after that before people are aware that God is three persons. They begin to get interested in the Holy Spirit too. Ideally this should happen as soon as they are Christians, but often it doesn't.

John Bunyan wrote one of the most forceful and most discerning sentences I have read: "Some think that the love of the Father and the blood of the Son will do, without the holiness of the Spirit of God, but they are deceived." In other words, a full, rounded experience of God will include the third person of the blessed Trinity, the Holy Spirit.

In this chapter we are going to look at four brief mentions of the Holy Spirit in the first half of John's Gospel. Every one of these is linked with water—the most ordinary thing. Water has two particular uses in our human life, and without it we would be in real problems. I had experience of being short of water in the Arabian Desert. You realise how vital it is to life to have water, and it is no accident that again and again the Bible links the Holy Spirit with water. There are two purposes for which I need water in my daily life: outside me I need it for washing, cleansing; inside me I need it for drinking and refreshing. These are the two aspects taken up by the Bible when it mentions water with a spiritual meaning.

The "outside" significance is more connected with baptism, which is total immersion in water as a means of cleansing, washing, getting rid of the dirt of the past. But the water inside, Jesus always describes in terms of the Holy Spirit. The one without the other is inadequate. You may have been baptised in water but that is only half of what you need. You also need to be full of living water inside, so that springs of living water are welling up to eternal life. We shall see this unfold as we go through John's Gospel.

Jesus came to the river Jordan to be baptised by his cousin John:

Then John gave this testimony: 'I saw the Spirit come down from heaven as a dove and remain on him. And I myself did not know him, but the one who sent me to baptise with water told me, "The man on whom you see the Spirit come down and remain is the one who will baptise with the Holy Spirit." I have seen and I testify that this is God's Chosen One.'

John 1:32–34, NIV

Here is a statement which you can criticise if you like: Jesus was and is a baptist, in the strict meaning of that term. That is not a cheap denominational plug because the word in the Bible does not mean a denominational label. The sooner it stops being used that way the happier I will be because it robs us of the real meaning of the word "baptist" just as the use of the word "brethren" as a denominational label robs us of the real meaning of that word.

Jesus was a baptist and so was John. That is where the word started, and it does not mean someone who has himself been baptised, because as far as we know John had never been baptised and that is why he said Jesus should be baptising him. We learn now in this first passage from this Gospel that Jesus is the baptiser, just as much as John was. Both of them were baptisers, but there is a profound difference between the baptisms they gave and it is described here in simple detail: John baptised in water, but Jesus is he who baptises in the Holy Spirit.

So they used different media in which to baptise people. John flooded you with water outside you, whereas Jesus floods you with living water inside you, but they are both soaking you in something else. This is the difference between a human baptism and a divine one, because one thing is quite clear: your preacher or pastor can baptise you in water but can never baptise you in the Holy Spirit. Only a divine person could ever do that for you.

So here, right at the beginning of John's Gospel, we have both these things clearly taught, clearly presented, and the interesting thing is that the early Christians taught that both were necessary. The one does not supersede the other, and for the entire history of the early church both baptisms were sought: baptism in water; baptism in the Holy Spirit. One was sought from another human being, the other was sought from a divine being, and both continued parallel so that when you study the letters that were written to the early church, you find that they are equally described as being *baptised* in water and *baptised* in the Holy Spirit. All the early Christians knew both, and realised that both were meant to continue together.

The important question arises: how do I seek this baptism

in the Holy Spirit? The answer lies in other passages in John's Gospel and we turn to the second passage for the first step towards being filled with the Holy Spirit:

> Now there was a Pharisee, a man named Nicodemus who was a member of the Jewish ruling council. He came to Jesus at night and said, 'Rabbi, we know that you are a teacher who has come from God. For no one could perform the signs you are doing if God were not with him.'
>
> Jesus replied, 'Very truly I tell you, no one can see the kingdom of God unless they are born again.'
>
> How can someone be born when they are old?' Nicodemus asked. 'Surely they cannot enter a second time into their mother's womb to be born!'
>
> Jesus answered, 'Very truly I tell you, no one can enter the kingdom of God unless they are born of water and the Spirit. Flesh gives birth to flesh, but the Spirit gives birth to spirit. You should not be surprised at my saying, "You must be born again." The wind blows wherever it pleases. You hear its sound, but you cannot tell where it comes from or where it is going. So it is with everyone born of the Spirit.'
>
> *John 3:1–8, NIV*

Step number one to being filled with the Spirit is to be born of the Spirit. You will never know what it is to be baptised in the Holy Spirit unless you have been born of the Holy Spirit. One of the categorical statements made by Jesus later in John's Gospel is this: the world cannot receive the Holy Spirit, *cannot—* that is categorical. Jesus was full of "cannots", and if you study all the "cannots" of Jesus you will discover some very profound spiritual truths. One is that the world cannot receive the Holy Spirit. If you are not a Christian you cannot have the Holy Spirit—full stop.

Secondly, we are told that unless you are born of the Spirit you cannot see the kingdom of God. You will never catch a glimpse of heaven. You will never see God's reign and power. You will never catch a hint of it. You are blind until you have been born of the Spirit.

When a baby is first conceived within its mother's womb, at first it cannot see the world in which it exists. It cannot touch the world outside the womb. When it has come out and been born, the baby can see, hear, touch and smell the wider world. Do you know there are people in your community today who are utterly blind and deaf to the kingdom of God? They can walk through the streets and they can see all sorts of interesting things, and they cannot see a thing that God is doing. They are spiritually blind and deaf. Until they are born again of the Spirit of God they will never begin to see and hear the things that God is doing in their town, even as the kingdom of God begins to break in.

Jesus was speaking to a man who was a preacher in Israel, in Jerusalem. Nicodemus was probably a theological lecturer as well as a teacher, and here is this man who should have been telling others the truth but he hasn't a clue himself. He is religious and theologically trained, he has got everything but one thing: he is spiritually blind and he cannot see the kingdom of God. Now he comes to Jesus by night. I don't know if that was because he was ashamed or afraid. He was the man in the dark in more senses than one.

Nicodemus had realised that he taught and nothing happened, but Jesus taught and signs from God came. How come? Here is a man who knows that theology is meant to work. Here is a man who knows the truth is meant to set people free, and nothing happens. "You're a teacher from God," he says. Where does he think he was a teacher from?

The difference between being a teacher in Israel and a teacher from God is that a teacher from God sees things happen. Jesus was showing Nicodemus what was wrong: let us go right back to the beginning; until you are born again you can't know this power; you can't see signs in your own ministry until you have got power, and it starts by being born of the Spirit.

Nicodemus was not trying to be awkward. I don't even think he was being just literal, but wondered how at his stage he could go back and start all over again. How can you begin life again?

Jesus was teaching Nicodemus that the power of the Spirit can do this. You see, the flesh can give you a fleshly birth. I was born of the flesh February 25, 1930 and all that I got from that birth was flesh: a nature that was blind to God, deaf to God; a nature that was self-centred and going to live in this world not in another. A nature that was born of the flesh was flesh. It took me many years to find out what flesh is, but as soon as I reached my teens I discovered that which is born of the flesh is flesh. Then, I don't know how it happened, but in 1947, in a sitting room, I was born of the Spirit and began to think, "Now the world is a different place."

I remember the following morning setting off to milk the cows on the farm. I had to get up at four o'clock and milk ninety cows—at that time it is not fun. But that morning I got up and I sang choruses to the cows while I milked them. I am quite sure this was a new experience to them, just as in Wales, after the Welsh Revival, the ponies down in the coal mines couldn't do their work. Why? Because men who had been affected by the Holy Spirit had stopped kicking them and swearing at them.

The cows I was looking after were the same as the previous morning. Why did they look different to me? You see, it *was* a new world. Being born of the Spirit opens up a spiritual world that was all around you.

"Lord, open the young man's eyes," prayed Elisha, and

the young man looked up and there were the chariots of God, and he had thought they were all alone. You do become aware of a new world. That is how it begins. You will never be filled with the Holy Spirit until you have been born into the spiritual world. That comes when you believe in Jesus Christ. It is as simple as that. Jesus was teaching Nicodemus, sitting on that dark rooftop with the evening breeze blowing their hair, and, to explain, he used the wind they could both feel. You don't know where the wind comes from or where it is going. You don't understand a whole lot about it but you know it has hit you, don't you? So it is with everyone born of the Spirit—you can't explain but you experience the effect. You cannot say how it all happened, what led up to it, you just know that one day the wind of God blew upon you, and you knew that life was going to be different and start all over again. You have been born again of the Spirit of God.

That, then, was the second passage. The first says there are two baptists, two baptisms, two things in which you need to be soaked—water and the Holy Spirit. So step number one is to be born of the Spirit and get into the spiritual world.

The next passage we move to is in John chapter 4.

When a Samaritan woman came to draw water, Jesus said to her, 'Will you give me a drink?' (His disciples had gone into the town to buy food.)

The Samaritan woman said to him, 'You are a Jew and I am a Samaritan woman. How can you ask me for a drink?' (For Jews do not associate with Samaritans.)

Jesus answered her, 'If you knew the gift of God and who it is that asks you for a drink, you would have asked him and he would have given you living water.'

'Sir,' the woman said, 'you have nothing to draw with and the well is deep. Where can you get this living water? Are you greater than our father Jacob, who gave us the well and drank from it himself, as did also his sons and his livestock?'

Jesus answered, 'Everyone who drinks this water will be thirsty again, but whoever drinks the water I give them will never thirst. Indeed, the water I give them will become in them a spring of water welling up to eternal life.'

The woman said to him, 'Sir, give me this water so that I won't get thirsty and have to keep coming here to draw water.'

He told her, 'Go, call your husband and come back.'

John 4:7–16, NIV

This is an amazing conversation, firstly because Jews and Samaritans did not speak to each other, and, secondly, it was not the done thing for men to speak to strange women in public. Here is a Jewish man, who is clearly an important teacher, asking a woman of very doubtful reputation for a drink of water. He never did get that drink of water, he had to go without it. The woman was too interested in the conversation! I have drunk from that same well and can testify that it was the best and most refreshing water I had ever drunk. In the hot climate of the Middle East, to reach Jacob's well and let the bucket down sixty feet and get that beautiful, pure water, is wonderful.

Jesus' words pointed to the truth that the woman had to keep coming to the well because there was a physical thirst that would never be satisfied. You have to go on drinking all your life, so she would have to go on coming for water, letting that bucket down. But Jesus could give her something to drink that would mean that she would have a spring inside – not one at the bottom of a well but right deep down within her. It would go on bubbling up so that she would be satisfied.

Now she tried to be flippant and light as people sometimes

are when you challenge them. Jesus didn't even have a bucket. How could he give her a drink? But this was a serious matter. Jesus could meet her deepest needs, spiritually, morally, emotionally. Now he told her to go and get her husband, and she said, "I haven't got one."

He reminded her that she had had five husbands and was now mistress of another man. He knew she was still seeking for something in her life that would satisfy and complete the longings of her being. She was unsatisfied, thirsty morally and emotionally.

Then she tried a typical dodge. I remember talking to a man as we were sitting on a packing case in the back of an old aircraft flying across the desert. We got talking about moral things and after a bit he began to admit that perhaps his life was not as straight as it ought to be, as I admitted mine wasn't. Then to steer the conversation he said, "Well what about all these different denominations? Who's right?" That is a very clever dodge and when you have heard it a few times, you are on your guard against it. It is a wonderful red herring because it's God we've got to deal with, not the denominations.

The Samaritan woman, when Jesus was getting a bit near the bone, tried to deflect the discussion, and turn it to the subject of a place of worship. The Samaritans say that you should worship God on this mountain, Mount Gerizim; Jews say you have to worship God in Jerusalem. Who was right? Jesus brought her back to the personal issue. God is Spirit, and you are to worship him in Spirit and truth.

The form of worship is not the really important thing, but whether it is worship in spirit and in truth, for then it is real. The time was coming when people would worship him anywhere – in Spirit. It doesn't matter about the place of worship.

Then the Samaritan woman changed the subject again

and spoke of the Messiah, who would tell the people all things, and Jesus said, "The man who's speaking to you is the Messiah."

That is when it all began. Three years later, revival hit Samaria and it had started with this woman. More and more people there believed, and three years later the Holy Spirit came in power. They were all baptised in water and then the Holy Spirit came, poured out upon them, in that very place. You can read all about it in Acts chapter 8.

So here is the second step. Step number one: you must be born of the Spirit. You won't even want the Holy Spirit until you are, incidentally. Step number two is to get thirsty, to become dissatisfied with your moral living and with your spiritual worship.

I have sat on commissions with theologians to discuss how to improve worship, and I think they are all beside the point. They discuss forms of worship, orders of worship, but if you just change your pattern on Sunday, all you might achieve is, like somebody who doesn't like the menu dished up in one order, getting the same food in a different order. If it's going to be real worship, it depends on whether people come in spirit. If you become dissatisfied with worship the answer lies within yourself. It lies in having a thirst. "Lord, I'm not living right, I'm not worshipping right, I'm not satisfied. I'm thirsty for more."

A few months later, we are at the Feast of Tabernacles in Jerusalem.

On the last and greatest day of the festival, Jesus stood and said in a loud voice, 'Let anyone who is thirsty come to me and drink. Whoever believes in me, as Scripture has said, rivers of living water will flow from within them.' By this he meant the Spirit, whom those who believed in him were later to receive. Up to that time the Spirit had not been given, since Jesus had not yet been glorified.

John 7:37–39, NIV

The great Feast of Tabernacles was the happiest feast of the Jewish year. It was their harvest festival, when they all lived in tents in the hills around Jerusalem, and they came in for the services at the temple. They remembered not only the food that God had given during the previous twelve months' harvest, but how, for forty years, two and a half million had found bread in the Sinai Peninsula where the Egyptian army didn't survive three days. God fed his people with manna from heaven, and they needed water in a land that is so dry there is no water, and God produced enough water for all those people and hundreds of thousands of head of cattle and sheep and goats, and he produced that water from the rock. So they thanked God for water, and that is why at every Harvest Festival I asked: "Is there a glass of water on the table?" We ought to thank God for water.

The climax of the feast came on the last day. The high priest took a gold and silver pitcher and walked down through the city of Zion, from the temple at the top to the pool of Siloam at the bottom, and he filled the container with water. He came back up the hill, chanting, "Let us draw water from the wells of Salvation" (from Isaiah 12). He came back up the hill with that pitcher of water, and when he reached the altar of burnt offering he poured out the water to God, to remember the water that gushed from the rock for forty years. That year when he did this, in the silence, as everybody listened to the water splashing on the altar, a voice rang out, "If anyone thirsts, let him come to me and drink," and it is a most dramatic moment. Jesus was declaring that he gave the water to their forefathers. He is the one who can draw water from the wells of salvation. He can produce in you a well of living water. You don't need to commemorate something in the past. I'm here, come to me and drink.

The only qualification added was this—that there would have to pass a little time before they could drink. Jesus was not yet glorified, he had to die, rise, ascend, and sit at the right hand of the Father before the Spirit could be poured out. Then they could drink.

Now we are on the right side of Pentecost, not the wrong side. We do not need to wait until Jesus is glorified. He has been glorified. Therefore the invitation is to come *now* and drink. If you say, "I'm thirsty", and I give you a cup of water and you hold it in your hand and say, "Thank you that really has refreshed me" it has done nothing of the sort until you drink, until you act, until you receive, until you take within yourself that water. A minister can preach about the Holy Spirit. But until you drink from Jesus that is just another sermon – interesting, but only a sermon.

So far we have seen two baptists and two baptisms, in water and in the Holy Spirit: water outside our body, living water inside, both soaking us in Christ. How? Be born of the Spirit, and then let that increasing thirst and dissatisfaction make you turn to Jesus and say, "Jesus, I come to you. I want to drink. Will you pour out your Holy Spirit on me?"

When he does, then take a deep drink. Do whatever he tells you to do and leads you to do, and drink of the Spirit. Then you will know a well of living water.

A ship was wrecked in the Atlantic. It went down and the crew took to a lifeboat, drifting for weeks. They had a little food, but their water soon ran out, and without water, food is of no use. They lay there increasingly weary and exhausted in the bottom of the lifeboat. Then one of them lifted his face above the boat edge, saw smoke on the horizon and said, "A ship, a ship!" They jumped up and tore off the remains of the shirts that were still clinging to their backs, and waved them and shouted.

The big ship turned and came towards them until it towered above the little lifeboat with these poor men in it. One of the men in the lifeboat shouted up to a sailor on deck, "Water, water." The sailor shouted down, "Dip your bucket over the side, mate." What a cruel joke – or was it? Half mad with thirst, this sailor dipped the bucket over the side, drank it and discovered it was fresh water. They were drifting off the mouth of the mighty Amazon river, which pushes fresh water right out into the Atlantic. They had been drifting in it and all they needed to do was dip a bucket over the side and drink. If ever there was a picture of the church of Jesus Christ, that's it – drifting along. Some say it's dying, just drifting along—trying to keep each other alive. People look at the church and they see it as a lifeboat full of dying people, not one that can save others. Jesus has been glorified and he is waiting for people to say, "I'm thirsty, Lord, desperately thirsty, and I'm going to go on coming to you until you give me something to drink deeply. I want living water inside. I am thirsty, and I want to be baptised inside, and I want within me a spring of water welling up to eternal life."

Chapter Six

THE HOLY SPIRIT IN JOHN 14–16

Very truly I tell you, whoever believes in me will do the works I have been doing, and they will do even greater things than these, because I am going to the Father. And I will do whatever you ask in my name, so that the Father may be glorified in the Son. You may ask me for anything in my name, and I will do it.

'If you love me, keep my commands. And I will ask the Father, and he will give you another advocate to help you and be with you for ever – the Spirit of truth. The world cannot accept him, because it neither sees him nor knows him. But you know him, for he lives with you and will be in you. I will not leave you as orphans; I will come to you. Before long, the world will not see me any more, but you will see me. Because I live, you also will live.

On that day you will realise that I am in my Father, and you are in me, and I am in you. Whoever has my commands and keeps them is the one who loves me. The one who loves me will be loved by my Father, and I too will love them and show myself to them.'

Then Judas (not Judas Iscariot) said, 'But, Lord, why do you intend to show yourself to us and not to the world?'

Jesus replied, 'Anyone who loves me will obey my teaching. My Father will love them, and we will come to them and make our home with them. Anyone who does not love me will not obey my teaching. These words you hear are not my own; they belong to the Father who sent me.

'All this I have spoken while still with you. But the Advocate, the Holy Spirit, whom the Father will send in my name, will teach you all things and will remind you of everything I have said to you. Peace I leave with you; my peace I give you. I do not give to you as the world gives. Do not let your hearts be troubled and do not be afraid.

'You heard me say, "I am going away and I am coming back to you." If you loved me, you would be glad that I am going to the Father, for the Father is greater than I. I have told you now before it happens, so that when it does happen you will believe.'

John 14:12–29, NIV

Imagine that your best friend was going to be executed tomorrow morning at eight o'clock, and you knew he was innocent of the crime for which he was going to be killed, and he sent an urgent message to you asking you to spend his last evening with him in his cell because he had some things that he wanted to say to you. I want you to imagine going to visit that friend with your heart breaking at the thought of his life being thrown away unnecessarily and wrongly. Imagine the attention you would give to everything he said that memorable night, things that you would remember as long as you lived. If you can imagine this, then I think that you can begin to feel as the twelve disciples felt on the night on which Jesus told them all this.

The very next day he was going to be executed for a crime he had not committed. He was going to leave them and they knew it. Their hearts were troubled to breaking point. There were a number of things Jesus wanted to say to them which he wanted them to remember. In this atmosphere he spoke to them about many things. He began by washing their dirty feet, he finished by praying for them. Such was the memory of that evening that sixty years later John, writing about it, could remember every single word. I think you would have done under the circumstances.

Among the many things that Jesus said was: "I am going ... I am coming...." This was what he was constantly saying. You would be very puzzled if someone about to be killed said that to you, so when the Son of God talks like this, it is no wonder the disciples said, "Whatever does he mean? He keeps saying he's going, but then he says don't worry, I'll be back again. I'm going and you won't see me any more but don't worry I'm going to stay with you. I'm going back to the Father, but don't worry, I'm making my home with you forever. I must say goodbye but you need never say goodbye." It seems so puzzling, and the more you study chapters 13–17 of John's Gospel the more puzzling does this become, until you understand something about the Holy Spirit and then the whole thing makes sense. Suddenly, through experience, you can read those chapters and you understand what he is talking about. In fact, the Lord Jesus was talking about three different ways in which he was going to go and come back – three different ways in which he would do this at different times. I will explain which are the three ways he was going to go and come again to them. In a sense they are all jumbled up – Jesus speaking of all three at the same time. Only later could they sort out the three strands. First, and this is the simplest, he was going to go from them in death and come back to them in resurrection – that's the first going and coming. That was to be a gap of three days away from them. He said: in a little while you will not see me and you'll have great sorrow, and then suddenly after a little while you'll see me and you'll have great joy such as a woman has, just after she's delivered her child. It is quite clear that the going and the coming in that case is the going in death and three days later coming in life again, so that they could see him and touch him. There are certain things he says

123

about going and coming which won't fit into that one, so we have then to think of a second instance. This is clearly about his going from them to heaven and his coming back again to earth. The gap between these two, the gap of his absence in this case, would be hundreds of years. He didn't tell them how long, and we still don't know how long because he has not come again. But when he says, "I go to the Father and I will come again and take you to be with me where I am," he is referring to his going to heaven not his going in death (for that was not his going to heaven). Now he was speaking of something that was to happen six weeks later when he ascended to heaven; and from heaven he will come again one day. Now that covers a lot of the other things he said about going and coming but it still doesn't cover all of them.

There is still a mysterious thing that he says, that in between that going and that coming – going to heaven and coming back to earth – he would still be *with* them. He would be making his home in them and really he would never go away. So he is saying in this case that they would not see him, but he would have come to them. This third going and coming is going in the flesh and coming in the Spirit. The gap this time between the two, the going and the coming, was to be ten days only.

Now these are the three comings and goings that Jesus talks about on the last night of his life. When you read these chapters, you must constantly bear all three in mind or you might get confused. Maybe I have got you thoroughly confused now, but I point this out to lay a foundation for what Jesus says about the Holy Spirit. It is with the third coming and going that we are concerned here. This is the most wonderful of all because it gets over this problem: if Jesus is in heaven, how can I have him in my heart here? If Jesus is at the right hand of the Father, how can we say that Jesus is alive and doing things in the world today? If you understand this third coming and going, then you will understand the answer to this problem.

Jesus' teaching meant: I am going, but don't worry I'm not; I'm leaving you but you don't need to say goodbye because I'm not leaving you; you will not see me again until I come back again from heaven, yet you will not feel that I am away from you. This is precisely how a Christian feels even if they cannot explain it. I know that this very day, right now, Jesus is at the highest point of heaven in the control room of the universe at the right hand of God the Father. Christians also know his presence in each one of his believers, and he is busy and alive in the world today.

The answer is that he has gone in the flesh and I have not seen his body. I am going to one day, but not until he comes back in the flesh. But he is already here in the Spirit, and he came to his disciples in a new way.

The best way to approach this is through two key verses The first is John 14:16. "I will pray the Father and he will give you another comforter [counsellor, helper, advocate, standby, friend, teacher; you could put almost any of those words in there] "to be with you forever." What a promise! The greatest gift that God ever gave to people was his only begotten Son. The second greatest gift is the Holy Spirit. The tragedy of it is that there are many thousands of Christians who have received the first gift but don't know anything about the second. Sooner or later in every Christian's life there comes an interest in the second gift, the third person of the Holy Trinity.

Jesus died for us, was raised from the dead for us, and, after going back to the Father, asked for another gift for us. It is interesting that throughout the New Testament the Holy Spirit is frequently referred to as the gift. Frankly, that's one of the loveliest words in the English language. Giving is tied up with God—God is a giving God and his gifts are lovely gifts, and the things that the Spirit does among mankind are still called "gifts". If there is one thing the word "gift" conveys to me it is that it is something that I did not deserve and did not earn. It comes to me because of the goodness of somebody else. I want to fix that word "give" and the word "gift" in your mind.

If you have come to know Christ, it is a sheer gift. It is only because God is generous that you did. If you know what it is to be filled with the Holy Spirit, it will be because God is generous and has given you a gift you never deserved. So let us be filled with gratitude that we have got a God who gives.

Consider that expression "another comforter". I don't know what the word "comforter" means to you. Something that soothes you, something that wraps you up nice and soft and warm? What does "comfort" mean? Unfortunately, it has changed its meaning, and today if you say, "I will comfort you," invariably you mean, "I will get you out of trouble. I will get you away from that situation. I will get you away from what is causing bother to you." But in fact the word "comfort" originally meant exactly the opposite. It meant to put someone right into trouble and give them the strength to face it. It comes from the Latin word *fortes* from which we get the word "fortitude" and even "fort". It means to be right in the middle of the battle and pushed into it.

The Bayeux tapestry illustrates the meaning. The tapestry is a sort of long comic strip from the days before newspapers. It depicts the battle of Hastings and other military history. It has a very interesting section depicting a battle royal going on, and bears the caption "Bishop Oden comforts his troops". His soldiers are lined up, facing the enemy across a narrow strip of land. The bishop is behind them, a sword in his hand and he is goading them with it, to get them into battle. That is the last thing you would have said was comforting them! In its modern usage the word might mean sending them away to a convalescent home on leave, but in fact "comforting" means prodding someone, stirring them up to battle – to make you strong and brave to face the foe. The big shift to the modern meaning of "comfort" is why most translations now try to get away from the word "comforter". The tragedy is that there isn't another word in English to translate the sense of the original adequately. One scholar has pointed out that "comforter" nowadays suggests a dose of something soothing, which is not what is meant. The Greek term *paraclete* is most intriguing: *para* means "beside", "by the side of"; *clete* means "to be called", so the whole word means: "someone you call to stand beside you; someone who would be with you in battle".

It is helpful to have Christian friends who are fearless in the cause of Christ and can stand with you. Is there someone like that in your life? You have a problem, a burden, or you have had some disastrous news, and you tend to think: if only someone would just come and stand beside me in this I would be alright. Most of us have someone like this and of course this is ultimately what marriage is – a man and a woman are called to stand beside each other, not just in church but all through their lives, facing things together.

The *paraclete* is someone you have called to stand by you, to give you courage when you are in some sort of battle. It was used of lawyers in the Greek world: when you got into trouble with the law and you needed an advocate, a counsel for the defence, the paraclete is the one who comes to stand by you in the heat of the battle and sees you through.

Jesus taught his disciples that when he got back to heaven he would ask the Father to give them a paraclete, a comforter, someone to stand beside them when they were in the heat of the battle, and this was the one who would throw them into the thick of the battle and then be with them in it – the divine Comforter, the blessed Holy Spirit. Here is the secret of the courage of the saints of God. They have had someone standing by them who gave them strength and courage.

The other word to notice is "another", and again I need to mention New Testament Greek expressions. The two words *heteros* and *allos* could both be translated "another". If you are describing another thing that is *different*, you use the word *heteros*. But if you are saying here is another which is exactly the same as the first, with the same things inside identical so that you couldn't tell the difference, you would use the word *allos*. Here is the most amazing thing Jesus said: "When I get back to heaven, I will pray the Father that he will give you *allos paracletos*, another standby exactly the same as the one you have had." Here we are touching one of the deepest and most wonderful truths that comes out again and again in the New Testament: the Holy Spirit and Jesus are so similar you cannot tell the difference. If the Holy Spirit is filling you, it feels just like Jesus filling you. They are not different in character, they are not different in outlook, and exactly what Jesus was to the disciples in the days of his flesh the Holy Spirit is to the Christian today. Whatever deed he did for them, the Holy Spirit does for us. This is why so often you find him described in the New Testament as the Spirit of Jesus.

This is why when a person is filled with the Spirit they talk so much about Jesus. They will say, "Jesus is real to me, more real than ever before," because to know the Spirit is to know Jesus. This is why Christians who are filled with the Holy Spirit have such a vivid relationship with Jesus Christ – another Comforter. The other key verse that helps us to understand this is at John 16:7, *NIV*:

But very truly I tell you, it is for your good that I am going away. Unless I go away, the Advocate will not come to you; but if I go, I will send him to you.

Now one of the childish things that the adult Christian puts away is the idea that it would be better for us if Jesus was in the flesh—it is not. It is to our advantage that he is in the Spirit now. Why? There are two very simple reasons. First, if Jesus were still in the flesh on earth he could not be everywhere. We might get him visiting us once in a lifetime, maybe for some special occasion, but until the twentieth century he could not have travelled around the world very quickly, and people would never have seen him, never have known him personally. Even during the days of his flesh, he was limited to one place. There is no recorded example of his ever being in two places at once, and that is because he was in the flesh. Sometimes I have to say in a letter: "Much as I would like to be with you, I can't be in two places at once. I have other things I must do."

We might take this a little further. Martha, the sister who lost a dear brother, once said to Jesus: "If you had only been here my brother would not have died." Her sister Mary said the same thing. Do you realise that Jesus only healed people where he was as he moved around? There was one case of healing at a distance, but it was because a near relative of the sick person could be where Jesus was. Everything that Jesus did in the days of his flesh he did because he was in physical contact with the situation. I read of no miracles performed in China or India or Africa by Jesus in the days of his flesh – none at all. He was localised because he was in the flesh. Do you wish he were in the flesh again now? Do you wish that he were in only one little place on earth and that the only things that happened took place there? I don't! It is to our advantage that he went away and sent another Comforter who could be with us all the time and in all places. The same could be said of the presence of the Lord with Christians in many different places, all worshipping at the same time. If

Jesus were still in the flesh, we couldn't do it.

Give thanks that Jesus prayed the Father, and his Spirit has come, and it means that I can be in touch with Jesus and so can others all round the world, and even in space! It is significant that the majority of American astronauts have been convinced Christians. This is the first great advantage: he can be everywhere.

On a little island called Patmos, in a dungeon there lay chained an old man called John, whose Gospel we are thinking about. One day, suddenly, the chains didn't matter. He was in the Spirit and Jesus was with him in that cell. Jesus took him in the Spirit and showed him heaven. John looked through an open door and saw the future. You can be in the Spirit today and you can know Jesus today. You can converse with him now, and all because he went away and prayed the Father to give another Comforter.

There is another advantage in having Jesus in heaven now. Just suppose that he was still in the body on earth, even in his resurrection body. I have pointed out already that he could not be everywhere. If that was so, there is something else that also follows: *he could never be inside us, he would always be outside us*. Now you can get very close to a person outside you, but not close enough. All the time that Jesus was in the body on earth, even after his resurrection as well as before, they couldn't get any closer to him than you can get to another person on earth. He was still outside them. They could have touched his hand. They could, as John did, lie against his breast at supper. They could be so close to him, but they could not get any nearer than that. This was a limitation on the relationship because what we deeply desire with each other is to get right inside each other. When a husband and wife live together for a long time they begin to get inside each other mentally, to such a degree that they begin to understand each other's deeper thoughts and feelings, but there is still a limit because they are still in body. But when Jesus went to heaven and sent his Spirit, his Spirit no longer remained outside the disciples but was now inside.

One of the things we learn from the words of Jesus in these chapters is this: you have known the Holy Spirit outside you; he has been *with* you. Of course he had, in the person of Jesus, the Holy Spirit had been near to them. They had been eating and sleeping and drinking with the Holy Spirit because the Holy Spirit was in Jesus. Jesus said, "He has been with you, but he will be in you." Now that is the difference — to have Jesus, the Spirit of Jesus, right *inside* me. Now things become possible that I could not have imagined. Such things can happen only if he gets so deep inside me that he begins to put his thoughts in place of my thoughts, and he uses my hands so that deep down inside I am not using them, he is. He begins to use my voice, and all this begins to open tremendous possibilities. "The works that I do shall you do also, and greater works than these shall you do" – this becomes possible, and the future opens up in a new way.

At the end of John's Gospel we learn that Mary Magdalene wanted to keep Jesus in the body. After his resurrection she was perhaps the first person to meet him face to face in the body. She fell at his feet and got hold of those blessed ankles and she hung on, as much as to say: they are never going to take your body away from me again. For she had just been asking this person she supposed to be the gardener, "Where have you put his body?" She was going to hang on to the physical Christ. Jesus said: "Mary, don't go on clinging to me for I have not yet ascended to the Father." Do you now understand what he was saying? As long as Mary was holding on like that, nobody else could have him. He would ascend to the Father, and then she and others could have him inside them. When Jesus came in the Spirit, anyone could cling to him as closely as they liked. Do you understand what he was saying? So don't cling to a physical Jesus. Don't wish that you had his body here. Don't wish that you had been like the disciples, able to walk the dusty lanes of Galilee – just praise God and shout "Hallelujah" that you can have his Spirit dwelling in your heart wherever you go, that you can keep Jesus all the time, that you can take him into the middle of the battle, that his Spirit will be your standby, strengthening you and giving you courage in the middle of the fight, giving you the victory that overcomes the world.

Chapter Seven

THE HOLY SPIRIT IN THE
CLOSING CHAPTERS OF JOHN

If the Holy Spirit is a strengthener, a standby, a person you would like to have with you in the crisis just like Jesus, then two things follow which are very important. First, the Holy Spirit is a *person*. Never talk of the Holy Spirit as "it". You would be amazed how often that is done in prayer or speaking. People say, "Give *it* to us." Never do that. If the Holy Spirit is another Comforter like Jesus, the Holy Spirit is *he*, a full personality who can think, feel, guide, teach, lead, speak, and be grieved, angry, upset — one who can be to you all that Jesus is.

It is interesting that in what we call the sects, who claim to have the truth and to be the only ones to have it—Jehovah's Witnesses, Christian Science, Mormons, Spiritism and so on, you will discover a remarkable thing. They refer to the Holy Spirit as a kind of force or atmosphere, an impersonal "it". That is to misunderstand what Jesus taught: he would pray the Father, and the Father would give another Comforter just like him. Therefore he is a person, someone you can know and can talk to. This is the first thing that follows from the word "another" — the personality of the Holy Spirit: *he*.

If somebody goes away from a service or meeting and says, "There was a nice spirit in the meeting," they will invariably spell "spirit" with a small "s" and they will not say "he", just "a spirit" or "a good spirit". But if a believer goes away from a service or meeting in which the Holy Spirit has been present they will talk differently. They will

133

say, "Wasn't the Spirit there this morning? *He* was there. *He* helped us to worship. Didn't *he* show us truth?" That is how they will talk if they know the Holy Spirit. Now the other thing that follows, if the Holy Spirit is another Comforter like Jesus—his deity; he must be God.

We know that Jesus is God. It took three years for people to find that out, but it was a doubtful, scientific sceptic who, having known Jesus well for those years, said, "My Lord and my God." For the first time in their lives those Jewish disciples realised that God was more than one person, and they called Jesus God, and they worshipped Jesus and prayed to Jesus. As Jews they knew you should only pray to or worship God, and now they worshipped Jesus and they prayed to him. The third step to which they came — and this led to the Christian doctrine of the Trinity – is that the Holy Spirit, if he is another Comforter, like Jesus, must be God. Therefore you can worship him, pray to him and praise him. Christians believe in Father, Son, and Holy Spirit, all of whom are persons, all of whom can be grieved and can be angry, all of whom love you, all of whom have compassion for you, and all of whom are God. So we say, "Father, Son, and Holy Spirit" and we praise all three freely.

Now go back to John chapters 14–16. Our Lord is going to die within twenty-four hours. What a man says in his last day of life is usually significant and memorable. The Son of God must have said many wonderful things ("If they had all been written down, the world could not contain the books"), but in these chapters we have the longest recorded discourse of our Lord's words in the whole of the Bible. I don't know if you realise this, but in the whole of the New Testament we have only got about six hours of our Lord's teaching. If you don't believe me, check this out and read all Jesus' recorded words. It will be a very useful and healthy thing for you to do. This passage in John is longer than the Sermon on the

Mount, which is the second longest. If you really want the teaching of Jesus you have got to go to these chapters. People sometimes say to me, "If everybody lived up to the Sermon on the Mount, that would be all we would need." However I have not yet met anyone who could live out the Sermon on the Mount—that's the snag! How could we? The answer lies in the last sermon Jesus preached: by the Holy Spirit. The heart of the Sermon on the Mount, many people say, is in the positive command "Do unto others, as you would have them do to you" — and that is fine. But think: how many of us have given our neighbours as much attention as we would wish to receive? How many of us have given those lonely people down the road as much friendship as you would wish to have if you were alone? How many hungry people in the world have you thought of as if they were you? There isn't one of us in any church who could say, "I have done what the Sermon on the Mount tells me to do in full." How will we ever get there? The answer is that we need another Comforter, another standby, to come and help us.

This is what our Lord spoke about in the last night of his earthly life. Father, Son, and Holy Spirit are identical in character; to meet one is to meet them all. We know that we should look to Jesus all the time, and then we will begin to reflect him. With couples who are very close together, to meet one is to meet the other, to hear what one thinks is to know what the other will think, to have the reaction of one is to know the reaction of the other. With Father, Son, and Holy Spirit, if you know the Father you get to know the Son and *vice versa*—if you get to know the Son you will get to know the Father. "He that has seen me has seen the Father." It is just as true of the Holy Spirit: if you get to know the Holy Spirit, you will get to know Jesus better and you will get to know God the Father better, because they all think alike, they all speak alike and they all have the same feelings towards you. If one is grieved by something you have done, the three persons will be grieved. If one tells you to do a thing, the other two will agree that is the right thing to do.

In John 17, a prayer that Jesus prayed at the end of this discourse, he says: "Father I am in you, you are in me. I just say the things you want me to say. I just do your will. We are one." Such closeness is lovely, and I don't think any relationship on earth could be as close. But, having said all that, Father, Son, and Spirit are so united, so identical in character, in outlook, and in feelings, I want to affirm that they have different *work* to do. Each of them gets on with that work in his own way. In John 14–16 Jesus explained three aspects of the work of the Holy Spirit: his work in relation to Jesus; his work in relation to disciples, and his work in relation to the world.

1. His work in relation to Jesus

The Holy Spirit is the one who brings Jesus to people's attention. Jesus said: "When he comes, the Spirit of truth, he will glorify me." This means: he will take my things and make them real to you; he will make people think about me. The Holy Spirit gets people talking about Jesus, draws their attention to Jesus. You might publicise the church, you could publicise a minister, but you will find it embarrassing and impossible to publicise Jesus without the Holy Spirit.

The Holy Spirit will indeed always glorify Jesus. I have noticed again and again that one of the marks of people having been filled with the Holy Spirit is that they start using the name "Jesus" much more frequently, much more openly, much more frankly. This is because the Holy Spirit at work in them is now going to use them to tell others about Jesus so that his name is on everyone's lips and widely known, and everybody knows that Jesus is coming one day and they are getting ready for him. You will not find this apart from the Holy Spirit. You will never hear people saying "Jesus is coming" except through the Holy Spirit.

Those who talk a great deal about being filled with the Holy Spirit can sometimes be denying that they are, because they are not talking about the right person. Sometimes churches have been divided over the Holy Spirit, and that is a tragedy. I have been asked more than once to go to such a church as a kind of consultant to try to help them to get over the problems. I first get hold of those within the church who have claimed to be filled with the Holy Spirit and said to them very frankly: "Who have you been talking about in the fellowship, the second or the third person of the Trinity? Have you been talking about Jesus or the Holy Spirit?" Invariably when trouble has come it is because they have been talking about the Holy Spirit instead of about Jesus. I have said: "No one in a church can ever object to someone who talks more about Jesus." So you use the power of the Holy Spirit to talk about Jesus, that is what he was given for you to do. He is a most self-effacing person of the Trinity. He doesn't want you to talk about him, he wants you to talk about Jesus. So this is the first work of the Holy Spirit in John 14–16.

2. His work in relation to disciples

I have noticed that the Holy Spirit is more concerned with our mind than our heart, with our thoughts than our feelings, yet again and again I have come up against people who think that to be filled with the Holy Spirit is primarily an emotional or ecstatic experience, giving you wonderful, bubbly feelings inside. One young lady, who was still seeking, actually asked, "How will I know when I'm filled with the Holy Spirit? Will I get a nice bubbly feeling inside me?" That may well come but Jesus never promised it, and it wouldn't worry me if it didn't come. The Holy Spirit is much more concerned that we think right, rather than that we feel right. That is very important, and again and again in John chapters 14–16 this comes out. He is described in 14:17, 15:26 and 16:13 as the "Spirit of truth."

Truth is what your mind understands, truth is what you think about, truth is what is real and what is true and right, and he is called the Spirit of truth because when he comes to someone, they see what is true and right. The world in which we live is a world packed with lies. That may sound a strong statement but it is the case: lies about God, lies about men, lies about the world in which we live; lies about the past and lies about the future. There are articles which are lies appearing in the media about Jesus and about God.

There is a lie going about that God won't punish sin. That is not true. Now the Spirit of truth, when he comes to a believer, brings truth. The believer knows that God must punish sin, but will also know that God pardons sin and that he is a God of mercy as well as justice. He will know the truth about himself, and there are not many of us who like that. To be able to know what you are really like in God's sight is a devastating thing. But to know yourself, the ancient Greeks said, is the beginning of wisdom. So in a world full of lies, the Spirit comes as the Spirit of truth. He will tell you what is true and bring you into all truth. When Jesus was on earth he could only introduce his disciples to a little bit of the truth. There were things that they could not understand at that stage, and things they could not yet believe. So there was more that Jesus might have told the disciples but didn't then. But the Spirit of truth would lead them into all truth.

Truth about the past—the Spirit would bring everything Jesus said to their remembrance. I have listened to scholars who said the New Testament books were written between ten and forty years later. How do we know the disciples remembered accurately what Jesus said? The answer is very simple: the Spirit of truth would bring to remembrance everything Jesus said—truth about the present and about the future.

How do we know how the world is going to end? How do we know the future? Do we consult a horoscope? Do we gaze into a crystal ball? Do we listen to the political pundits? The answer is that the Spirit of truth shows everything, and we have in the Bible an account of the future with everything you need to know about the end of this world and the beginning of a new one, and it was the Holy Spirit who did this. The Spirit of truth would bring believers into the past truth, the present truth and the future truth. The Gospels are the past truth brought to their remembrance, the epistles are the present truth for them in their church life, and the book of Revelation is the future truth – that pretty well covers it, and it is the New Testament. The Spirit of truth brought the Bible into being. It is not the production of a bunch of men who thought they would write down their thoughts, it is the production of the Holy Spirit and that is why it is all truth.

If the Holy Spirit is another Comforter like Jesus you would expect him to be a great teacher. Let me tell you now about a young man who was a Pilot Officer in the Royal Air Force. I remember Trevor sitting one night on a deckchair with me, outside the officers' mess in the blistering heat of the desert. He told me frankly he wasn't interested in religion, but we looked up at the stars, and somehow when the desert stretches before you into infinity, it is easier to think big. We talked about God and I gave him a book to read about God, and he came back and said, "That's interesting." Finally, he started coming to the little hut where we had our church. Then, one night, Trevor came to know Jesus Christ and he was soundly converted. But after the service, when I was talking to him, he said to me, "Padre, I've got to leave tomorrow. I have been posted to one of the desert outposts for six months, with fifteen men." So the day after he was born again of the Spirit, he was cut off from Christian fellowship for six months. I told him straightaway about the other Comforter who would go with him into the desert, and who would teach him the things that he couldn't come to church to learn, and off he went.

Three weeks later I had a letter from him which said that he had led someone else to Christ, so there were now two of them meeting and worshipping together. So it went on. For six months he had no one to teach him. For six months he had no one to take him through the Bible. For six months he had nobody to help him but the Holy Spirit, and the Spirit was enough. The Holy Spirit undertook for him in that situation. Trevor later built motorways – and preached around the Midlands, leading people to Jesus Christ.

If ever you find things difficult to understand, ask the Holy Spirit to teach you. Each time you read the Bible say, "Holy Spirit you wrote this; now, as I read it, teach it to me."

Why is it that a group of people can sit in the same building listening to the same preacher, and two people who had been sitting next to each other can go out and one can say, "Well I got nothing at all this morning and I didn't understand what he was on about" (which does happen quite frequently) and somebody sitting next to them can go out and say, "Well I really learned something this morning that I never knew before and I shall be able to live by that." Why is it? I'll tell you. One has the Holy Spirit and the other doesn't. One has a teacher in his heart who is able to take the word that the preacher is reading and speaking about, and plant it deep down in the soil of the heart where it germinates, and during the week something will happen, something will grow, and something very practical will result.

3. His work in relation to the world

What can the Holy Spirit do for the people outside the church? First of all, Jesus says quite bluntly in John 14:16 that they cannot *receive* the Holy Spirit. They cannot have him, they cannot be *indwelt* by him, they cannot have this Comforter. They cannot have this strengthening. They cannot have this fortress experience. It is as simple as that.

The tragedy is that these people, when they come to the crisis, when they find themselves in the battle, when they find themselves in the heat of it, they must face that alone without the blessed Comforter to stand by them. That draws out our compassion and our pity – to live without the Holy Spirit must be miserable. But what can he do for them? John 16:8 is the key verse now: "When he comes he will convict the world of sin and of righteousness and of judgment. Of sin because they do not believe in me, of righteousness because I go to the Father and you will see me no more, of judgment because the ruler of this world is judged." Now if ever you need the Holy Spirit to understand the word of God you need him now. You need his teaching. There are three things that are true which you will never convince anyone else are true without the Holy Spirit: sin, righteousness, and judgment. Let us break that down. You can convince people of vice and of crime, but not of sin. You can convince them of vice if they have vices. You can convince them of crime if they have broken laws, but to convince them of sin is impossible. You have tried. I have tried. We have said to somebody, "You're a sinner." They have either slapped our face or given us the cold shoulder or said: "I never did anybody any harm in my life" Fancy saying that! I found the best thing to say to a person who says "I've never done anybody any harm" is to say, "I wish I could say that," and that is true. No Christian could ever say that, because they have been convinced of sin.

It is amazing that people without any vices and without any crimes in their life (and that is possible) don't realise that doesn't mean they are not sinners. They may be thoroughly respectable, thoroughly good living, decent, hard-working folk, and yet they are sinners in God's sight. Why? Well, do you know what the worst sin of all is? Murder? Adultery? What do you think the worst sin is? No, the worst thing you can ever do is not to believe in Jesus. It is to throw God's love back in his face and say, "God I don't really care. God, did you send your Son to the earth to die and be raised for me? I don't care, I can manage without him."

Think of the millions in England who have heard about Jesus but do not believe in him. Now you will never convince anybody that is a sin. You will never convince your nice neighbours who are so kind to you when you are in trouble. It is hard enough to convince yourself they are sinners sometimes, isn't it? Only the Holy Spirit can convince you that nice neighbour is a sinner needing a Saviour, and only the Holy Spirit can convince them. Sin is the first thing a person needs to be convinced about if they are going to come to the Saviour. If you don't believe you are a sinner you will never believe in a Saviour because you don't think you need one. If you don't think you have got any sins you won't come to Jesus.

The second thing you need to be convinced of is righteousness — that there is such a thing as perfect goodness, and that it is by that standard that your sin will appear at its most clear. How can you convince people that there is such a thing as perfect goodness? I remember a hairdresser saying this to me while we were chatting: she said, "No one's perfect." But there is someone who is perfect. There was once a Man on earth who was absolutely perfect. When you have convinced people that they are sinners, something else follows. What happens when badness meets perfect goodness? What happens when sin comes face to face with righteousness? The answer is *judgment.*

Have you ever tried to convince a person that one day they will stand before God and answer for every idle word they have uttered and every thought they have had, and every feeling that passed through their minds? Have you ever tried to convince anyone that they are going to be judged for their whole life, and that things they have forgotten for years will be brought up again? Have you ever tried to convince somebody that this is true? You never will. People today don't believe there is a judgment, they don't believe in hell, they don't believe in anything like that. How will we convince them? The answer is the Holy Spirit will convince the world (not the church) of sin and righteousness and judgment. When someone is convinced of those three things they are ripe for the gospel, ready for the Saviour. They want to know how they can escape. How can I get out of this terrible dilemma? I am bad, God is perfectly good. When I meet him face-to-face I shall have to run from him. How can I get out of this? Then you can tell them: "Jesus died for you. Jesus died that you might be forgiven. He died to make you good, that you might go at last to heaven, saved by his precious blood." That is when the gospel comes in.

Sometimes I think that in the church we have many half-converted people who have never been convinced of sin, never been convinced of righteousness, never been convinced of judgment, and therefore they never really loved the Saviour as they might. But when the day comes in your life when you tremble and say, "God, I can't face you. I can't face the judgment, I'm not ready, I'm not good, I'm a sinner" – then God reaches down so tenderly and he lifts, and through Jesus Christ he saves.

Chapter Eight

THE HOLY SPIRIT IN THE ACTS OF THE APOSTLES

There is a tremendous difference between theory and practice, between reading about something and then experiencing it. One has heard of the man who wrote a book on how to bring up children and outlines six different theories in the book, but he had no children at the time and he finished up with six children and no theories and he found it very different in practice! Before our marriage, my wife and I read certain books on marriage, which is a very good thing to do. We came to the point where we said, "We're not going to read any more, too many things can go wrong, we shall get cold feet about the whole process." But how different it was to read about it in a book and then to be married and to work it out together. I remember reading a lot of books about the land of Israel and being thrilled about what I read, but the day came when I went, and I discovered that to walk around there is completely different from reading a book.

There are those who have read a great deal about the Holy Spirit. They have read the Bible, read other books, been to conventions and heard preachers and speakers. They have a lot of head knowledge, but that is as far as it goes. It is as different again to have personal experience of the Holy Spirit as it is to read a book about marriage and then get married. In the last chapter we left the disciples at the point where they had head knowledge of the Holy Spirit. They had been well taught by the greatest teacher in the world, Jesus Christ himself. They could have sat a theological examination on the subject. They could have answered doctrinal questions with the right answers. If you had asked them who the Holy Spirit is, they would have said, "He is the Comforter." If you had enquired, "What is his work?" they would have said: "To comfort the believer and to convict the unbeliever." This is where many Christians are today. They know *about* the Holy Spirit; they have heard about him. But if one asks them, very personally, "How much do you know in your own experience?" they would have to confess a considerable amount of ignorance.

I once had the privilege of visiting Chartwell, Sir Winston Churchill's home, with our church secretary and his wife. For once I had very little to contribute to the conversation. I managed to think of one little thing that I had once read about Churchill, which I found that our church secretary didn't know, but the difference was that he knew him personally. He had been to see him many times so he could tell me all about him. Even though I had read many books, even though I had read many stories, even though I know a lot *about* Churchill, I never *knew* him. So my knowledge really was quite out of place as we walked around.

It is not enough to know *about* the Holy Spirit, the blessed third person of the godhead. We need to know him in personal experience if he is ever to be to us what Jesus intended. He intended the Holy Spirit to be active personally, powerfully, in our lives. When we turn to the Acts we turn from the doctrine to seeing him powerfully, personally at work. In the preceding chapters of this book I have been giving you the doctrine and telling you about the truth, the teaching about the Holy Spirit, which our Lord has given. But as soon as we get to Acts, I cannot do that any more.

As long as the Holy Spirit is talked of as a doctrine then everybody is happy because you can keep a book on the shelf. You can keep a doctrine in a compartment of your mind. But as soon as we begin to talk of the Holy Spirit as a dynamic person whom we need to know, not just to know *about*, then difficulties arise. People get tense, worried and afraid. Why should they be afraid of the Spirit? He gives love, peace, power and a sound mind.

As we move from the doctrine in John's Gospel to reading about the dynamic person we see at work in the book of Acts, we find that the disciples have passed a boundary. Of course they weren't living as printed words in a book! They were real people in a real situation. *Now they were able to speak from the heart whereas before it would have been from the head alone. They were now able to convey to others an experience instead of just lecturing.*

The book of Acts is called the "Acts" of the Apostles and it is certainly about some apostles (Peter, Paul, James and John), but it could be described as acts of Jesus, things he continued to do and to teach. It is interesting that the Gospels cover thirty-three years and the Acts cover thirty-three years, as much as to illustrate that our Lord's ministry continued. But it is even more true to call Acts the "Acts of the Holy Spirit". If you underline the words "Holy Spirit" in Acts, you discover that over forty times in the first few chapters, the Holy Spirit is mentioned by name, and by implication many other times too.

First, though, consider the last mention of the Holy Spirit in John chapter 20.

On the evening of that first day of the week, when the disciples were together, with the doors locked for fear of the Jewish leaders, Jesus came and stood among them and said, 'Peace be with you!' After he said this, he showed them his hands and side. The disciples were overjoyed when they saw the Lord.

Again Jesus said, 'Peace be with you! As the Father has sent me, I am sending you.' And with that he breathed on

them and said, 'Receive the Holy Spirit. If you forgive
anyone's sins, their sins are forgiven; if you do not forgive
them, they are not forgiven.'

John 20:19–23, NIV

Now one thing is patently clear: they did not receive the Holy
Spirit at that moment. What was he doing to them when he
knew perfectly well they would have to wait another couple
of months before they did receive the Holy Spirit? Why
did he do this, and why did he say this on that evening in
particular?

Among other things, he wanted them to know the secret
of real peace. You will never know real peace until you find
that peace is a fruit of the Holy Spirit. Twice he said to them:
"Peace be with you." With doors bolted and barred, for fear
of the Jews? Yes. They must have the Holy Spirit if they were
going to have peace and go out with peace in their hearts.

Jesus was giving them three things at this stage, which
would prepare them for what would happen two months
later. First, he was giving them a sign by which they would
recognise the Holy Spirit when he came. The literal word
translated "breathed" is strong: he *blew* on them. Jesus had
blown on them once, so when they heard the sound of a
rushing, mighty wind, they would recognise that it was Jesus
in heaven blowing on them, breathing again.

Secondly, he was giving them a connection between the
Spirit and himself. The Spirit who would come was *his*
breath, *his* Spirit, his blowing upon them. So they never
made the mistake of separating too far the Spirit and Jesus.

Thirdly, he was giving them a command: "Receive". It
is an imperative verb. Why did he say that? Because, with
the best will in the world, a gift can be refused. Sometimes
I have wanted to help someone, and I have said, "Here you

are," and they have said, "No, I couldn't take that." "Go on. Here you are. I want to give it to you; I want to help you." "No, I couldn't." One wants to say, "Receive. Take what I'm giving. Don't refuse, I'm wanting to help." The Holy Spirit does not force himself or any of his gifts on any Christian. You can resist the Spirit; you can turn down his gifts. You can keep him right out of your life and out of your church if you wish. It is within our human power to resist the Spirit, and when he wants to fill us, to refuse and to grieve him in so doing.

I have found that one of the reasons many people back off from asking to be filled with the Spirit is the fear that he will make them do something they are not willing to do. The answer is that you need never fear any such thing. The Holy Spirit doesn't force anyone to do anything, but when God breathes, when the Lord Jesus blows, then those who are willing to receive – actively to take what he is giving – will know great love, great joy, great peace and great power, but those who sit tight and say "I'm scared, I don't want this, I want to be in charge of myself, I don't want to be taken over by him or anyone else" can go home without anything happening.

I remember once in younger days, amongst students, we were getting interested in hypnotism and decided to try it out. So one of the young men said, "I can do it," and he started dangling watches and so on. Most of us that he tried it on were quite determined not to go under. We didn't want to be the first, until one poor student was willing to go under and was under the influence. It is right to have a healthy fear of hypnotism because it puts you in the control of a man who is not perfect, who could do things to you that were wrong and damage you. But why should one fear coming under the control of the Holy Spirit? The very word "holy" removes your fear that anything can happen that can harm, hurt, damage or destroy.

Jesus said "Receive", so let the Holy Spirit come, don't resist. So the first step was a sign, a connection and a command.

The last mention of the Holy Spirit in Luke's Gospel and the first mention of him in Acts is in the same upper room. Jesus told them to wait in Jerusalem until they had been baptised in the Holy Spirit with power, and that then they would be his witnesses to the uttermost parts of the earth. He said it just before he went back to his Father in heaven.

There are two points to make about this. It is quite obvious they still had not received the Holy Spirit in power, even at this stage. And it is also quite obvious that they would know when they had. There are those who think the Holy Spirit comes so quietly that you don't even know he slipped in. This is utterly alien to the New Testament. When he comes, you know it, and they would know it, and that was why he was able to tell them to wait until he came, because they would know perfectly well when he came. They would be left in no uncertainty. But the two key words in these passages, at the end of Luke and the beginning of Acts, are: "power" and "wait".

We need to know that there are two important Greek words: *exousia* (authority) and *dunamis* (power; ability). It is quite different having the authority to do something and having the ability to do something. The word translated "power" in Acts 1, and at the end of Luke, means "ability". They already had the authority, but they didn't have the ability.

When you apply for a provisional driving licence, you have the authority to drive a car, but you do not have the ability and you may buck along the road and veer around. The poor person sitting with you will be reaching for the handbrake!

Here is the authority of Jesus: he said to the disciples on the Mount of Olives, "All authority in heaven and on earth is given to me; therefore, you go and make disciples of all nations...." But they were to wait until they were given the ability, in the Greek language, the *exousia*. They now had Jesus' authority to preach anywhere, at any time, in any place. They were to go and preach to every creature, but to wait until they got the ability. So this is the difference that the Holy Spirit makes—he turns the Great Commission into the "great compulsion". The Great Commission is to go and make disciples of all nations. The great compulsion is that the Holy Spirit will send you.

I have heard a number of sermons preached from Acts 1:8 and all have misquoted the text, and it is a misunderstanding. It is often read as though it says: you shall receive power to witness. But that is not what Jesus said. He said both that "you shall receive power" and that "you shall be my witnesses". If they would wait for the ability, they would be his witnesses. It would happen spontaneously. It will no longer be an outward, imposed "must", it would be an inward "must", constrained by the Holy Spirit. When they had received the ability, the power, they would do it, they would not need to be told to. They won't need to be exhorted to go out and evangelise or to be pushed to the ends of the earth. When they received power, they would be witnesses to Jesus. If you just set out on the authority of Jesus, it is a must, a demand, something that you ought to do and try to do. But if you wait for the power, then it is something you want to do, you are bursting to do, you must do from inside, and that is the difference.

I suppose many of us have exhorted people to win others for Christ, to go out and talk about Jesus, telling them that we must go and preach the gospel to every creature. But I have noticed that it doesn't achieve much, telling people to

151

witness, because that is just giving them authority to. What people are wanting is the ability to, and alas they often look in the wrong direction for it and ask for classes and training courses, handbooks and manuals in which they can look up and find out which category their neighbour is, and then they know what to say to them next time they meet them. But the ability doesn't come that way. A person filled with the Holy Spirit will overflow into the lives of their neighbours. The ability will be there. They will have an entirely different method from anyone else. They will develop that which will fit their own personality. It will be a spontaneous outgoing which is so different from, "We must hold a crusade, we must evangelise, we must fulfil the Great Commission." Wait until you receive the ability, the power – and seek that power.

This brings me to the second key word, which is often misunderstood: "wait". This sounds as if they had to do nothing until something happened. I have known some who have thought that "wait" was a passive word. In the Bible "wait" is an active, busy word that means doing something, not sitting down in an armchair doing nothing until something happens. Just to help you to realise that this is what the English word "wait" means, next time you go to a café and call the waiter I hope it's not someone who is sitting doing nothing! A waiter is somebody who is busy – active, serving.

Let me illustrate this from Acts 1. Did they do nothing between Jesus ascending from the Mount of Olives, and Pentecost? Did they all sit around doing absolutely nothing, as we would say: "waiting?" Nothing of the sort; they were very busy. For one thing they were busy organising. They were busy making up the gap in the apostles. They were busy electing officers. They were busy organising the church, getting it ready for the power when that came, so that it was well managed, so that it was according to the Word of

God. They were studying the Bible so that they might have a knowledge of God's will. They were praying during those ten days. They gathered together for prayer, 120 of them. They held a prayer meeting every day for ten days.

When a church is really waiting for the power of the Holy Spirit it will be terribly busy. It won't just be sitting in pews doing nothing. People will be gathered around the Bible, studying it in groups; people will be praying hard in groups. People will be organising the church, getting the machine running efficiently, getting ready so that when God sends the power, the force to be mobilised is there. Waiting always includes activity. That is why the Bible tends to say not waiting *for* the Lord, but waiting *on* the Lord. I wonder if you have learned how to wait on the Lord. Most people can wait for the Lord and just sit and wait for him to do something. Anybody can do that. But wait on the Lord by busily doing the things that can already be done, and above all, be drenching it all in an expectant prayer. "Lord, we're getting the organisation ready, but pour out the power, give us the ability."

Here is the difference I notice: the church in the New Testament was just as active before Pentecost as after. But before Pentecost everything they achieved was inside the church; after Pentecost most things they achieved happened outside. Now this is the difference the power of the Holy Spirit makes. You can be terribly busy, you can organise, you can be reading your Bible and you can be praying. You can do all this within the church, but what is it that sends a church out into the streets, into the neighbourhood, into the houses of neighbours, with a dynamic that changes lives? It is the difference between living before and after Pentecost. It is the difference between having the authority to preach and having the ability—the power.

That was step number two for them, and step number

three, of course, came on the day of Pentecost. For a fuller study of that portion of the Acts of the Apostles, please refer to my book on ACTS in my New Testament Commentary series. But there are a few points we need to note here. First, Pentecost was a *definite experience*. There can be no question about that. Everybody knew it happened. It was so clear. Nobody could have been in any doubt that the Holy Spirit had come. If a person says to me, "I'm not sure whether I've been filled with the Spirit or not," I would just say very humbly, "Then I think you must go on seeking, because if you had been there would be no doubt."

Something happened to them and they heard something, saw something and did something. Whether or not the particular manifestations they had, which have happened to others, happen to us, if we are filled with the Holy Spirit then it will be as definite to us as it was to them. It happened to *all* of them and to *each* of them, and I love the combination of those two words. It was not that everybody was swept into something by mass hysteria. It happened to each of them together so it happened to all of them. It was an individual thing. The tongues of flame touched each of them. The Holy Spirit deals with people as individuals. He doesn't sweep masses into experiences that will die away as quickly as they come. He brings each individual, and sometimes a group of individuals together, into his power. When it comes together, it is a very wonderful moment.

I want to point out that they were filled to overflowing and the overflow for the human body is the mouth. Every single time in the New Testament the Holy Spirit came, that is where the overflow showed that they were full. You will never know you are absolutely filled until you overflow, and you can't overflow until you are filled. If our Christian experience is so low down that we have to dig deep into our own experiences to give a bit away to somebody else, we shall find very quickly in Christian service that we are getting dry and stale ourselves. As when the woman touched the hem of Jesus' garment, if you ever help someone spiritually, goodness has gone out of you. It is a costly business witnessing and helping people. Goodness goes out of you when you are serving others in the name of Jesus. That is why you need to be overflowing rather than dipping down in the bottom of your own little well, and this is what happened here.

I notice that they overflowed to God first, and the world cannot understand this. The world can only understand overflowing to other people. The world can only understand money or service to people. They cannot understand a service of worship. "What do you do, wasting your time in there singing hymns and things? You should be out in the streets helping people – much more use." They cannot understand that we are called to love God first. But when you are filled with the Holy Spirit, your overflowing is to God long before it is to people. You will praise him before you preach. On the day of Pentecost they were filled and they began to speak and extol the mighty works of God – not to men, because nobody had yet gathered to hear them – but it flowed out in praise to God. When a person is flowing in praise to God, then they will flow in preaching to men and women.

The other big thing that I notice about the day of Pentecost is that it led straight into effective evangelism because people could see in ordinary people the power of God at work. These were not professional preachers but Galileans, fishermen, men and women, old men, young men, maidservants, menservants, regardless of age, class, gender. When people see ordinary men and women who are filled with the Holy Spirit, they wonder at this. How do they do it? How is it they are so full of God? They have not been to theological college. The answer is that the Holy Spirit is no respecter of persons.

When we study the next few chapters of Acts, we discover that the real boss in the early church was the Holy Spirit. I know that Peter was the first pastor (not the first pope; that means "father" and Jesus had warned disciples not to call each other "father") but he did call Peter a "shepherd", which is "pastor". Peter was not the *leader* of the church, he was the pastor.

It is right that the church should have officers appointed for particular tasks, and so they had a pastor and deacons. But the pastor didn't lead the church and nor did the deacons. The church meeting didn't lead the church either, as if it were some kind of new democracy in which the church members could all have their say, and "any other business" was the kind of complaint section at the end of a church meeting!

So who was in charge? In Acts 3, I find the Holy Spirit gave them power to give that man health in his legs. In chapter 4 I find that when the apostles were put on trial for their lives, the Holy Spirit gave them holy boldness and wisdom to defend themselves in court most effectively. In chapter 5 I find that when church members sinned they were not sinning against the members, the deacons or the pastor, they were sinning against the Holy Spirit, and he dealt with them through Peter. In chapter 6 I see that when the deacons were selected it was not a matter of finding the most popular men in the church, it was: "Seek out seven men full of the Holy Spirit and of wisdom."

The Holy Spirit equipped them for their task. In Acts 7, I find that the first martyr who died for Jesus went to his death filled with the Holy Spirit, and he had a vision of Jesus in heaven next to the Father. The Lord was waiting to receive Stephen. In chapter 8 I find that the mission spread for the first time beyond the confines of Israel and went into Samaria. A city was filled with joyful, believing baptised people who were then filled with the Holy Spirit and they became a church. Did you notice this? The church in Samaria was started by the church members from Jerusalem, not by the ministers. The apostles stayed in Jerusalem, but the disciples, the rest of them, were scattered abroad. The Holy Spirit was doing this. In Acts chapter 9 we have the account of Paul converted on the Damascus road. When did you last hear a preacher mention what happened three days later? A Christian called Ananias, who had been filled with the Holy Spirit, came to Paul three days after he had been converted and said he had been sent to baptise him in water and to lay his hands on him, that he would be filled with the Holy Spirit. That is how Paul began, not just by a Damascus road conversion, not just by being baptised in water. I am quite sure Saul wasn't perfectly sanctified after just three days (from what he wrote later, I know perfectly well that he wasn't) but he could be filled with the Spirit now to get it all going. Ananias knew that Saul believed in Jesus, and he baptised him and helped him to get filled with the Spirit, and then he would be able to get on with the work that he had been given to do.

In chapter 10, in Caesarea there was a man who was not even one of the people of God (though the Samaritans had some Hebrew blood in them). Cornelius was a Roman regimental sergeant major, a Gentile. There he was, in an army camp in Caesarea. Peter comes and preaches, and during the sermon the Holy Spirit is poured out on this soldier – not a very mystical or sentimental kind of person, the backbone of the Roman army. Cornelius would have been a tough and courageous man and now he was filled with the Holy Spirit. What a mighty Christian he would be!

In chapter 11 we are in Antioch, spreading further afield. It was the place everybody made for if they wanted to sin. Right there in that place, growing like a cluster of chaste snowdrops on a foul rubbish heap, a little group of Christians met. And there came Barnabas, full of the Holy Spirit, to see what was going on and to help them.

In that place Agabus, full of the Holy Spirit, prophesied a famine a few years before it happened so that they could start collecting beforehand. That is really something, isn't it? We collect for disaster relief after we have heard of it, but in those days the Holy Spirit said there was going to be a famine and they had better start saving up now. The Lord can see what is coming. Needs are anticipated when the Holy Spirit is in charge. When men are in charge they can only see the need after it has come.

In one church where I was pastor a long time ago, there had been a man of God ministering, and he had been filled with the Holy Spirit. The church building only got half full at that time—they never used the gallery. He said, "We must buy the four cottages on one side of the church, two cottages, the fish and chip shop and the pub on the other side, and the two cottages at the back." They said to him that the church wasn't full, to which he replied: "The Lord tells me that it's going to be needed." He persuaded them to buy when cottages were going for about five hundred pounds each. The time came when we needed that land to expand, to pull those cottages down and get more building up for the Lord and expand the work. That man's vision thirty or forty years previously, when there was no sign of it being needed, meant that we had got the land to do it. The Holy Spirit can plan ahead where people can't.

In chapter 12, Peter is imprisoned and, following a prayer meeting, it is by the power of the Holy Spirit that he is released. In chapter 13, Paul and Barnabas are set apart. The Holy Spirit tells the church at Antioch to send people out as missionaries. Nowadays we usually wait until someone says "I feel called." Why should we wait for that? Why should not the Holy Spirit say, "Send that one out"?

The early church did not have most of the things we think we need. They didn't have any ministers trained in Christian theology – though they had those who had done a three-year course with Jesus, and that was worth many times more than the theology that I studied! They did of course know the scriptures (the Old Testament). They didn't have any buildings (which is not to say that buildings aren't sometimes useful). They didn't have much finance. "Silver and gold have I none," said Peter to the beggar. They didn't have any organisation with impressive headquarters in some big city. What did they have? They had the *dunamis* (power), they had the ability, they had the Holy Spirit. God can honour dedicated natural gifts. He can use a building offered to him. He can use energies and an organisation. But only in the church where members are filled with the Holy Spirit (not just knowing a doctrine about him), does God do things like this.

It is my sad conviction that the church today has become obsessed with matters of authority and governance, and has forgotten the essential matter of ability. Jesus first gave the authority to disciples, then the ability. "All authority in heaven and on earth is given to me." We want it for ourselves. Ministers have said to me, "Oh, if I had a bit more authority, if I didn't have to try and persuade all the church meeting to do something and have to wait until the deacons could agree; if I had more authority I could get on!" Jesus has the authority, it is we who lack the ability. So how do you get the ability? Is Pentecost once for all, or can it be repeated? Are these things part of what might be called "the first stage" – the first part of the rocket that boosted the church into orbit, which has now dropped away and we can now forget? Or does what we have been thinking about here belong to the continued essence of the church?

Here I must be personal. I was brought up a Methodist,

but I do not recall hearing in those days anybody talking to me about the Holy Spirit filling someone or being poured out, or falling upon them. I have friends among the Brethren and I thought, "Now surely they will know the answer to this question," but I was puzzled by what they had to say. I got from them a picture of the history of the church as having been something like a journey into space where there is a terrific blaze of power at the beginning, followed by a very quiet and monotonous voyage, with the sense that we are not likely to see anything terribly exciting until we get near to the Lord's second coming, and an idea that now that we have the Bible we don't need this supernatural power of the Holy Spirit as much. Well that was the impression I got in those days, and maybe I am being unfair!

The next group of friends I talked to were Anglicans. They said to me, "Oh yes, you can be baptised in the Spirit today, but you were when you were converted, and that's all you'll get. When you were born of the Spirit that's the same thing as Pentecost." Yet when I was born of the Spirit nothing happened like Pentecost to me and it happened unconsciously if it was concerned with the Holy Spirit because I never thought about him then. They did tell me that I could be filled with the Spirit if I emptied my life of everything that was wrong, which I am afraid was so discouraging – to hold this carrot before me, that at the end of the road, when I was perfect, I could be filled, and that I couldn't be filled until I got everything else out. That put this experience so far out in the future that I just gave up and stopped thinking about it. If it is a reward at the end of the road for a long life of getting better, then most of us can forget about it for the time being.

Then I talked to some friends among the Baptists and found they were so preoccupied with baptism in water that they had never discussed baptism in the Holy Spirit, and in not a single statement in Baptist history was anything said about it.

So I was left with only one alternative. It was to ask what God said about the subject. I spent many months going through the Bible and saying: God, what's your answer to this question? I am bewildered by all these people from different backgrounds who tell me this, that and the other, and I don't feel that any of them have told me what I have noticed in the New Testament. Will you speak to me? Is Pentecost something that is once and for all, that it is done with, the stage one of the rocket, and should I read it as history and forget about it now as far as I'm concerned? Was I baptised in the Spirit when I was converted even if I didn't realise it at the time, or is there something more that you have got for me and for every Christian today that explains why the church is not as dynamic and powerful as it was in Acts?

What follows is the fruit of what I found from God's Word alone, not from other people. First I am going to give you the conclusion I came to, then I am going to describe the steps by which I was led to it. The conclusion was that Pentecost is a definite experience, available to every believer who will ask until they are given and seek until they find and knock until it is opened to them; that it is an experience quite distinct from being born again, and that it is a blessing which God intended all of us to have, for the promise is to you and your children and to all that are afar off, as many as the Lord our God shall call to him, which I would think includes me and includes every true son of God. How did I come to that position? Mainly through reading Acts, but partly through looking at one or two other passages. I went back to Luke chapter 11:

'If you then, though you are evil, know how to give good gifts to your children, how much more will your Father

in heaven give the Holy Spirit to those who ask him!'
Luke 11:13, NIV

It struck me as a new discovery that the giving of the Holy Spirit is not automatic but must be requested. Now if that is so, then it is quite clearly not conversion, for two reasons. First of all, it is quite obvious that an unbeliever can't ask for the Holy Spirit. He couldn't receive him anyway, and it is unlikely he would even bother to ask or be interested. If the believer has already received the gift automatically at conversion, he doesn't need to ask for it. So who is this verse for, if automatically at my conversion I received this gift of which Jesus speaks so I don't need to ask? On that interpretation this verse would not make sense.

I came to the conclusion that Jesus was giving lessons in prayer to his believers, his disciples. He has just given them the Lord's Prayer, which I believe is for Christians to use. Now he has told them to ask for the gift of the Holy Spirit. So there must, I thought, be some gift for which I should be asking, that I don't have yet as a believer—some blessing, some outpouring the heavenly Father longs to give me, but isn't giving because I am not asking, not wanting. That was the first step in a search that led a long way.

Returning to John 7:39 took me a step further. I discovered there that there is a difference between *believing* in the Lord Jesus and *receiving* the Holy Spirit, and that there can be a considerable gap between the two events. For Jesus has been saying, "If anyone thirsts, let him come to me and drink. He who believes in me, as the scripture has said, out of his heart shall flow rivers of living water." This he said about the Spirit those who believed in him were to receive or, in quite literal translation of the Greek: "Which those who had believed in him were going to receive." In other words, they believed without receiving this gift. They had already believed in Jesus. They did not yet know this river of living water flowing out of their heart. Many Christians today are in the same position.

Then I turned to Acts 2. The question which now troubled me was: *when* were these 120 people converted? I discovered that every Christian I know, and every commentator I could read, were agreed that the 120 people who were baptised in the Holy Spirit on the day of Pentecost had all been converted before then. Opinion differed as to when they were converted. Some said before Jesus died; some said after he died. But they are all quite sure that on the day of Pentecost the 120 people were converted believers praying for the gift and promise of the power of the Holy Spirit. So, to me, here was absolute proof that these two things are different and distinct from one another and that there was something more waiting for me in God's providence that I had not enjoyed at my conversion, something more that I could ask for, something more that I, as a believer like the 120, could pray for and seek until I found.

Then I began to gallop through the rest of the book of Acts because I read that on the day of Pentecost Peter said to his hearers that they could have what the disciples had just got. The promise that had been fulfilled in them, the gift given, was to others as well. There is no limit in time and space on this – it is for everyone whom the Lord our God calls. I began to ask whether there was any proof in the Bible that Pentecost was more than a once and for all event that you could then celebrate annually.

Returning to chapter 8, I remembered those events we mentioned earlier, in Samaria. We recall that there was persecution in Jerusalem. The safest place for the Christians to run to was Samaria because the Jews would not go there. They were led in their flight by a Spirit-filled deacon called

Philip. Those Christians didn't hide in back streets. They went out into the main streets, and everywhere they went they preached. (See Acts 8:4.) The result was that revival broke out. It wasn't planned, but miracles happened; men and women were healed of their sicknesses. People believed in the Lord Jesus. There was much joy in that city, and Philip baptised them in the name of the Lord Jesus. Now there are many people who would have been quite content with all that and might say of such events: "That's wonderful – crowds of people believing in Jesus, repenting of their sins and being baptised in water." But God was not content with that, and even though the city was full of joyful, baptised Christian believers, God says: "but". (His "but" is in vv. 14–16.)

Now when the apostles at Jerusalem heard that Samaria had received the Word of God, they sent to them Peter and John, who came down and prayed for them, that they might receive the Holy Spirit, for he had not yet fallen on any of them but they had only been baptised in the name of the Lord Jesus. Then they laid their hands on them and they received the Holy Spirit.

How did they know they had not yet received the Holy Spirit? Here is a further thought that struck me. It must have been that until that time, every other Christian had had his own Pentecost or they would never have noticed that there was something missing in those Samaritans. If nothing spectacular had happened from the day of Pentecost until this moment they would have accepted their faith as sufficient. But here, for the first time, was a group of Christians who believed in Jesus, who had repented of their sins, who were filled with joy, who had been baptised in water in the name of Jesus, but nothing had happened to them – there had been no manifestation of supernatural power filling their lives. Again it is clear from this passage that you can repent and believe and be baptised in water and be filled with joy without having received this gift. It is quite clear that something is missing if you are in this condition. Peter and John, those wise men of God, came down. They were going to pray, to help those believers to seek. They wanted to share everything they had. The sentence says, "And as they laid hands [literally] on each one, the Spirit fell on that one." And as they prayed for the next, the Spirit fell on the next and it went right down the line of those believers like that. Now then, I don't know what happened when the Spirit fell on them. Something happened so clearly that a man standing by, one who had played about with black magic and who had now professed faith in Christ and been baptised (a man called Simon) was amazed when he saw what happened to each person. He went to Peter and offered money if he could have the power so he could give it to other people. They would think Simon was an even greater miracle worker than they thought before. Peter said, "To hell with you and your money. Do you think you can buy things from God? It's a gift. It's not something you can buy or pay for; it's a gift to be received. Unless you repent, your money will perish with you." (The word "perish" is the same as the word for "hell" elsewhere.)

The point I want to make is this: not only were these Samaritans happy, joyful, baptised believers in the Lord without this gift, but, when they received it, it was so utterly clear that even somebody else standing there knew they had received. We must acknowledge that Simon saw something more definite there than he would see in many of us.

Somebody once said to me, "I need to be filled with the Spirit to get rid of sin in my life. It's no use telling me that if I do, then I can have the Spirit. I want to start with him so that I can be like this." That seems to me more scriptural. Pentecost happened in Acts 2, not Acts 28. It didn't happen at the end of their pilgrimage, it happened at the beginning to get them going.

In Acts 10 we have another remarkable account of two men who normally would never have met, except for Jesus. Jews and the Gentiles did not usually have much to do with each other. Peter had a dream in which the Lord made it clear that he, Peter, who had despised unclean things, animals and people, now had to get all that out of his mind because, as we saw earlier, he was to go to the Gentile Cornelius, and tell him about Jesus. At the same time, the Gentile was having a dream, and God told him that was Peter coming to see him. So Peter came and met this Gentile. They had a meal together, the first time this Jew Peter had ever eaten a meal with a Gentile. They started talking, and Peter preached to this man and his household. The slaves of the centurion came in and packed the room, and Peter told them about Jesus. These Gentiles had already repented of sin, they were serious and feared God. Now they believed in Jesus. As Peter was preaching, Pentecost happened all over again. The Holy Spirit fell on this company. Peter would not have baptised a Gentile in the name of Jesus until this moment, but now how could he refuse? If God baptises them in the Holy Spirit, how could Peter refuse to baptise them in water? He did so.

Once again, we see these are necessary to the full Christian experience: repentance from sin, believing in Jesus, baptism in water, and receiving the Holy Spirit—four definite things which God wants every person to have. One thing we notice here is that the order was slightly different from elsewhere. It was normally: repent, believe, be baptised, be filled with the Holy Spirit. Here, the last two are reversed. Why? Simply because they would never have got baptism in water from Peter unless God had shown the apostle that he had to acknowledge what had occurred. God, in his mercy, reversed the sequence, convincing Peter that these people were indeed his, and that he could go ahead and baptise them. It is the only case recorded in the New Testament in which those last two events were reversed. Everywhere else it is: one, repent; two, believe; three: be baptised in water; and four, be filled with the Holy Spirit and receive the promise. So here was Cornelius. Again we see everybody knew that the Holy Spirit had been poured out upon these people. How? Because they did exactly the same that had been done on the day of Pentecost—they opened their mouths and they praised God in other languages.

Peter, when he got back to Jerusalem, got into serious trouble from the Jewish Christians who had heard about him baptising Gentiles. Peter's answer was that they too had been baptised in the Holy Spirit. How could he refuse? They praised God that God had given life to the Gentiles. Notice that *life* was linked with the gift of the Holy Spirit. It is one thing to have the promise of eternal life, and another thing to have abundant life – and it is the abundant life that they had been given now.

The clearest passage of all, and the one which helped me to see most clearly what God had said about the matter, is in Acts chapter 19.

While Apollos was at Corinth, Paul took the road through the interior and arrived at Ephesus. There he found some disciples and asked them, 'Did you receive the Holy Spirit when you believed?'

They answered, 'No, we have not even heard that there is a Holy Spirit.'

So Paul asked, 'Then what baptism did you receive?'

'John's baptism,' they replied.

Paul said, 'John's baptism was a baptism of repentance. He told the people to believe in the one coming after him, that is, in Jesus.'

On hearing this, they were baptised in the name of the Lord Jesus. When Paul placed his hands on them, the Holy Spirit came on them, and they spoke in tongues and prophesied. There were about twelve men in all.

Acts 19:1–7, NIV

Paul had found some disciples who knew that Jesus is the Christ and they had the scriptures in their hands. They had been taught by a man called Apollos, who was well versed in the scriptures and who also believed that Jesus was the Jewish Messiah – and that was as far as it went. Paul knew what was missing. He got these twelve men together and he asked them this question: when you believed in Jesus, did you receive the Holy Spirit? He was not asking a theological question, he was asking a simple question about their experience. They didn't know what to say. They had heard about Jesus, but had never even heard about the Holy Spirit. Nobody had taught them. Here is the basic reason why so many Christians are running on three cylinders instead of four: because they have never been taught about the Holy Spirit. They have never read about him; they have never studied; they have assumed that if they have believed in Jesus, that was all that was needed.

It is vital to tell a person beginning the Christian life about the Holy Spirit, and that baptism in water is not the whole story. Those believers had had the baptism of John. They had repented of their sins, because John's was a baptism of repentance; and they said that Jesus is the Christ but had they believed in him? They obviously had not been baptised properly. No wonder they had not received the Holy Spirit. So of the four things which are clearly seen to be part of Christian beginnings, they had only got one of them. So Paul taught them about Jesus and they now believed in Jesus properly. They had repented and believed, so then he got them baptised in the name of Jesus in water. They now had three, but there was one more thing they still didn't have. Once again, we have a picture in the New Testament of Christians who had repented and believed and been baptised, and still lacked. It is so utterly plain. Every Christian reader of the New Testament has agreed that by that v. 5 they were converted people; Paul would not have baptised them unless they believed in Jesus and had been converted, but still he prayed for them, he laid hands on them, and they received too. Once again, supernatural manifestations were given. They spoke with tongues and they prophesied. To speak with tongues is to praise God in a language you never learned, and to prophesy is to give a message from God in your own language. Both of these are things that you cannot do by nature. Everybody knew that those twelve were now full of the Holy Spirit and had been anointed and sealed and confirmed.

It is very strange that this laying on of hands and praying for the Holy Spirit became crystallised and then fossilised in a rite called "confirmation". Many people go through the rite and the outward form of it, but never get the inward reality – they have never had supernatural manifestation and have never shown the power. The outside of a thing is worse than useless if it isn't balanced by the inside. Mind you, I heard of a bishop who confirmed someone and uttered the words, praying that the Holy Spirit would come upon the person being confirmed – and he did! He was poured out on this candidate for confirmation. The bishop nearly jumped out of his mitre, having never seen such a thing, but it worked that time. I believe that what we need is more of the "confirmation" that God gives.

Conversion is a human thing. You convert yourself, God doesn't convert you, so the Bible says. Jesus said, "Except you convert yourselves, you'll never enter the kingdom of heaven." Or he says you can convert a brother and cover a multitude of sins. Conversion is the human side and it consists of repenting, believing and being baptised. God's act is when he pours out the Holy Spirit and says, "This is a child of mine. Here is my seal upon this man, this woman. I pour out my Spirit upon this child as a guarantee that he is mine. I fill him with my Spirit and give him my power. I fulfil my promise" – that is divine confirmation and this seems to me the lesson from the book of Acts and what it says about the Holy Spirit. Even if you have repented, even if you have believed in Jesus, even if you have been baptised in water, ask God to confirm you by pouring out his Holy Spirit upon you.

This was the point I reached in my own Bible studies and then I discovered two things. First of all, I found a widespread prejudice (and I deliberately call it that) against a gift of God. People began to say, "You in the tongues movement...." What a ghastly phrase! They began to say, "Oh, you don't like that sort of thing, do you?" Why do people despise a gift of God? I find that in the majority of cases in the book of Acts, this was precisely the way in which God chose to confirm a man or a woman. I find that this was precisely the gift which he used time and again to show that he was supernaturally in control of a person so that he could speak languages and utter praise in tongues that they had never heard or learned. That proves it, but I found this prejudice, people warning and saying all kinds of odd things. I said, "God, I don't care – I want what you've got for me, I want to be confirmed, I want to be filled, I want to be baptised, whatever happens. I just want you and I'm going to ask until I receive, and I am going to seek until I find."

There was just one more question that was a blockage in my mind and I had to sort that out first. It was this: all this happened way back in the apostolic days, the early days.

Are those people right who say these things don't happen today, but that they were just for that period and have now vanished? I came to the conclusion that the only person I would accept as saying this and from whom I would believe it to be true would be God himself. So I said, "God, I'm going to go through the New Testament to find if you ever said anywhere that these things were of the past and would pass away." I found one passage in which God said these things would pass away, where he said tongues will pass away, where he said prophecy would pass away. It was in 1 Corinthians 13. Eagerly, I looked up this passage and said, "When, God, will all these things pass away?" I read: when the perfect has come, when I know God as well as he now knows me, when I no longer see through a glass darkly. I thought: Lord, that has not come yet. So they have not passed away yet. All that the New Testament says concerning the Holy Spirit is for us today. These are the last days, in which we live. So I found that throughout the New Testament there was not a single word of God to suggest in any way that these things were not for today.

One of the things which the coming of the Holy Spirit made gloriously possible was the gift of prophecy for any believer. In the first half of the book of Acts it is the gift of tongues which seems to be singled out more than any other, perhaps linking that with the gift of boldness. But when we come to Acts 11 the gift of prophecy begins to be exercised, and this goes on through the rest of the book. There are nine references to it in the book of Acts, which I want to take you through and comment on briefly. We have already noted the prophecy of famine by Agabus in Acts 11:27. He wasn't a preacher, he wasn't a teacher, it wasn't his job to get up and give sermons. Agabus was a man filled with the Holy Spirit, and he could prophesy. Now you notice that Barnabas and Saul were the treasurers of the relief fund and were sent with the money to Jerusalem. Those two figures appear again in Acts 13.

> Now in the church at Antioch there were prophets and teachers: Barnabas, Simeon called Niger, Lucius of Cyrene, Manaen (who had been brought up with Herod the tetrarch) and Saul. While they were worshipping the Lord and fasting, the Holy Spirit said, 'Set apart for me Barnabas and Saul for the work to which I have called them.' So after they had fasted and prayed, they placed their hands on them and sent them off.
>
> The two of them, sent on their way by the Holy Spirit, went down to Seleucia and sailed from there to Cyprus.
>
> *Acts 13:1–4, NIV*

Barnabas and Saul had been called of God to the mission field, they knew it and other people knew it, but they had not yet gone. Why? Because they were waiting for the Holy Spirit to tell them when to go and where to go. Once you have heard a call to be a missionary, when and where become the main questions. They did not have the answer. Now you notice it was while a group of five prophets and teachers were worshipping that the Holy Spirit spoke – through prophecy. I used to think in my naivety, before I ever understood what prophecy was, that they must have had a kind of impulse, they took a vote on it, or somebody had a kind of thought about this, and that this was how the Holy Spirit normally spoke. I know much better now.

These were prophets and we are told that they were prophets, so when they worshipped they expected the Holy Spirit to take someone's mouth over and put words in that mouth. The Holy Spirit said: separate for me these two; I have called them, now you send them. They were to be separated from their homes, from that local church, from their daily work, from everything that engaged them now, to this work. Send them out! So it says, not by the ECMS, the Early Church Missionary Society, if there was such a thing, which I don't think there was! Nor being sent out by the Antioch church with their blessing, but: sent out by the Holy Spirit. They had no doubt as to who had sent them out—there had been a word of prophecy.

The third reference is in the same chapter. When they arrived at Cyprus they got an interview with the Governor. They were really getting places with him. He was interested, and if the governor became a Christian, wouldn't it be wonderful. Then it all went wrong because a man who dabbled in magic who was the court conjurer or magician came along and he was furious. He saw his job in jeopardy and he started trying to persuade the governor not to listen.

But Elymas the sorcerer (for that is what his name means) opposed them and tried to turn the proconsul from the faith. Then Saul, who was also called Paul, filled with the Holy Spirit, looked straight at Elymas and said, 'You are a child of the devil and an enemy of everything that is right! You are full of all kinds of deceit and trickery. Will you never stop perverting the right ways of the Lord? Now the hand of the Lord is against you. You are going to be blind for a time, not even able to see the light of the sun.'

13:9–11, NIV

Now there is a prediction, and a pretty horrible one. Paul was full of the Holy Spirit and knew from personal experience that God could blind a person. He knew that this was a fitting punishment for those who deliberately set their face against God. If ever there was a description of the most terrible things you could do it is here: to make crooked the straight paths of the Lord. Here is a straight road from God into someone's heart. God is wanting to come straight down that road into that life. You take the road and you twist it, you bend it, you put stiff hills in it so that God has difficulty getting through to that person — this is a terrible thing to do. God had a straight path into a man's heart and this magician was making it crooked. Sadly, I have known many people who have done that. Somebody was getting interested in the gospel, they were getting near, and somebody else in their family makes crooked the straight path of God and dissuades them from going an inch forward, makes it more and more difficult for them to consider accepting Christ. The point I am making is that Paul, full of the Holy Spirit, predicted the man's future. Sometimes a prophecy has to speak of punishment, and many of the Old Testament prophecies did.

The next reference is at 15:32. Do you realise how many references there are to prophecy in Acts? There is more about prophecy than baptism in water, yet we pay great attention to baptism. Let us do the same to prophecy.

Judas and Silas, who themselves were prophets, said much to encourage and strengthen the believers. *NIV*

These two men only appear in the pages of scripture this once. We know nothing else about them. But we do know that a prophet is able to strengthen his brethren. He is able to make a church strong. He is able to comfort a church in the deepest sense, and the gift of prophecy is given to strengthen the Body of Christ.

Now to 16:6, when Paul's plan went wrong.

Paul and his companions travelled throughout the region of Phrygia and Galatia, having been kept by the Holy Spirit from preaching the word in the province of Asia. When they came to the border of Mysia, they tried to enter

Bithynia, but the Spirit of Jesus would not allow them to.
So they passed by Mysia and went down to Troas.

16:6–8, NIV

How did the Holy Spirit stop them? The word "forbid" means "Don't go." It does not mean to put an impulse in their heart – a sort of feeling that they shouldn't. The word translated "forbid" is saying: "Don't do that." It is quite clear again that Paul, who we are told had the gift of prophecy as well as the gift of tongues, had been waiting on the Lord and the Holy Spirit spoke, giving very clear guidance. Why did the Holy Spirit say no? The answer is that shutting this door and shutting that door, he was driving them forward. Whenever God shuts a door in your face, don't look at the closed door or you might not see the one that he is opening.

Sometimes guidance from the Holy Spirit comes in quite a negative way. Door after door will shut like that. God is saying don't consider any of these side turnings; there's a door ahead that I want you to use. The door in front of them at this stage was the door into Europe, and the gospel came to Europe as a result of this negative prophecy.

Let us move on to chapters 20–21. Paul is nearing the end of his missionary journeys and there are three verses to comment on.

And now, compelled by the Spirit, I am going to Jerusalem, not knowing what will happen to me there. I only know that in every city the Holy Spirit warns me that prison and hardships are facing me.

20:22–23, NIV

Later, they have landed at Tyre:

We sought out the disciples there and stayed with them

seven days. Through the Spirit they urged Paul not to go on to Jerusalem.

21:4, NIV

When they had moved on to Caesarea:

After we had been there a number of days, a prophet named Agabus came down from Judea. Coming over to us, he took Paul's belt, tied his own hands and feet with it and said, 'The Holy Spirit says, "In this way the Jewish leaders in Jerusalem will bind the owner of this belt and will hand him over to the Gentiles."'

21:10–11, NIV

In three different verses we encounter ordinary men and women who predicted, before it ever happened, that if Paul went to Jerusalem he would be bound, imprisoned and afflicted. Paul still went. He said, "I'm going to Jerusalem bound by the Spirit. I've got to go." But in this way the loving heavenly Father prepared this man for all that lay ahead, so that when it happened it did not find him unprepared. As our Lord set his face to go steadfastly to Jerusalem, knowing that he would be killed there, so his follower and servant Paul set his face to Jerusalem knowing perfectly well what was going to happen. He would never have known if the gift of prophecy had not been given. From time to time God wants to prepare his servants for something that lies ahead so that it may not find them unready or unable to meet the crisis when it occurs.

Leaving the next day, we reached Caesarea and stayed at the house of Philip the evangelist, one of the Seven. He had four unmarried daughters who prophesied.

21:8–9, NIV

He was one of the seven, and stayed with them. And he had four unmarried daughters, who were prophetesses, or who prophesied. These daughters had the gift of which I have been speaking, and which is such a useful thing to the church of Jesus Christ. I am tempted to say I wonder if they remained unmarried because they prophesied, because this could be an embarrassment to their husbands – being married to a woman who could make revelations, personal ones at that. But that is mere speculation, I don't know if it was actually the reason. But true to the promise of Acts 2 the gift of prophecy was poured out on women. I don't believe in women preachers or women teachers, which I think is unscriptural. The same scripture that tells us not to have women preachers is perfectly clear that women will prophesy in a church, and Paul allows this, indeed encourages it (see 1 Corinthians 11.) I find that in Christian circles people go to extremes on this issue of women taking a public lead. There are those who say that women must keep absolutely silent and do nothing, and you get those who say they can do anything. The scripture balance is very clear: not preaching and teaching, but praying and prophesying. Where that is observed you have a wonderfully balanced ministry and fellowship. It is utterly clear in the New Testament. So if the Holy Spirit gives a woman a prophecy it is not from her mind so she is not exercising authority over anybody else (she would be if she preached or taught), she is simply God's mouthpiece, and there were prophetesses in the Old Testament too.

The final reference is in the last chapter of Acts. Paul is now a prisoner, in chains in Rome. To that prison there comes a group of Jews who have heard that a Jew is in prison and they want to know why. They have come to visit their fellow Jew and he talks to them, telling them about the kingdom of God and about Jesus, and they don't like it.

Some were convinced by what he said, but others would not believe. They disagreed among themselves and began to leave after Paul had made this final statement: 'The Holy Spirit spoke the truth to your ancestors when he said through Isaiah the prophet:

> "Go to this people and say,
> 'You will be ever hearing but never understanding;
> you will be ever seeing but never perceiving.'
> For this people's heart has become calloused;
> they hardly hear with their ears,
> and they have closed their eyes.
> Otherwise they might see with their eyes,
> hear with their ears,
> understand with their hearts
> and turn, and I would heal them."

'Therefore I want you to know that God's salvation has been sent to the Gentiles, and they will listen!'

28:24–28, NIV

Here we have Paul quoting a prediction made by Isaiah centuries earlier. When the truth came to the Jews they would say: "We're not interested. We don't want to understand, we don't want to hear, we don't want to turn and be healed." Then he adds a prediction of his own in the Holy Spirit: the gospel which you have rejected I predict will be accepted by the Gentiles. That prediction was fulfilled.

We have seen that the gift of prophecy is concerned primarily with the future, about predicting things of which only the God who knows the end from the beginning has knowledge, and revealing those things to the people of God as far as they need to know the future to prepare for it.

Now we come to the crucial question. We can see that this gift goes right through the New Testament. When we study 1 Corinthians 12–14, that is all about the gift of prophecy. When we study the letters to Timothy, Paul says, "Timothy remember the gift that is in you through the laying on of hands by prophetic utterance." When we come to the last book in the Bible, the great book that unveils the future, the writer describes his own book as "this prophecy". But is this gift still around? Is there any reason why it should not be? I know that prophecy is going to pass away. Tongues are going to pass away. Knowledge is going to pass away. When will these things pass away? When we don't need any more communication, when we are in heaven and see God face to face, when we know even as we have been known. We won't need knowledge then, we will have it all. We won't need prophecy or tongues then because we shall all be with him in glory.

Chapter Nine

THE HOLY SPIRIT IN ROMANS

Therefore, since we have been justified through faith, we have peace with God through our Lord Jesus Christ, through whom we have gained access by faith into this grace in which we now stand. And we boast in the hope of the glory of God. Not only so, but we also glory in our sufferings, because we know that suffering produces perseverance; perseverance, character; and character, hope. And hope does not put us to shame, because God's love has been poured out into our hearts through the Holy Spirit, who has been given to us.

Romans 5:1–5, NIV

There is a problem which only Christians have. It is one which every one of the disciples of Jesus had, and they all had it together on the same occasion. Jesus asked them all to ensure that he got a little bit of privacy on the last night of his life and they were quite incapable of doing this. He left them at the gate of the garden of Gethsemane and told them to watch. He was going to pray and he wanted them to watch to see that he was not disturbed, and when he came back after a short interval they were all asleep. Jesus said one thing which pinpoints the problem every Christian has, which may be summed up in our Lord's words to them: "The spirit is willing but the flesh is weak."

This tension, this civil war, this wretched frustration is the tension between what we ought to be and what in fact we are. A Christian has accepted higher standards than anyone else in the world. A Christian has accepted the ideal of God and his laws as the guide for his life and is quite determined to live like that, and then sooner or later discovers that he does not live like that, and that God's standards are way above him.

It is a critical point in the Christian life when you experience this. Sadly, many Christians settle the tensions by settling for less than God's best. Middle aged Christians in particular often get out of this problem by reducing their standards and saying, "Well, no-one is perfect and if I just try to do my best, that surely that will be good enough for God." But the real Christian knows perfectly well that my best is not God's best, and that there is a huge gap between these two things. Now Romans chapters 5, 7 and 8 deal with this problem.

The spirit wants to do certain things but cannot make the body do them. As Paul puts it, with my mind I serve the law of God, but my members seem to serve another law altogether. I want to be God's best, yet I can't be; I want to love God with all my heart, soul, mind and strength, but I find myself loving all kinds of other things. I want to live an upright, straight, honest life but I just cannot make it. This despairing cry of Romans 7, "Oh, wretched man that I am," is the cry of every true Christian sooner or later. If you have never known this agony then ask yourself, "Am I really a Christian? Have I really accepted God's standards or am I simply trying to do my best rather than his best?"

Romans 5:1–5 deals with this problem in the aspect of love. The real problem is this: on the one hand my head says that as a Christian I ought to love everybody, but on the other hand my heart doesn't, and this is the tension. With my head I accept that I ought to love my neighbour as myself. It is impossible, it seems to me, to love everybody in the world. My heart says it is impossible, and I am even going to go further and say that my heart by itself can't even love everybody inside my own church, never mind my own community, or my own nation. The world that God has made – that is utterly beyond my heart. My head says, "I must love everybody," my heart says, "I don't like him and I don't like her...." Is this not part of the tension of the Christian life?

A man asked Jesus, "Who is my neighbour?" He may have been hoping Jesus would say, "Well, the man who lives next door to you and two doors away, and the person who lives opposite." But he didn't. Instead, Jesus gave the example of someone the man would not even have spoken to: a Samaritan. Your neighbour may be a Jew if you are a Samaritan. The implication is that your neighbour is anybody in the world who is in need of your agape love. Quite frankly, my heart is just not capable of that.

You can tell the difference between a church where the members live in Romans 7 and a church where members live in Romans 5 and 8 by this: in a church where the human heart lives on its own love, the church will divide into groups, cliques, small factions of those who like each other, those who have enough in common, those who live in the same kind of house, those who have had the same kind of education, those who like the same kind of music, those who have the same cultural interest. Those groups will often get together in each other's houses, but only with their own kind. By nature this is what our hearts are capable of: we are capable of loving those we like, no more. There is a limit to those we like.

What is the answer to this terrible tension? "I know I should love that person but I don't like them. My heart closes up when I meet them. They're so irritating, they're so different. They're so awkward. I can't love them." Must we go on in this tiny circle of those we like all our lives? The answer is in the Holy Spirit. In this lovely little passage we have a glimpse of the answer to this tension. We are shown faith, hope, and love; Son, Father, and Spirit; and we are shown present, future, and past.

Our past is dealt with through faith in the Son, Jesus Christ. Our future is dealt with through hope in God; but our present is dealt with through love in the Spirit.

Paul shows here that those who really know what the Holy Spirit means will discover that he will do something in this matter of loving and liking, that he will pour God's love into your heart through the Holy Spirit given to you. The very word "pour" means in a super abundance, a bucket full of love, not just eking out a little bit of love for someone, but he will pour God's love into your heart, and this is the answer. No human being has enough love for more than a few people, and a particular few of a particular kind.

So you look around when you are young for someone you could love and someone you could live with for the rest of your life and the circle is quite limited. I don't think it is limited to one but it is limited by your capacity as a human person to love someone else, and their capacity to love you. You might fall deeply in love with someone who couldn't love you, and unrequited love is a very big problem. Or they might fall in love with you and you just don't see anything in them—that's human love.

Many people say, "Surely God will accept us if we do our best." Immediately they have lowered God's standard to theirs. The real answer is this: "My love isn't big enough, but, Lord, *your* love is big enough; could you give me some of *your* love?" God's love is so big that he doesn't just give you a little tumbler full for you, a thimble full for somebody else. *God's love is poured out into our hearts through the Holy Spirit given to us.* In other words, even as a Christian you will find that your heart has too limited a love to love even everybody in your church. That is where you need to love people first. Charity begins at home for the Christian.

The first people you are called to love are the brethren.

Romans 7:6 (NIV) reads like this:

But now, by dying to what once bound us, we have been released from the law so that we serve in the new way of the Spirit, and not in the old way of the written code.

Then *7:14–8:13, NIV*

We know that the law is spiritual; but I am unspiritual, sold as a slave to sin. I do not understand what I do. For what I want to do I do not do, but what I hate I do. And if I do what I do not want to do, I agree that the law is good. As it is, it is no longer I myself who do it, but it is sin living in me. For I know that good itself does not dwell in me, that is, in my sinful nature. For I have the desire to do what is good, but I cannot carry it out. For I do not do the good I want to do, but the evil I do not want to do – this I keep on doing. Now if I do what I do not want to do, it is no longer I who do it, but it is sin living in me that does it.

So I find this law at work: although I want to do good, evil is right there with me. For in my inner being I delight in God's law; but I see another law at work in me, waging war against the law of my mind and making me a prisoner of the law of sin at work within me. What a wretched man I am! Who will rescue me from this body that is subject to death? Thanks be to God, who delivers me through Jesus Christ our Lord!

So then, I myself in my mind am a slave to God's law, but in my sinful nature a slave to the law of sin.

Therefore, there is now no condemnation for those who are in Christ Jesus, because through Christ Jesus the law of the Spirit who gives life has set you free from the law of sin and death. For what the law was powerless to do because it was weakened by the flesh, God did by sending his own Son in the likeness of sinful flesh to be a sin offering. And so he condemned sin in the flesh, in order that the righteous requirement of the law might be fully met in us, who do not live according to the flesh but according to the Spirit.

Those who live according to the flesh have their minds set on what the flesh desires; but those who live in accordance with the Spirit have their minds set on what the Spirit desires. The mind governed by the flesh is death, but the mind governed by the Spirit is life and peace. The mind governed by the flesh is hostile to God; it does not submit to God's law, nor can it do so. Those who are in the realm of the flesh cannot please God.

You, however, are not in the realm of the flesh but are in the realm of the Spirit, if indeed the Spirit of God lives in you. And if anyone does not have the Spirit of Christ, they do not belong to Christ. But if Christ is in you, then even though your body is subject to death because of sin, the Spirit gives life because of righteousness. And if the Spirit of him who raised Jesus from the dead is living in you, he who raised Christ from the dead will also give life to your mortal bodies because of his Spirit who lives in you.

Therefore, brothers and sisters, we have an obligation – but it is not to the flesh, to live according to it. For if you live according to the flesh, you will die; but if by the Spirit you put to death the misdeeds of the body, you will live.

On a visit to Omaha Beach, one of those beaches in Normandy where allied troops landed in World War II, I saw the very well-defended place where many young conscripts died. At one stage so many had died with so little progress up the beach that the commander might have halted the assault. But then there was a breakthrough, the troops reached the top and they were able to move forward. Taking that example, we might think of Romans 7 as the beach and Romans 8 as the cliff top above it. There is fighting in both. But whereas in Romans 7 it is a losing battle, in Romans 8 it is a winning battle. In Romans 7 there is an atmosphere of death (you can see the word "die", "death", "dead" all the way through). It is death to be on this beach only to get so far into the Christian life – you think: better not to have come. But when you get up on to Romans 8, up the cliff, there is still a fight but now the language is: "In all these things we are more than conquerors." It may perhaps be stated that the majority of Christians are still on the beach of the Christian life, still living in Romans 7 and they haven't come out on top in Romans 8.

What is the problem in Romans 7? It is that the battle is too great. It is civil war, which is terrible, but there is one thing even worse than civil war – a man at war with himself. That is the battle in Romans 7. It is a kind of "split personality" that only the Christian has. The person who is not a Christian doesn't have this fight. He has moments when he would like to be better, but he soon comes to terms with them and he usually lowers the standard enough for him to reach it and then he is in a state of psychological equilibrium. So the man who lives next door to you who never goes to church is probably much happier than you are as a Christian. He probably has far less tension and frustration than you have if you are living in Romans 7.

This is a greater wretchedness than anything you knew before you knew Christ: my mind serves the law of God; I have accepted that standard, it is the only right way to live – *his* best, not mine – but my members just can't make it. I know what I ought to do but I find myself doing the opposite. "I really want to do good but what I don't want to do I find myself doing." That is the agony of a divided soul. The man who is not a Christian doesn't accept the law of God. He says, "It's too high a standard."

We can give thanks to God that chapter 7 is not the last word on the subject. If it were, then Christians would be the most miserable people on earth. We would be more wretched than anybody else, because the Christian on the beach, who has only got so far (to accept God's standards, but not to discover how to keep them) is the Christian who will neither enjoy sin nor salvation. Can you imagine anything more miserable than that? Because these are the only two things you can enjoy in life ultimately. You can enjoy the pleasures of sin for a season. Don't let anybody tell you it's misery to sin. For a time it might be great fun—and that is probably part of the difficulty of it. But the man who is in Romans 7 can't enjoy sin because he knows it's wrong, and he can't enjoy salvation because it doesn't seem to mean too much to him – and he is stuck in the middle. If you want to know why so many Christians have long faces you have probably hit on it here, because they are more miserable than they were before they were converted. They are on the beach struggling for their lives, and sometimes the tension is so much to stay there that something cracks. In the middle of D-Day on the beach, on the Omaha beach, a soldier was seen singing softly to himself, crying at the same time and sitting out in the open, throwing pebbles into the sea. The tension of the struggle had snapped him. It was too much.

It seems in Romans 8 as if the thunderclouds clear away and the sun comes out. It seems as if you have got up that cliff and the enemy is on the run. You are still fighting, still in a desperate struggle, but now you are more than a conqueror. It seems in Romans 8 as if you have come out of a cemetery into a garden where things are springing up with life. Instead of the words "dead, death, dying" you have got the words "life, living, alive". Have you noticed the change? The difference is this: in chapter 7, in the discussion or description of the struggle, the Holy Spirit is not mentioned. But 19 times in chapter 8: "Spirit, Spirit, Spirit".

In other words, once again the answer to this tension is the Holy Spirit. You will never get out of it by yourself. "So then," says Paul, summarising the struggle at the end of Romans 7, "I myself serve the law of God with my mind but with my flesh I serve the law of sin." There is no hope of doing anything else but that until we understand what the Spirit can do for us. What can he do for us? A Christian is the only person in a position to serve one of two masters. He can't serve them both at once. He can either serve the flesh or the Spirit. Now a person who is not a Christian doesn't have that choice. He can only serve the flesh, and that is why he is not free. But a Christian is free to choose either. Sadly, many abuse their freedom and choose the flesh, but he can choose the Spirit. If he chooses to live in the Spirit then he will discover that this tension goes.

Look at it in more detail. God has done what we could not do—that is the simple message of Romans 8. We were weak in the flesh. God has done what we could not do. Through his Son he has dealt with the *penalty* of our sin. But through the Spirit he deals with the *power* of it. The object of this is that the law of God might be fulfilled in us. In other words, that we might come up to God's standards. You will never lift yourself up to it but he, by the Spirit, can enable his commands to be fulfilled in you. You will never keep even the Ten Commandments by yourself. There is no point in trying. You might manage six out of the ten—I know of a man called Paul who kept nine out of ten. But I am afraid that when he got to number ten it floored him. You will never keep ten out of ten – which is God's pass mark – except by the Holy Spirit.

Does this happen automatically? No, Romans 8 tells us that there are three things we must do if we are going to know this victory. There is something you must do with your feet, something you must do with your head, and something you must do with everything in between, which just about covers it. With your feet, "Walk after the Spirit"; with your head, "Set your mind on the things of the Spirit"; and with everything in between, "Mortify the deeds of the body that you may live."

So there is no sudden flash in the pan experience which will suddenly get you up on the cliff and keep you there, on the victory side. I don't want to be discouraging but I want to be realistic. Many Christians I meet are hoping that one single experience will help them to have the victory. Well it may help but it won't give them the victory permanently. They go to conference after conference, they go to this place, that place, always seeking for something that will suddenly put it all right, and forever after they will have no bother. I know of no experience that once, by itself, puts you right in this regard.

Take the first word: "walk". If you walk after the Spirit then you will find you are in the victory, in Romans 8. But walking is not a thing you can do once, in a split second, in one single experience. To walk is to go on, step-by-step, in the right direction. What it means simply is this: at moment after moment in your daily life you will come to a fork in the roads, and the flesh will say, "Come my way," and the Spirit will say, "Come my way." If you are going to know Romans 8 every time, you come to the decision that you must walk after the Spirit. Every time he leads you, you will need to follow to know the victory. The Christian can do this; the person who is not a Christian couldn't possibly do it, because the Spirit would not walk in front of them and show them where to go. The Christian who wants to live in Romans 8 every day of their life will need to step out after the Spirit.

It may be quite literally where you go with your physical feet. You may be in a situation where the flesh would take you down one street of a town or city, and the Spirit would take you in the opposite direction. You may have to walk after the Spirit. You would have known the power of the flesh. But the word "walk" is also a metaphor and it means every time you come to the crossroads of decision and the Spirit says, "This way," and the flesh says, "That way," you will need to take the right step at that point if you are going to stay in Romans 8. Take one wrong step and you will be back in Romans 7. You will feel wretched and unhappy, and you will say, "Why should I be like this?" But every time you take a step in the right direction after the Spirit, you will know Romans 8 and you will be more than a conqueror — so that is what you do with your feet.

The second thing we are being told here that we must do to live in Romans 8 is what we do with our minds. Again and again the Bible makes it quite clear that the real place where battles in your life and mine are fought and won are in our thought life. The pictures hanging on the gallery walls of our memory are going to be crucial in the battle. Before the allied armies invaded Normandy they had seen photographs taken by midget submarines. They had been told about what they were going to face and had memorised it all. So people who had never set foot in France knew all about the Normandy beaches – they had mentally fought the battle and invaded the land long before they got there, and they were ready for it when they arrived.

Therefore we must realise when we are in the place of temptation, the place where the battle is fiercest, it will depend on what we have done with our mind before the battle begins as to whether we win it or lose it. If you set your mind on the things of the flesh then when the crisis comes you will follow the flesh. Jesus said this again and again but he was only repeating the book of Proverbs: "As a man thinks, so is he." The real person you are is not the person people see, but the person who thinks, the person who meditates. To be very practical, that covers our reading, our entertainment, newspapers, magazines we browse through, everything that enters in and becomes a thought. If someone is going to set his mind on the things of the flesh, then don't let him expect to live in Romans 8. But if he sets his mind on the things of the Spirit, when the crunch comes he will live in Romans 8. Paul says in Philippians, "Whatever is good, whatever is true, whatever is honest, whatever is lovely, whatever is gracious, whatever is of good report, think on these things and the God of peace will be with you."

Paul also writes that to set the mind on the flesh, on the one hand is death, it kills your spiritual life. You may go to church on Sunday but you won't feel it's alive. It will go dead on you. Your prayer life will go dead. Your Bible will seem to go dead. Why? There is nothing wrong with the church. There is nothing wrong with the Bible or your prayers. What is wrong is that your mind has been set on something else for so long that it has killed your mind – but to set the mind on the things of the Spirit is life and peace.

To set the mind on the things of the flesh is war because the flesh is hostile to God, it is in rebellion toward God. The flesh has declared independence against God, and it cannot come to terms with him. Jesus taught that if you have wished anybody dead, you are a murderer. You have set your mind on the things of the flesh. You may never have committed adultery, and you are horrified at the thought. But have you ever looked at somebody wrongly? If the wrong thought has been in your heart then you are an adulterer. Jesus consistently went right through the act to the thought life that lay behind it. This is where the battle is lost or won.

So if you are going to live in Romans 8, the first thing is to walk after the Spirit. Every time you come to a choice, take the Spirit's path and not the path of the flesh. Secondly, even before you come to such a crisis, make sure that your mind is being set on the right kind of thoughts. Otherwise, when the temptation comes, your thought life is already so much in that temptation that you can't resist it.

The third thing you are to do is with everything in between your head and your feet, and it is to mortify the deeds of the body. Every Christian is called to be a murderer, not of other people but of himself or herself. Once again there have been those who thought this was meant literally. Martin Luther flogged himself with a whip until he fell unconscious in his monastery cell. Others have done this. But we are meant to take this in a deeper sense. We are to be as serious as Martin Luther was in cutting out – "killing" – anything at all that is against the Spirit. Jesus said that if your eye is looking at something it shouldn't, cut it out. He didn't mean blind yourself, he meant cut out what you are looking at. Mortify the deeds of your body.

Sometimes the cells in people's bodies go wrong and it becomes vital that a surgeon or radiotherapy treatment kills that before it spreads the damage. You must kill that life before it ruins the whole body. As a surgeon would be desperate to kill that ugly, evil thing growing in the body, so we are told in Romans 8 that by the power of the Spirit as soon as there is an evil thing growing in your body, mortify it, put it to death, get rid of it before it spreads. By the Spirit you can go on living, before your spiritual life dies on you.

There is a paragraph (vv. 9–11) which I think we must look at. There are two key words – little words, but since this is the Word of God every word matters: "in" and "if". You might overlook those words but they are important: "You are not in the flesh. You are in the Spirit if the Spirit of

God really dwells in you" – *in, if.* There are two statements being made here. The first is that if you are not a Christian you couldn't possibly know Romans 8, because if any man has not the Spirit of Christ he is not one of his. To reverse that statement, you couldn't possibly claim the power of the Spirit if you don't belong to Christ. The Spirit is not of you because Christ is not in you. Until Christ is in you, until his Spirit has come into your heart, has been invited in, you could not possibly know Romans 8. But there is something more than that because not every Christian is living in the Spirit. They can be living in the flesh, or as Paul puts it in 1 Corinthians, you are either a carnal Christian or a spiritual Christian. There are still those two sorts of Christian, and a carnal one is still in the flesh even though he belongs to Christ. A spiritual Christian belongs to the Spirit.

"Now you are not in the flesh if the Spirit really dwells in you." Some people may quarrel with my words here but I think not with the sentiment: I believe that the Spirit does not dwell in every Christian, not in the proper meaning of the word "dwell". If the Spirit really "dwells" in you it means he is there all the time and in every part. If somebody dwells in your house then they are there, they can use every room and they make themselves at home. They are in the kitchen as well as the front room; they are not just an honoured visitor. They dwell there and therefore they are welcome to the whole house. They share all the life; they are there all the time.

Now to many Christians the Spirit is something of a visitor. Now and again they feel his touch, now and again he comes to them, now and again they feel, "Oh, the Spirit is really near me now." But he is just a visitor because they keep him in the front room. Maybe they keep him on Sunday, but on Monday: "Well that room isn't quite fit for him to dwell in, so we'll hope that next Sunday we'll have a touch of the

Spirit again." If the Spirit really dwells in you, Monday as well as Sunday, every day of your life, every part of your life, if he really does dwell there, then he gives life. Your spirit is alive because of *righteousness*. I know that sentence is in Bible language but let me put it into simple terms. The only person who is really alive is the righteous man or woman, the person who is living right.

I have heard so many people tell me they have the impression that if you really want to taste life, then you have got to do all kinds of sin. They think that if you really want to be alive you have got to do what God says is wrong. Don't you believe it! That way is death and war. Those who think that to really live you have got to do wrong just don't understand the Bible. God says that the Spirit makes us alive because of righteousness. Even your mortal body gets the effect. Even though your body is dead because of sin, the Spirit who raised up Jesus, if he really dwells in you, will quicken your mortal bodies. This body will have new vigour in this life, and in the next life it will have a new body altogether. Even in this life the Spirit quickens your mortal body so that you are vigorous and healthy. I am not saying that every Christian will enjoy perfect health, but I will tell you this: that those who live in the Spirit will have more physical energy than those who do not, because the Spirit quickens your mortal body as well as your spirit.

So finally Paul teaches: why live according to the flesh? What do you owe the flesh? Brethren we are debtors not to flesh. What did the flesh ever do for you except bring you to wretchedness, death, and despair? We are debtors to the Spirit. We owe the Spirit our life here and hereafter. Then let us live according to the Spirit because we owe the Spirit everything we have that is worth having. We owe the flesh everything that we have that is not worth having. So why live according to the flesh?

Here then is the problem: we want to do good but can't, we want to love everybody but can't, we want to live but can't, and we find that spiritual life is going dead. What's the answer? It is to walk after the Spirit, to set the mind on things of the Spirit, and by the Spirit to put to death the deeds of the flesh, and then we shall live and be more than conquerors through him who loved us.

We are told again and again not to be conformed to the world outside, but we are. Therefore Christians have stopped singing and talking about heaven. The world has said to the church: we are not interested in the future, we are interested in the here and now. But Christians are the only people in the world who can offer the world hope by talking of the future.

In the Bible, hope is a vital ingredient of real life. Faith is the virtue that makes you sure of the past, and "hope" appears in Romans 5, "...we rejoice in our hope of sharing the glory of God. More than that we rejoice in our sufferings, knowing that suffering produces endurance, and endurance produces character, and character produces hope, and hope does not disappoint us because God's love has been shed abroad in our hearts through the Holy Spirit which has been given to us." That is the first mention of hope and the first mention of the Holy Spirit in the epistle to the Romans, and it is not a coincidence. You will never have hope except through the Holy Spirit. There is another word link in that passage I want to point out because it comes up later. Hope is related to suffering, and hope is the one thing that enables you to suffer and to cope with trouble. Your hope for the future is vital if you are going to cope with suffering in the present. It is the anchor in the storm of trouble.

Hope comes up again in Romans 8 and so does the Holy Spirit. So hope and the Holy Spirit go together, but the other thing that comes up in chapter 8 is suffering. The Bible is absolutely honest and makes no bones about it: if you are going to live in the Spirit you are going to suffer. If you are going to have the victory that we have been thinking about, you will suffer for it, and you desperately need hope if you are going to cope with suffering. Recall this passage:

For those who are led by the Spirit of God are the children of God. The Spirit you received does not make you slaves, so that you live in fear again; rather, the Spirit you received brought about your adoption to sonship. And by him we cry, 'Abba, Father.' The Spirit himself testifies with our spirit that we are God's children. Now if we are children, then we are heirs – heirs of God and co-heirs with Christ, if indeed we share in his sufferings in order that we may also share in his glory.

I consider that our present sufferings are not worth comparing with the glory that will be revealed in us. For the creation waits in eager expectation for the children of God to be revealed. For the creation was subjected to frustration, not by its own choice, but by the will of the one who subjected it, in hope that the creation itself will be liberated from its bondage to decay and brought into the freedom and glory of the children of God.

We know that the whole creation has been groaning as in the pains of childbirth right up to the present time. Not only so, but we ourselves, who have the firstfruits of the Spirit, groan inwardly as we wait eagerly for our adoption to sonship, the redemption of our bodies. For in this hope we were saved. But hope that is seen is no hope at all. Who hopes for what they already have? But if we hope for what we do not yet have, we wait for it patiently. In the same way, the Spirit helps us in our weakness. We do not know what we ought to pray for, but the Spirit himself intercedes for us through wordless groans. And he who searches our hearts knows the mind of the

Spirit, because the Spirit intercedes for God's people in accordance with the will of God.

Romans 8:14–27, NIV

Here is life in the Spirit and there is a tension in this life between the present and the future, between the suffering that we have to go through now, and the glory that is waiting for us, and this produces in the Christian a tension which nobody else has. Only we who have received the firstfruits of the Spirit groan inwardly longing for the future. A Christian is torn between two things: he wants to stay here and he wants to go there.

If you want to know what life is like in the Spirit: you will *cry*, *groan* and *sigh*. I am impressed again and again by the fact that when the Holy Spirit really gets hold of a person it is usually out of that person's mouth that things start to happen. On the day of Pentecost that certainly occurred, and almost every time later you find that when people are filled with the Spirit something tends to come out of the mouth. In other words, you make *sounds*.

Why these sounds and what do they mean? Take the *cry*. When we are in the Spirit, and the Spirit is guiding our life Monday through to Saturday as well as Sunday, when we are walking after the Spirit, when we are being led by him, we *know* that we are sons of God. God is not the Father of all people—the Bible never says so. All men are not brothers because they are not all his sons, and that is the tragedy. If all men became his sons they could become brothers, but to talk of the brotherhood of mankind is a ridiculous dream because it is obvious we are not in that relationship. Read any newspaper and you will see that. Why do we still believe we are? Until we become sons of God, we can't be brothers, and the first step is, through the Holy Spirit, to become *sons of God*.

We may take this a little further. In a Roman family a boy did not become a son until he was between fourteen and seventeen years of age. I don't know if you know the Roman habit of sonship, but Paul is writing to the Romans so we know this is what he means. A man might have a large family, all of them his own. Maybe some were by his wife and maybe some by his slave, but all were his children. There came a day when the father would look at the boys and he would say, "I am going to adopt this one." It was his own child yet he was going to "adopt" it. He would then take this child through a legal ceremony with witnesses, and that child then became his son and heir. The family property and the family name would come to this boy. He was now the son, having been adopted.

Until that point the boy was controlled not by his father but by a slave whom he feared, who made him do the right thing, and punished him when he did wrong, but the day he was adopted the boy would be virtually given the key of the door and was told, "You are no longer under this slave to make you behave; from now on you must behave yourself. You are self-disciplined now." Furthermore, from that point for the first time in his life the boy was allowed to call this man "father" – and this was adoption. Now he was the inheritor of all his father's property, and he was free from external control; now he was controlled by the restraint of love and respect for his father. There was no slave to tell him what to do. Paul is saying: don't you realise that when you live in the Spirit you are living the life of an adopted son of God; you have not received the spirit of fear, such as a little child has, you have received the spirit of sonship and adoption, and now for the first time you can cry, "Abba, Father". Proving that Paul was thinking of the Roman ceremony of adoption, he says that you will need witnesses to prove that you are now a son, and the Holy Spirit bears witness with your spirit that you really have been adopted by God, you are now his son, and you are walking a life of sonship.

I would emphasise that the word "cry" here means to shout out involuntarily. Most people do this when they are afraid. The word Paul uses here Greeks would have used for a shout, meaning to shout out instinctively without intending to do so. It is used of the disciples when they were on the Sea of Galilee in a boat and they saw Jesus walking on the water, and they were afraid because they thought it was a ghost. It says that they cried out with fear. If you have ever screamed with fear, that is the word here. But there are two things which may make you cry out spontaneously: fear or love. When our children were young they would see me and, without planning it, without intending to, they just shouted, "Daddy!" That is what this means: someone who looks up at God and suddenly finds themselves shouting, "Daddy, Father!" There are many people who believe in God. But their relationship is not that. They don't instinctively cry out "Father!" Until you know the adoption as sons you are bound to be afraid of God if you really believe in him, because you would always be afraid as to whether you really came up to his standards. When you have been adopted by him as only the sons of God have, it is the Spirit who gives us this.

The Spirit is bearing witness with your spirit that you are a child of God, so this is a double witness, both shouting together, "Abba, Father", and this double testimony proves you are a child of God, a brother of Jesus. The Spirit of Jesus is talking to his Father through your lips. "Abba, Father," is just what he used to say, and that is one thing the Spirit does. When the Spirit does that, then you are sure you are a child of God. Jesus the Son of God talked spontaneously to the Father like that, and here you find yourself talking the same way—this is the witness of the Spirit.

God the Father is going to give Jesus every kingdom of

the world, indeed the whole universe. All things are to be summed up in Christ. Do you realise that if you are a son of God, you are the son of a multimillionaire, you are the richest person on earth? Everybody else will have to leave behind when they die every bit of the universe they possess, and the lawyers will tuck away their trust deeds in some cubby hole. But you are going to be a joint heir with Christ. You can share all the future with Christ if you share the present. If you share this life of suffering, you can share that life of glory – if you take up your cross daily and follow him.

Do you know what difference this makes to suffering? It means, as literally as Romans 5 puts it, and maybe you didn't notice it there, that we rejoice even in our suffering. Other people put up with it and bear it wonderfully, but Christians rejoice during it. Christians say that this momentary light affliction works an exceeding weight of glory for me – the sufferings of this present time are not worth comparing with the glory that is going to come. How can this be? Suffering produces endurance, and endurance produces character, character produces hope, and hope does not disappoint us because God's love is shed abroad in our hearts through the Holy Spirit. What does that mean? Quite simply: only a mature character who knows how to suffer will have hope. Hope is not produced overnight. Hope is produced through suffering if the Holy Spirit is in that suffering. Hope doesn't disappoint us; our hope is to share the glory of God. How do we know we are going to have that? The answer is: because we share the love of God now. We have got the first down payment, the deposit, the first instalment. All these are terms we are familiar with. So Paul says that we have the first fruits of the Spirit. We have started sharing God's love, and that is why our hope of sharing his glory does not let us down. We are as sure of his glory as we are of his love, and so we are sure of the future.

Suffering is something we share with the whole universe. When we enjoy the beauty of creation we may find it difficult in a sense to believe what Romans 8 says about nature, but what Paul wrote is perfectly true. Nature itself is wrong, even the beautiful world around us has gone wrong. Nature itself is waiting for something to happen. It is groaning like a woman in labour. The groans and the pains of the whole universe are waiting for something tremendous to happen, and Paul says here that nature is subject to *futility*, and that means going around in a circle. The earth is going in a circle, the moon is, the sun is, the galaxy – everything is going in cycles, getting nowhere fast. Even nature is in a cycle – the flowers that are blooming today will be dead tomorrow. Things are born and die. This is the futility to which the whole universe is subject. It is subject to decay, and everything is decaying all around us. You are constantly fighting decay in almost everything you possess, and it is subject to pain— there is an awful lot of pain in this natural world.

The one part of me that I share with nature is my body. It is subject to the same futility – it is born and it dies. It is subject to the same decay. My hair is getting thinner. I have to visit the dentist more frequently. It is subject to pain, and I know what pain is, and so do you. The amazing hope for the future is that one day I will be given a new body that is free from death, free from pain and free from decay. When I get that body, the whole universe is also going to get a new body – there will be a new heaven and a new universe, new earth with no decay, no pain, no futility.

The whole creation is groaning, and when I groan nature groans, and when nature groans I groan. When nature shows how wrong it is, I groan and say how wrong I am. We all groan together. A Christian who knows there is going to be a new universe will groan, he longs for it to happen, and it is very frustrating because we don't see any sign of it.

Bodies are dying all around us and the universe is decaying all around us and we don't see it coming.

It may be frustrating, but we were saved in this hope: the hope of a new body in a new universe. If we could see it now we wouldn't need to hope for it, and if we hope for what we don't see, we wait for it patiently. It is absolutely certain to come. We were saved in the hope of getting a new body as well as a new inside. I have already got a new inside—God has put within me his Spirit, he has made me a new person in Christ Jesus, but I still shaved the same chin a week after I was converted as before. I have still got the same old body I had when I was a sinner. I have still got the same old body that I had when I did not love God at all. I am only half saved. What God has begun he will continue until it is completed, and one day he is going to save my body.

The whole creation is groaning – what for? Waiting for the same thing as we are waiting for: the redemption of our bodies. God is going to save the physical universe one day; that is our certain hope. Nobody but the Christian knows that this is going to happen. No scientist can tell us what is going to happen to nature in the future, but the Christian has this certain hope – he is going to get a new body to live in a new universe, and he groans.

Now that produces a problem of prayer when you are feeling the weight of this body, and we do from time to time, when you are ill, when you are tired, when something goes wrong medically. Then you may feel "Oh it's just all part of this dying universe. Here I am, I'm getting older. I was born too soon, I can't run upstairs now. I can't get around as I used to." When you feel like that, you wonder what you should pray about. Sometimes you feel like saying, "Lord, give me back my health and strength." Or sometimes you feel like praying "Lord, take me out of this."

I have known older people say to me very sincerely "I'm

praying that the Lord will take me." The simple truth is that when we are groaning like this we don't know how to pray as we ought. The tension of being in a body that is still part of a dying universe increases with the years, and old age can be a frightening thing from this point of view because you are more and more conscious that your body is part of this groaning universe.

You don't know quite what to pray – "Lord, give me a few more years' strength," or "Lord, take me to be with yourself." It is at that point that the blessed Holy Spirit comes in to help us in our weakness. We know not how to pray as we ought, but he takes the sighs that are too deep for words and he intercedes for the saints according to the will of God. We don't know what the will of God is, so all we can do is sigh.

Don't worry, you can sigh prayers as well as say them, and a prayer that is sighed is a real prayer. A Christian who is feeling the burden of this body tied to this dying world should simply sigh and say, "Holy Spirit, I don't know how to pray as I ought, so just take this sigh and turn it into a prayer."

If you realise that one day you are going to have a new body in a new universe, you will sigh very deeply. There will be moments when you groan, moments when you say, "Lord, you promised me a new body; you promised that I'll be free from tiredness and disease and pain one day, why can't I have it now?" God has a very good reason for not giving it to you now, if he doesn't. So you say, "Lord, give me hope. I'm not asking to see it. I wouldn't need to hope for it if I saw it, so I am going to wait patiently for this hope."

There are three other things in the letter to the Romans which you can check for yourself – concerned not now with our relationship to God but our relationship to others and our human responsibility – and they are concerned with our hope. In 9:1, "I am not lying, I am speaking the truth in Christ ... my conscience bears me witness in the Holy Spirit." Your conscience is moulded by society and by yourself. It is not therefore infallible and your conscience will depend on your upbringing among many other things, but once you are in the Spirit he makes your conscience accurate. One of the things you can't do to other people is to lie to them; the Holy Spirit doesn't let you. "My conscience bears me witness in the Holy Spirit, I am not lying...." Paul is there speaking of his hope for the future of Israel.

In 12:11 he says, "Never flag in zeal, be aglow with the Spirit, serve the Lord, rejoice in your hope, be patient in tribulation, be constant in prayer." Notice that as in a great musical symphony the theme keeps coming up again and again in the epistle to the Romans: hope; tribulation. The way to cope with trouble is to fix this anchor of hope. Will your anchor hold in the storms of life? Yes it will if it is Christian hope.

The final mention of the Holy Spirit in Romans is at 15:13, "May the God of hope fill you with all joy and peace in believing so that by the power of the Holy Spirit you may abound in hope." Earlier in this chapter, v. 4 says that by the encouragement of the scriptures we might have hope.

If you want to be a man or woman of hope then you must be well versed in the Bible because it tells you what is going to happen in the future. But that by itself is not enough to make you abound in hope – because how do you believe it? Who convinces you that what the Bible predicts will come to pass? The answer is: the Holy Spirit convinces you, and by the power of the Holy Spirit you can abound in hope.

So when people say to you "I don't know what things are coming to," just say to them quietly, "I do." When people ask where in the world we are going, you say, "I know where the world is going." People may say, "I don't know if the world will end with nuclear war – or what?" you can say, "I know how it will end." People say, "I don't know where we go when we die." You say, "I do." People will say, "I don't know if there's a God." You say, "I know there is." People will say, "I don't know if God can control this world." You say, "I know he can." The world is crying out for people who abound in hope. Love without faith and hope? It is just inadequate to live by.

Chapter Ten

THE HOLY SPIRIT IN 1 CORINTHIANS

For the message of the cross is foolishness to those who are perishing, but to us who are being saved it is the power of God. For it is written:

'I will destroy the wisdom of the wise;

the intelligence of the intelligent I will frustrate.'

Where is the wise person? Where is the teacher of the law? Where is the philosopher of this age? Has not God made foolish the wisdom of the world? For since in the wisdom of God the world through its wisdom did not know him, God was pleased through the foolishness of what was preached to save those who believe. Jews demand signs and Greeks look for wisdom, but we preach Christ crucified: a stumbling-block to Jews and foolishness to Gentiles, but to those whom God has called, both Jews and Greeks, Christ the power of God and the wisdom of God. For the foolishness of God is wiser than human wisdom, and the weakness of God is stronger than human strength.

Brothers and sisters, think of what you were when you were called. Not many of you were wise by human standards; not many were influential; not many were of noble birth. But God chose the foolish things of the world to shame the wise; God chose the weak things of the world to shame the strong. God chose the lowly things of this world and the despised things – and the things that are not – to nullify the things that are, so that no one may boast before him. It is because of him that you are in Christ

Jesus, who has become for us wisdom from God – that is, our righteousness, holiness and redemption. Therefore, as it is written: 'Let the one who boasts boast in the Lord.'

And so it was with me, brothers and sisters. When I came to you, I did not come with eloquence or human wisdom as I proclaimed to you the testimony about God. For I resolved to know nothing while I was with you except Jesus Christ and him crucified. I came to you in weakness with great fear and trembling. My message and my preaching were not with wise and persuasive words, but with a demonstration of the Spirit's power, so that your faith might not rest on human wisdom, but on God's power.

We do, however, speak a message of wisdom among the mature, but not the wisdom of this age or of the rulers of this age, who are coming to nothing. No, we declare God's wisdom, a mystery that has been hidden and that God destined for our glory before time began. None of the rulers of this age understood it, for if they had, they would not have crucified the Lord of glory. However, as it is written:

'What no eye has seen,
what no ear has heard,
and what no human mind has conceived' –
the things God has prepared for those who love him
– these are the things God has revealed
to us by his Spirit.

The Spirit searches all things, even the deep things of God. For who knows a person's thoughts except their own spirit within them? In the same way no one knows the thoughts of God except the Spirit of God. What we have received is not the spirit of the world, but the Spirit who is from God, so that we may understand what God has freely given us. This is what we speak, not in words taught us by human wisdom but in words taught by the Spirit, explaining spiritual realities with Spirit-taught words. The person without the Spirit does not accept the things that come from the Spirit of God but considers them foolishness, and cannot understand them because they are discerned only through the Spirit. The person with the Spirit makes judgments about all things, but such a person is not subject to merely human judgments, for,

> 'Who has known the mind of the Lord
> so as to instruct him?'
> But we have the mind of Christ.

Brothers and sisters, I could not address you as people who live by the Spirit but as people who are still worldly – mere infants in Christ. I gave you milk, not solid food, for you were not yet ready for it. Indeed, you are still not ready. You are still worldly. For since there is jealousy and quarrelling among you, are you not worldly? Are you not acting like mere humans? For when one says, 'I follow Paul,' and another, 'I follow Apollos,' are you not mere human beings?

What, after all, is Apollos? And what is Paul? Only servants, through whom you came to believe – as the Lord has assigned to each his task. I planted the seed, Apollos watered it, but God has been making it grow.

1:18–3:6, NIV

There is a great difference between being clever and being wise. Some of the cleverest people in the world have been fools, and some of the simplest people in the world have been very wise. The world has achieved brilliance without wisdom, power without conscience. We have more education and more knowledge than ever before. Knowledge is growing so rapidly that we cannot now keep up with it. We have to let computers process and remember it for us. Our young people get educational opportunities such as our grandparents could never have dreamed of. The human race is clever but so often foolish.

1 Corinthians 1 tells us that there are two sorts of wisdom. There is the wisdom of God and the wisdom of man. The two are incompatible, and to the one the other appears foolish. To God, the cleverness of man appears folly; to man, the wisdom of God is foolishness.

This letter of Paul was written to a place that was materially the most prosperous in Greece, and perhaps in the Roman empire, yet it was a place that morally was so degraded that they called anyone who was given to debauchery "a Corinthian". Even as late as the Regency period in England, if a man played the fool, painted the town red and broke every moral rule, he was called a Corinthian. It has dropped out of our language now, but that is what it meant.

Materially they had everything. Their architecture still influences our own buildings. Walk around London and see the Corinthian pillars supporting many buildings. Their art and sculpture still inspires, filling our art galleries. Greek philosophy is still at the heart of education in this country, and most people still think in terms of Greek ideas.

Yet if you read the history of Corinth, you will find that it was filled with vice. There were a thousand professional prostitutes paid by the city council to ply the streets. There was idolatry right through the city. Homosexuality was more common than normal relationships between men and women. In that place where people were brilliantly clever, there was a free port with all the trade going through. It was in this prosperous business centre that God's wisdom was made manifest. God did certain things that were so wise that people thought they were foolish.

In the middle of that town in which people lived purely to make money and enjoy what money could buy, God planted a little church. In eighteen months' work by one missionary, a church came into being to which his letter is written. In that church were people who had been (and I am quoting now from 1 Corinthians 6:9–10): "Homosexuals, fornicators, idolaters, murderers," and Paul says, "Such were some of you." The little church was full of them and they were changed and had become new men and women.

I am going to take you into that little church in your imagination. It probably met in a warehouse or somebody's house down by the docks. We are going to look at three things which seem utterly foolish and yet were the wisdom of God. First, we are going to listen to the sermon. In Greece, noted for its orators, people would turn out in their hundreds to hear the latest speaker – the debater who could be clever in his arguments, who could twist the words of his opponents round and could answer them. They were very fond of listening to debates, heckling, hearing a brilliant speaker make his point in brilliant logic. But if you came into the little church at Corinth you would hear a sermon about a man who was God; a man who was executed at the age of thirty-three, nailed to a block of wood as though he had been a criminal, a man who rose again from the dead—a message to insult anybody's intelligence. You can imagine those Greeks who loved listening to logic and argument and philosophies saying, "Utterly ridiculous! Utter folly! You expect me to believe that a man walking around the earth was the God who made the earth? You expect me to believe that a man dying on a cross saved the world? You expect me to believe that he rose again from the dead three days later and proved that he was the Son of God?"

This preacher is not trying to convince the intellect. He was just preaching what seemed to some a very silly message, but the wisdom of God is wiser than men. It is through this message that people's lives got changed. It was the word of the cross that to those who believed became the power of God. To others it seemed silly. One of our temptations in this sophisticated, educated age is to trim Christianity to the modern intellect, to cut out from our preaching those things that offend the intelligence of educated people; to cut out the miracles; to say this didn't happen and that didn't happen.

If we do that, we will just develop preachers' fan clubs. We don't see people saved because God, in his infinite wisdom, has chosen to save people through the word of the cross. Wherever people have preached about the cross, others have been saved. Now why is this wise? Why didn't God make the word that saved people an intelligent, intellectual word of which you could convince a person by argument? I just thank God he didn't, for the simple reason that seeing is not believing. I know people say, "Seeing is believing" but it is nothing of the kind. If you see a thing you have to accept it. There is no need for faith, no need for believing at all. If I have seen a thing, I accept it.

There are two ways in which you can see things: through your eyes or with your mind. The Jews want signs and the Greeks want wisdom. God says: "You don't see. You believe." How wise! Why? Because it makes heaven different from a school—because it doesn't make exams the test of whether you get to glory; because it means that anybody, even the simplest in the world, can come and believe.

Maybe for that reason it is sometimes harder for the clever to trust Christ. The wise men had a much longer journey than the simple shepherds to the babe of Bethlehem. "Except you become as a little child...." Where you cannot see, you need to put your hand into the hand of God and believe. God says that the Son of God died for you and, if you trust him, you can be saved. However foolish that seems – you trust and it will work. You don't need to be brainy. You don't need to have read theology and philosophy. It is simple enough for a little child.

Look around at the faces of the congregation in Corinth. What do you notice? They are very ordinary people, most of them. There were very few of noble birth, very few clever intellectuals. There were some, because the kingdom of heaven is open to them as well, but not many. Who was responsible for choosing the members of that church? The answer is that God was. He called them; he chose them. Why should God choose such a mixed bunch?

A worldly wise man once said to me, "Take my advice, don't bother with ordinary people, go for the important people, vital people in industry, commerce and university, then you will get the rest." That is worldly wisdom, which sounds so plausible, yet God in his wisdom chose a bunch of slaves, dockers, sailors, as well as men and women of the streets. He put them in the church, used them to change the world. God deliberately chooses nobodies to show the somebodies that he is somebody—how wise! In this way, it becomes obvious that what we are and what we have is Christ's. Christ is our wisdom, our sanctification, our redemption; Christ is everything we have got. It must be clear to other people that all we have is Christ. The church is so pathetically weak. There are very few noble people, very few wealthy people; very few influential people in an average church. Thank God. God wants people who are nobodies and he makes them somebodies. He takes a parlour maid and makes a Gladys Aylward; he takes a cobbler and makes a William Carey. God takes ordinary men and women and makes them extraordinary.

Take a look at this preacher at Corinth this morning. Now Greece loved tall, handsome orators with a lovely accent and suave, gracious manners. Alas, so do some churches today, but when you look into the Corinthian pulpit what do you find— according to tradition we have a little bald-headed Jew with bowlegs, who has a peculiarity in his eyes so that people don't find his presence impressive. He admits this in one of his letters. He says, "I know I don't have much of a presence when I am with you face to face." He knew this. He was a man they would not have looked at twice. He said: I came in fear and trembling. When I came to you, I just came to you with a simple message. I wasn't trying to persuade you with oratory; I wasn't trying to be brilliant. I just came to tell you the simple message, but when I spoke, something happened. This is what made the difference between this little Jew and all the Greek orators. When they spoke, everybody said, "How interesting," and they went home exactly the same. But when Paul spoke, the Spirit's power was demonstrated and people were changed. Why does God choose people like this to preach? Why does God choose all kinds of people to talk about the gospel? That your faith might be in God and not in man, that's why. How wise.

One of the best books I have ever read on baptism is by a professor in Germany. He had studied theology and philosophy and he didn't know Jesus Christ. One day a Salvation Army woman washing his front doorsteps led him to the Lord Jesus. How foolish of God to use a person like that for him! Surely you must set a professor to catch a professor? Oh no, God is wise, because that professor's trust will be in Jesus, not in a human being. The danger is that people put their trust in an orator, in a man, and therefore Paul says, "I just came to you with a simple message." The intellectual would say, "Nothing much in that," and go away without thinking any more, but God is wise.

I think that God still wants a very foolish message preached. He doesn't want lecturers. I remember a man saying after I had gained a theology degree, "We're emptying the church by degrees you know," and I can understand what he meant. God wants men and women who will preach an apparently foolish message—Christ, and him having been crucified. He wants a congregation of anybody, so that he can show his power. He is not wanting preachers who are great. He wants preachers who trust the Holy Spirit to do it instead of thinking they can do anything.

You might get the impression from all this that I am anti-intellectual or that Paul is, and that he is saying there's no place for instruction, no place for education and for teaching people. You could not be further from the truth if you jump to that conclusion. There is a wisdom to be imparted, given and taught. That is why the church must always place emphasis on teaching and instruction, but it is a wisdom that is different from the school and the university. So teaching methods in a church will be different. In both school and university the lecture method, for want of a better term, is on the way out. Now you don't say things *to* people, you let them find out. This is the big new switch that has come in recent years. Well this may be very good in secular education, but God has still chosen the foolishness of preaching, and he always will. The modern educationalist might say, "Do away with sermons. Let people find out another way. Preaching is over," but it is not, and instruction is still necessary, though it will depend on what sort of a person you are.

Anybody with a bit of patience and a good teacher can receive the wisdom of the world to a degree, but the wisdom of God is only received by one of three groups of people. Here are the three groups mentioned in 1 Corinthians 2 —the spiritual people, the natural people, and the carnal people. Only one of those three groups can be instructed in the wisdom of God. The spiritual people are the first mentioned.

Now there are two ways in which everybody else comes to knowledge, either through their senses, particularly the eye gate and the ear gate, or through their imagination, through their deductive mind leaping to conclusions. All knowledge comes one way or the other. All scientific knowledge comes either through the senses or through the imagination, some concept, but now let me affirm this: "What eye has not seen; what ear has not heard; what has never entered into the heart of man to imagine, God has revealed to us through his Spirit."

There are things we know which no scientist will ever discover. God has taught us, because the Spirit of God knows the thoughts of God. Nobody else does. I don't know what you are thinking at this moment. I might be surprised. I don't know how you are reacting to what you are reading. You might be revelling in it or you might be rejecting it – I don't know, but your spirit knows what you are thinking. Your spirit knows the inside of you. I don't know what God is thinking this morning. I couldn't possibly know, but his Spirit knows. Now just supposing I can have his Spirit, that means I would know. I would understand things that nobody else understands. When everybody else would ask, "Why did this happen? Why did God allow this?" – my spirit could feel, "I know he knows" – and I am content that he understands. That is a wisdom that is not given to everybody because many are incapable of receiving it. Unless someone has the Spirit of God, I cannot as a preacher, Sunday by Sunday, impart any wisdom to him at all – maybe cleverness but that is no use to him. Wisdom is so different, and a person will never become wise until they have the Spirit of God in them. One may become very educated, very clever, and cleverness will say, "I can make a great profit out of this deal," but wisdom says, "What shall it profit a man if he gain the whole world and lose his own soul."

Cleverness can learn how to make a living; wisdom learns how to live. Cleverness can cope with this life, most of it, but wisdom will prepare for the next. It amazes me again and again that after I have tried to preach the Word of God, someone will come up and say, "Oh, I got so much out of that this morning – I understand so much more than I ever did before," and somebody else will go out of this same service and say, "Well I got absolutely nothing – what was he on about?" The answer is that you can impart wisdom and interpret spiritual truths to those who are filled with the Spirit.

So never drag a person to the church on the grounds of all that you got from the preacher. I will guarantee what will happen if you do, because I have done it. I have listened to a preacher who ministered to my soul and I got so much and I said, "You must come along," and I dragged them along. Then they sat there coolly, and said afterwards, "Well I don't know what you get excited about—nothing there." The problem is that we talked about a preacher instead of about Christ. What a mistake! That is the wisdom of man, to try that. It is the "foolishness of God" to say wisdom is only there for the spiritual.

The second group of people mentioned are the natural people, sometimes translated "the unspiritual." The Greek work translated "natural" is *phusikos* or *psuchikos*, meaning a person who can go to the limit of human insight and knowledge. The natural man *cannot* understand the things of God. It is not that he is being obstinate or deliberately silly. I need to remember this constantly, as you do. I was having a long, earnest discussion with a very intellectual young man who seemed so blind and obtuse about things that are so clear, so obvious – that this is the world in which we live and that somebody must have put it here. I had to say within my heart again and again, "He can't see; he is a natural man. He has nothing more than his reason, and reason can't take him all the way." Therefore the natural man's judgments on spiritual things are worthless. His judgments of spiritual people are worthless. He will say all kinds of things about people of God, but don't trust his judgments. He can't understand, so we are told that the spiritual man is judged by no one. The natural man cannot understand the Christian. It sounds too simple – either spiritual or natural people. There is a third group—carnal people. These are people who have become Christians, who are born again of the Spirit, who belong to Jesus Christ, but who can't take wisdom. They can't take meat, they have to have milk. The reason is that they are still babies in Christ, and spiritual babies can't be given wisdom. You don't send a baby to school at first! They can't learn the wisdom of God. The proof of this kind of person is that it is someone who is still allowing the old mental habits to govern their thinking.

I will give you an outstanding example of it because it was happening in Corinth. Paul could not impart wisdom to some Christians because they were still thinking as they did before they became Christians, saying, "I am of Paul", "I am of Apollos," "I am of Cephas." Let me translate that for you into modern English. You don't put your faith in a man. Pastors come and go. We are just your servants for the Lord's sake. Your faith is in the Lord Jesus. That is growing up, and when you get away from this human angle of thinking and instead think about the Lord, and you put your faith in him, you get wisdom. It will be imparted to you. You will get wisdom in increasing measure as you listen to the Word of God. So Paul says, "I had to feed you on milk." I have the feeling, putting it into modern English, he was saying: with you lot, I'll have to give you children's talks and not sermons. Spiritual babies love the children's message, but not the sermon. We impart wisdom to those who have the Spirit—food, meat. We try to put a bit of gravy on it now, but it is meat we need to become strong, to get off baby food and start growing.

When we can't see, we can believe; when we can't understand at the human level, we can trust. When it seems as if the other world is so unreal and this world is so real, we can ask for the assurance of what eye has not seen, and ear has not heard, and what has never entered into the heart of man even to imagine – the glory that shall be revealed in the future we may be assured of by the Holy Spirit.

The wisdom of God is folly to man, but to those who are being saved, to those who believe the word of the cross, it is the power of God to change lives. We now move to 1 Corinthians chapter 12.

Now about the gifts of the Spirit, brothers and sisters, I do not want you to be uninformed. You know that when you were pagans, somehow or other you were influenced and led astray to dumb idols. Therefore I want you to know that no one who is speaking by the Spirit of God says, 'Jesus be cursed,' and no one can say, 'Jesus is Lord,' except by the Holy Spirit.

There are different kinds of gifts, but the same Spirit distributes them. There are different kinds of service, but the same Lord. There are different kinds of working, but in all of them and in everyone it is the same God at work.

Now to each one the manifestation of the Spirit is given for the common good. To one there is given through the Spirit a message of wisdom, to another a message of knowledge by means of the same Spirit, to another faith by the same Spirit, to another gifts of healing by that one Spirit, to another miraculous powers, to another prophecy, to another distinguishing between spirits, to another speaking in different kinds of tongues, and to still another the interpretation of tongues. All these are the work of one and the same Spirit, and he distributes them to each one, just as he determines.

Just as a body, though one, has many parts, but all its many parts form one body, so it is with Christ. For we were all baptised by one Spirit so as to form one body – whether Jews or Gentiles, slave or free – and we were all given the one Spirit to drink. And so the body is not made up of one part but of many.

Now if the foot should say, 'Because I am not a hand, I do not belong to the body,' it would not for that reason stop being part of the body. And if the ear should say, 'Because I am not an eye, I do not belong to the body,' it would not for that reason stop being part of the body. If the whole body were an eye, where would the sense of hearing be? If the whole body were an ear, where would the sense of smell be? But in fact God has placed the parts in the body, every one of them, just as he wanted them to be. If they were all one part, where would the body be? As it is, there are many parts, but one body.

The eye cannot say to the hand, 'I don't need you!' And the head cannot say to the feet, 'I don't need you!' On the contrary, those parts of the body that seem to be weaker are indispensable, and the parts that we think are less honourable we treat with special honour. And the parts that are unpresentable are treated with special modesty, while our presentable parts need no special treatment. But God has put the body together, giving greater honour to the parts that lacked it, so that there should be no division in the body, but that its parts should have equal concern for each other. If one part suffers, every part suffers with it; if one part is honoured, every part rejoices with it.

Now you are the body of Christ, and each one of you is a part of it. And God has placed in the church first of all apostles, second prophets, third teachers, then miracles, then gifts of healing, of helping, of guidance, and of different kinds of tongues. Are all apostles? Are all prophets? Are all teachers? Do all work miracles? Do all have gifts of healing? Do all speak in tongues? Do all interpret? Now eagerly desire the greater gifts.

1 Corinthians 12, NIV

There are two kinds of gifts people have—natural gifts and spiritual gifts, and God needs both in his service. Natural gifts are those we possess before we are Christians. There are gifts which we can then dedicate to the service of God when we are saved, and which we can use in his service. It is lovely when a person with natural gifts uses them for God. I suppose the most obvious illustration is a gift of music. That is a gift you either have or you don't. Most of my family are tone deaf. Some have that natural gift, and they can cultivate it, train it, and can put it at God's disposal. Some also have an amazing natural gift for improvising and arranging.

Some people have gifts of finance. I can't understand where they get it from, but some people just seem amazing with figures. Some people have a gift of organisation; some people can knock a nail in straight; some people have gifts of craftsmanship. I am thrilled when all these gifts are used for God and dedicated in his service, but they are all natural gifts. Some people might include the gift of the gab in that list – you can think what you like about that, but there are many gifts.

It is not God's will that the church should be limited to natural gifts. If it were, that would mean that there are those who will feel that they have nothing to contribute, or very little because it is quite obvious that natural gifts are very patchy, and when you listen to a great singer you think, "What a wonderful and rare gift." It is God's intention to divide gifts among other people who may have few or no natural gifts. I think everybody has at least one. If a church is limited to natural gifts, it will be severely limited in its development. It will depend on having a lot of gifted people in the congregation, and an average congregation doesn't have a lot of gifted people, as we saw at the beginning of 1 Corinthians 1.

So what is the answer? It is that God has had a wonderful idea, if you like, of giving supernatural gifts to the church. Since God is no respecter of persons and is not partial and has no favourites, he can give spiritual gifts to anyone who will receive them. This is the glory of it! You may say, "Well, I'm not gifted." That is your fault and your fault alone. If you think that is a hard assertion, let me point to these spiritual gifts. With natural gifts, it is not your fault if you are not gifted, but spiritual gifts are for everybody.

That is why 1 Corinthians 12 says again and again: "to everyone". It is God's will to give supernatural gifts, but the biggest difference is this. These spiritual or supernatural gifts are never found among the unbelievers, they are only given to Christians. These gifts you will not find in the most gifted person in the world who is not a believer. They are special gifts for God's people. Now Paul begins by saying, "Regarding spiritual gifts, I do not want you to be uninformed," but I meet plenty of Christians who don't want to be informed about them and think it is the last thing they want to hear about. "Don't talk to me about those things. I'm not interested" or, "I don't want to know." Paul wanted believers to be informed, to know about these gifts, so they could want them and have them.

There is only one kind of coveting that a Christian is ever allowed. He is not allowed to covet someone else's car, house or job, nor even someone else's natural gifts. "Thou shalt not covet." Yet there in the New Testament is one clear command: "Covet earnestly the spiritual gifts." If you see somebody else with a spiritual gift, then you are allowed to covet it earnestly, by the authority of the Word of God.

Many Christians are ignorant and uninformed about spiritual gifts and there are two reasons for this. Many Christians are ignorant because they lack any experience of spiritual gifts. They have never heard or seen them operated. They have maybe been in a church where only dedicated natural gifts have been seen and heard, and therefore lack of experience leads to ignorance. 1 Corinthians 12–14 becomes meaningless if you have no experience of these gifts. It is like reading the Highway Code before you have got a car—very interesting, but no earthly use to you. Many people don't study these three chapters closely for precisely this reason. You even miss the point of that wonderful chapter 1 Corinthians 13 if you don't have any experience of spiritual gifts because that is all about them: "If I speak in the tongues of men and angels...." There is the first spiritual gift mentioned, "... but have not love"; "If I have prophetic powers," there's the second; "and understand all mysteries and all knowledge," there's the third; "... and have all faith so as to remove mountains." These are spiritual gifts. Later in the chapter it says that prophecy will pass away; tongues will cease; knowledge will pass away. The whole chapter is about spiritual gifts, and so even this passage, which many Christians love, loses its meaning if you are ignorant of spiritual gifts.

A second kind of ignorance is like that at Corinth, which is quite different. This is the ignorance of those who have every spiritual gift in their church and don't know how to use them. That can cause difficulty, trouble, division, unhappiness and is an even worse kind of ignorance because the gifts of God are then used to break down the fellowship instead of to build it up. So Paul says that he does not want them to be uninformed because they are getting the spiritual gifts and don't know how to use them properly.

In particular, they were ignorant of two things: *how* spiritual gifts are given, and *why* spiritual gifts are given. He speaks in the first half of the chapter about the inspiration of these gifts—how they come. In the second half of the chapter he speaks of the integration of these gifts—why they are given– for the upbuilding of the body.

We will look at the first half, the inspiration of these gifts. How do they come? How do they become part of a church's life? There is one very big difference between the natural and the supernatural gift and it is this: the natural gift can be exercised whenever the person wishes. If you have a gift of singing, even if you don't feel particularly like opening your mouth and singing you can do so. Whatever is your natural gift, you can use it at your will. You can control it and you can cultivate it, you can develop it and so on; but a spiritual gift cannot be exercised unless you are moved by the Holy Spirit to do so. There is an immediate and a direct inspiration necessary for the operation of a spiritual gift.

Some musicians and artists will say, "I can't compose unless I'm moved, inspired" It is interesting they use the same word, "inspired", as if there must be some spirit that moves them to do something before they can. There is an element of truth in that, but the inspiration of which I am speaking is different. The inspiration of secular music and art comes from the human spirit. When the human spirit moves the person, they express in some wonderful work of art or music, but when God's inspiration comes, it is the Holy Spirit, not the human spirit that moves.

Paul now deals with something that has to be said in every church where spiritual gifts are exercised. He tells the believers that they may be moved by the wrong spirit. It is very important to realise that there are three kinds of spirit that move people to do things—God's Holy Spirit, the human spirit, and the evil spirit of Satan and his followers. A person can feel profoundly moved, but they can be moved in the wrong direction if the spirit that is moving them is either their own spirit or Satan's spirit.

As soon as people are being moved by spirits to do things, the danger comes of the wrong spirit moving them. One of the horrible things happening at Corinth was that when they were all saying things moved by the Spirit and people in the congregation were speaking out the praise of God, some people were saying, "Hallelujah, Jesus be praised, Jesus is Lord," and some people were saying, "Jesus be cursed, Jesus be cursed." The whole thing shatters us to realise this and Paul has to correct them.

Now it is very important, if you have been moved deeply, to ask *what* spirit moved you, because the direction in which you will move afterwards will depend on which spirit. Paul reminds them that when they were heathen, even though they worshipped dumb idols they were deeply moved. I have seen with my own eyes some dervishes. I have seen people working themselves into a frenzy, moved by evil spirits, shouting all kinds of rubbish and speaking in tongues; shouting horrible things, working themselves up, moved either by their own psychological spirit or probably by demonic spirits. They have been so moved that they have been doing and saying evil things.

You have got to watch this and Paul is teaching that you can always tell by the content of what people say when they are moved by a spirit. If they say anything against Jesus, it is not the Holy Spirit moving them. It may seem strange that somebody in church would curse Jesus but there were plenty of people in those days who did. The Jews did, they said: "Cursed be he that hangs on a tree," and that was Jesus. The pagans cursed him because wherever people talk about him, idol makers go out of business. Plenty of people were cursing Jesus, but when somebody got inside church and cursed Jesus, then the evil spirits were moving people. The real test of a service of worship is not were you moved by that service, but who moved you?

That is why one wants to beware of even human spirits trying to work people up. "Come on everybody, slap hands and shake hands with the person sitting next to you. Let's have the music full blast and let's have a great time inside." That could be simply psychological spirits, and it wouldn't move you in the right direction. It would just move you, shift you along a bit, maybe shift you in your seat a bit, but it doesn't move you. You can always tell when the Holy Spirit is moving someone because Jesus is glorified, Jesus is honoured, Jesus is Lord. The devil will never say "Jesus is Lord" because it is his death knell now to say that. Nobody moved by an evil spirit ever says, "Jesus is Lord."

A lady, after her conversion, became a spiritualist medium and went to a spiritualist church. Her pastor saw her some months later and asked, "Why did you do this?"

She replied, "It's alright, it's a Christian movement."

He said, "How do you know that?"

"Well," she continued, "I talk to the spirits and I say to them, 'Jesus is my master,' and they say, 'and he's ours too.'"

The pastor, knowing his Bible, said, "Next time you get through to the spirits, say to them, 'Jesus is Lord.'" She did, and she lost all power to contact spirits. She went back to church, and she is saying, "Jesus is Lord" now.

You can see the difference. You must be sure that it is the Holy Spirit moving you if spiritual gifts are going to be exercised. Otherwise your utterances could come from your spirit or from evil spirits, and that would not be edifying or helpful to the church. It could break the church up, and it could destroy what God is seeking to build.

So Paul is reminding Christians not to bring their pagan

inspiration into the church. Don't have evil spirits controlling your mouth. Speak in the Holy Spirit. Then you will say, "Jesus is Lord", words that only the Holy Spirit says. I have noticed that even those who have a respect for Jesus but who are not Christians never call him "Lord". They may talk about Jesus, or the "pale Galilean", or even the suffering servant, all kinds of titles, but you watch how often a person talks about the Lord Jesus. When you hear the word "Lord" you will know the Spirit is helping that person to speak about him.

Now Paul moves on to something else and teaches that the one thing that you can't use as a test for spiritual gifts is whether it always happens the same way. There will be a variety of gifts, variety of service, and variety of working. There is no fixed pattern for the Holy Spirit's working. Man's pattern of working is always the same. That's why we tend to get into either ritualism or "rutualism" when it is men running the show, and why when the Holy Spirit takes charge, there's a breaking out of familiar patterns— things happen unexpectedly that are new and fresh. There are varieties of gifts, varieties of workings and varieties of service. I discovered in the biology laboratory that there are no two blades of grass the same, no two grains of sand the same, no two clouds the same, no two snowflakes the same in the whole universe. There is variety in what God creates, and when God the Holy Spirit gets busy something will happen that doesn't fit into our preordained pattern. When God the Holy Spirit moves people, he moves them in varied directions. A wonderful variety comes in, yet this variety is from the same God. Look around at a crowd of people. Isn't everybody different? Even identical twins when you get to know them, are different. God has made a wonderful variety of people, and here we all are, such a mixed-up, crazy bunch of people with different problems, different hopes, different dreams, different homes, different children. Yet a group of believers has the same Spirit, the same Lord, the same God, and we are all one in Christ. It is God's will to fit together everybody, so that in heaven there will be people from every kindred and tribe and tongue. For now, there are different spiritual gifts, used in different ways, for different purposes, so expect infinite variety when the Holy Spirit is in a church; expect the dull, dead, sameness when the human spirit, even with dedicated natural gifts, is solely in charge.

Exactly what kind of spiritual gifts does God give to the church? This is not an exhaustive list, but there are nine different ones mentioned here, all of them beautiful, and we will look at them one by one. The first thing that strikes me is this: out of nine gifts listed here, five are gifts of speech. The one gift that God uses to build up a church is the gift of words. The world is more interested in deeds and says, "If the church would stop talking and do something, we'd have more respect for it." God in his wisdom, which is foolishness to men, uses preaching and uses speaking to build people up. It is part of God's plan that the majority of the supernatural gifts he gives should be gifts of speech, because one thing that no other creature in the world can do is to put thoughts into words. We are not just animals.

"Man shall not live by bread alone," so deeds by themselves are not enough. God wants to give you the gift of uttering words that will build other people up and help them. Isn't this one of the biggest problems in the church – to get people talking? If you're going to know the joy of fellowship, it is important to get everybody to speak to each other, believing that, as you do, you help each other. By sharing your blessings and burdens and insights, you build each other up. A church made of one man who can talk the hind legs off a donkey and a whole congregation who never open their mouths is not the kind of church that God wants.

The first two spiritual gifts mentioned are gifts of speech. First of all, it is not the gift of wisdom that is listed here – it is the gift of the utterance of wisdom – and that means you don't need to be clever, you don't need to be educated, all you need do is let God use your mouth to utter wisdom. His will be the wisdom, he will supply the wisdom, and the gift of the utterance of wisdom is this: when the church is faced with a huge problem; when there is a great difficulty; when nobody can see what to do – then somebody can get up and, given the gift of wisdom by the Spirit, can say, "This is what God wants us to do." As soon as they have said it, if it has been an utterance of wisdom, every believer present will say, "Well, why didn't we think of it? That's just the right answer to this problem."

Solomon asked for this gift and was faced with what I would have thought an impossible question—two women arguing over one baby; the kind of situation that most of us would run a thousand miles from because you feel you'll upset both of them whatever you say. He asked for a gift of wisdom and God put into his mouth one sentence that solved the whole thing. Any church member, any believer in Jesus filled with the Spirit, could give an utterance of wisdom to the whole church. How we need that gift!

The second gift is a gift of the utterance of knowledge. Now this doesn't mean that you have got a brain packed with theology. It is to be able to say something about someone or something that only God knows. Elijah had this gift. He knew exactly what the king of Syria said in his bedroom. It is a gift of supernatural knowledge that you could not have got from anywhere but God. I have been present when this gift has been exercised, when somebody has told the church something that nobody knew except God, and it has proved to be a helpful piece of knowledge, something that has helped the church to face the future. It may be a bit of knowledge about the future.

The third gift is the gift of faith. Now this is not the normal saving faith of the Christian. This is a special gift of faith, when a Christian's faith is strained and they can't just believe that a thing will happen, and somebody in the church says, "I believe it will happen. I know it'll happen. I'm certain it's going to happen," and the one person's gift of faith helps everybody else to believe it is going to happen.

The fourth gift mentioned is a gift of healing. That means to heal a physical disease without medicine or surgery, and these gifts are given from time to time to someone for somebody else. It is a gift of health which God wants to give someone else through this Christian. Praise God for that! I wouldn't be speaking, teaching and preaching – indeed I wouldn't be on earth – if that was not a real gift.

Then there is the gift of miracles, and this gift is power over things: the power to change nature, the power to change the weather, and this gift is still given to God's people.

The gift of prophecy is to give an immediately inspired word from God to his people. The gift of prophecy can be exercised by anyone. Anybody may have a word direct from God to give to the people—a word of encouragement, a word of prediction, a word that will challenge them, a word that will bring them up with a start and make them think of God. Any Spirit-filled believer could give a word of prophecy.

The gift of discernment is very simply the gift of knowing, when a person is moved to say or do something, whether it was God, the human spirit or an evil spirit doing it—God, the flesh, or the devil. There was a service where a man got up and spoke in tongues, and the pastor stood up and said, "Brother, the Spirit tells me that you're doing that in the flesh, not in the Spirit, so sit down and shut up; it's not helpful," at which the man sat down promptly. You can imagine in that situation there is going to be no abuse of gifts where the gift of discernment of spirits is there. A person will really seek the Lord's will before they exercise a gift, and that pastor has that gift frequently.

Then there is the gift of tongues, which is not ecstatic gibberish, but the use of a language you have never known, to praise God. The point of praising God in language you never learned is that it gets your thoughts and your mind out of the way. That clears one of the biggest blockages to free prayer and enables you to pray and praise with a liberty you don't have in your own language. It is a lovely gift but it can be counterfeited by psychological gibberish and demonic tongues.

The last gift is the interpretation of tongues, because if someone speaks in a tongue in the presence of others, it is no use to them because they don't understand a word of it. So another supernatural gift is given to translate that for the others present, so they know what beautiful thought has been expressed, what lovely praise has been offered.

We notice that it is within the will of the Spirit himself as to who gets what gift. It is not our decision. I can't say, "Well, I'm going to have this gift," and you can't say, "You're going to have that." It is the Holy Spirit who gives these gifts to people as he wills for the common good. He doesn't do it for harm, he doesn't do it to hurt, he does it to build up. No one else will decide.

This is the difference between the exercise of gifts and the sort of thing that a preacher does in his study. He decides what part he is going to take, what part others are going to take. There may be an order of service, but I believe that every church needs opportunities of fellowship where there isn't a set order of service; where the Holy Spirit has room to say, "I'm going to give Mrs. So and so or Mr. So and so a gift today that they may exercise for the common good."

Finally I come to v. 13. How do you start exercising gifts?

It is clearly there in that verse but I am going to alter one word in it because I am afraid the translators of my version have got it wrong. You can check me by finding someone who knows Greek and asking what the Greek says. Paul says, "In one Spirit you were all baptised," not "by", the Spirit doesn't baptise you; you are baptised in him by the Lord Jesus. The interesting thing is that again in the Greek language, which Paul used, the verb, "baptised" and "drink" are both a peculiar form of verb, which means something that happened once. You were baptised once, and made to drink once of this one Spirit, and he is referring to one specific experience in the past life of himself and the Corinthians. He is saying: don't you remember? That's how it all began. You were baptised in one Spirit; you were made to drink of one Spirit.

Just as you are baptised in water, but if you keep your mouth open you will drink of it – as one poor lady I baptised did. She opened her mouth wide and as the text in Psalms says, "Open your mouth wide and I will fill it." I am afraid that as she was baptised she opened her mouth and the water got inside as well as all over her outside. Paul is reminding believers of an experience comparable to that. They were clothed with the Spirit, plunged in the Spirit. The Spirit was all around you and you opened your mouth and you drank of that same Spirit.

Have all Christians had that experience? The answer as far as I can see is that if they had they would all be in a position to exercise spiritual gifts. That is when it all began—the day you were baptised in the Holy Spirit and drank of that Spirit, you began then to exercise spiritual gifts, and I can only share with you my deep conviction that one of the reasons we don't see more spiritual gifts than we do is that there are many believers who have never been made to drink in that way.

When they are, then more than natural gifts begin to be

operated. When you become a Christian all your natural gifts are there. You lay them on the altar and you say, "Lord, can I sing? I'll sing for you," but when you are baptised in the Holy Spirit and made to drink of the Spirit, you find that you can exercise gifts you never had before and use them for the common good and the upbuilding of the one body of Jesus Christ.

Chapter Eleven

THE HOLY SPIRIT IN GALATIANS

I want to look at the work of the Holy Spirit in Galatians and see what Paul says about it there. It is one of the key letters in the New Testament related to our subject. What the Magna Carta is to England and the Declaration of Independence is to the United States, the letter to the Galatians is to Christians. Here is our charter of Christian liberty. To know what freedom really is, this is the book you have to read.

The word "freedom" is widely used today. There are freedom fighters, people protest, march for freedom, and they want everybody to have freedom. But when I talk to people who talk about freedom and ask, "What do you mean by it?" I get all kinds of answers. President Roosevelt said that real freedom would consist in freedom of speech, freedom of worship, freedom from fear, and freedom from want. That is one definition. Some people say we must be free from capitalism, free from imperialism, free from all the other "isms" that there are. But that is not how this book defines freedom. Paul here is fighting for the liberty of the Christian. Real freedom consists in only two things: being free from legalism on the one hand, and free from license on the other. Now those are words that are not in normal conversational use so I am going to have to explain them.

In the first half of this little letter he deals with *legalism*, which means the control of human beings by law, by rules and regulations outside themselves, telling them what to do, making them do certain things, and punishing them if they don't. Every society has found it necessary to have a legal profession and to write laws telling people if you do that you'll be punished for it. There are laws that I've got to keep when I go out in my car. I'm not free to do anything I want. I am not free to drive on the wrong side of the road just because I want to and the view looks nicer on that side. I stopped at one crossroads in London and counted fifteen different road signs that I was expected to read, telling me which way to go, what to do, and where to go before I moved on. Behind me were a lot of hooting drivers who wondered why I was waiting. This is a picture of legalism. It is not freedom. You are hedged by rules and regulations.

Now religion can get like that. Paul had lived in a religion that was legalistic, full of rules and regulations. It is a miserable, hard kind of religion, and it becomes more and more oppressive. Paul had been a Pharisee, a Hebrew of the Hebrews, a religious Jew, and he knew what this meant. The Jews of Paul's day had 1,281 different rules about Sabbath observance. You couldn't go for a walk more than a thousand paces, couldn't drag your stick in dust or you were ploughing. There were all kinds of petty rules and regulations—and that's legalism. We must be very careful that we never let Christianity become a legalistic religion.

Paul fought this battle all his life. There were misguided Christians who wanted to put new converts under a list of rules and regulations, but he was fighting for their liberty. When we become Christians life is no longer a matter of petty regulations, and trying to live up to them. To help them to see that Christianity is not a matter of keeping rules he writes to his converts who are beginning to live by rules:

You foolish Galatians! Who has bewitched you? Before your very eyes Jesus Christ was clearly portrayed as crucified. I would like to learn just one thing from you: did you receive the Spirit by the works of the law, or by believing what you heard? Are you so foolish? After beginning by means of the Spirit, are you now trying to finish by means of the flesh? Have you experienced so much in vain – if it really was in vain? So again I ask, does God give you his Spirit and work miracles among you by the works of the law, or by your believing what you heard?

3:1–5, NIV

In other words, how did you start the Christian life? I will guarantee this: nobody ever became a Christian by trying to keep the Ten Commandments or by trying to do all the things that a Christian is supposed to do. Nobody ever found the power of God by trying desperately to achieve a certain standard of behaviour. Paul had once thought that if you want to get through to God you kept the commandments, and that is what he means by the works of the law. But he came to a point where he realised that that road is increasingly frustrating. You get more and more tied up in knots because there are so many regulations, and the one thing that you discover when you try and keep them is the weakness of the flesh. You can't make it.

That is a real problem because you feel more and more guilty. That is what legalism does. If you think Christianity is a matter of keeping the rules, trying to live according to the laws, then you are condemning yourself to discovering that the flesh or nature is just too weak and can't keep them. There are too many rules and we are just not disciplined enough to get up to the standard.

Paul here is saying: how did you discover power? How did you find out that your religion is not something you're meant to carry but something that's meant to carry you? Did you discover that by trying to keep the law? Or did you discover it as soon as you stopped trying and started trusting, and heard with faith? This means: how did you ever know the power of the Holy Spirit? As soon as you stopped trying and started trusting. As soon as you stopped trying to pick yourself up and let him take over. Now these are the two kinds of religion that you meet in the world. I would call one the "rowing boat" religion and the other the "sailing boat" religion. The "rowing boat" religion is a terrible business. You are pulling for all your worth, trying to get there, and you never see God because when you are rowing your face is usually turned the wrong way. You can't see where you're going and you keep pulling and you don't know where you're getting to. Maybe you are going around in circles and don't know it.

A "sailing" religion is where you set the sail of faith and wait for the wind of the Spirit to blow; it is the wind of the Spirit carrying you along, the power of the Spirit. If you are in a rowing boat you discover the weakness of the flesh pretty quickly. If you are in a sailing boat you will discover the power of the wind. If you are *trying* to be a Christian this is precisely what will happen: you will discover the weakness of the flesh. You can't make it. If you are *trusting* to be a Christian, you discover the power of the Spirit blows you along, carries you along, and gets you where you need to go; your eyes are facing forward and can see your destination.

Having begun that way, these "idiotic" Galatians (that's not my phrase it is Paul's so I can use it), having started the Christian life by trusting were now trying. They were in danger of going back to rules and regulations. Circumcision was the particular one that Paul was worried about. But he knew that was the thin end of the wedge. If you start doing that because it's one of the laws then you have to keep the rest. If you once start trying to keep the Ten Commandments you ought to keep all the others, and you are really sunk. Having started by trusting with the hearing of faith why are you going back to the works of the law, making it so hard for yourself? Many Christians do make Christianity hard for themselves by going back to legalism. So they must be told: you are no longer under the law. It is no longer a matter of obeying rules and regulations. At this point Paul was frequently misunderstood. Whenever I have said this, following Paul, I have been misunderstood. People jump to the conclusion that what the Christian is saying is, "You can now do what you like," and that is license and it is not liberty.

Let me give you some down to earth examples about two areas of Christian living in which Christians have made the mistake of making rules and regulations for themselves. Take Sunday observance. Here is an area of Christian behaviour about which our forefathers very often made rules and regulations. Sunday became a legalistic day and therefore an unhappy day, a day in which it was hedged around with restrictions in which you locked certain cupboards, put away certain toys, didn't do this, didn't do that, and it became sheer legalism. It is very interesting that those who had that view of the Sunday began to call it the "Sabbath", which is a Jewish regulation not a Christian one. As soon as you say, "You are not under legalistic rules and regulations for your Sunday behaviour," somebody is going to jump into license and say, "Good, that means I can do what I like on Sundays," and it doesn't mean anything of the sort – that is license to do what you like.

Take another sphere: I am a total abstainer, and I deliberately choose to be that, but you will never hear me saying that I think every Christian ought to sign the pledge. In the Sunday school to which I went we were confronted with a pledge to sign every November. I got the impression (I don't know if they intended to give it) that you couldn't possibly be a Christian unless you signed that pledge. But it is not a rule of Christian living that everybody has to be a total abstainer. As soon as I said that in one church, some of our young people thought that I had said it's perfectly all right for Christians to go on a pub crawl and to drink if they want to and I had said no such thing. There are some people who if they can't have legalism, with rules and regulations, think the only alternative is to do what you like.

In Galatians 5 and 6, Paul deals with this opposite error. To do what you like is not freedom. It is as much slavery as legalism. In other words, if you reject the rules and regulations and jump over into the opposite extreme and do what you like, that is sheer slavery. Under legalism you are a slave to other people; under license you are a slave to yourself. But either way you don't know what freedom is. If you are living a life that is about doing whatever you like, then, frankly, you are even more a slave than someone who is under law. Sooner or later you will find yourself put back under the law, if only to stop you misbehaving.

Everyone who jumps into the license category will come into trouble with the law sooner or later, because that way lies anarchy. I have the feeling that a very great deal of the talk about freedom today is really talk about license, which is not freedom at all. It is fighting for freedom to do what I like, to do what I want, and that is slavery. So at the end of Galatians, Paul is talking about the slavery that comes if you feel free to do what you like, and it becomes slavery to your own passions and desires. That is the very worst kind of slavery. Isn't it amazing that those who throw off the shackles of legalism so often voluntarily put their hands in the handcuffs of license and become just as much slaves?

I think of a couple of drunken men on the top of a bus, going home in Newcastle-on Tyne, and they were obviously very worried about the reception they were going to get from their respective spouses at home. One finally turned to the other and said, "Well I'm going to say to her, 'I'm free aren't I? I'm free.'" But he wasn't. He was a poor, besotted slave. He couldn't see through one Saturday night without getting into that condition. He was in the absolute grip of it. Now do you see the difference? What then is the answer?

In the second half of Galatians Paul is dealing with those who don't know how to use their freedom properly. So he teaches on walking in the Spirit. Here is a crucial passage:

You, my brothers and sisters, were called to be free. But do not use your freedom to indulge the flesh; rather, serve one another humbly in love. For the entire law is fulfilled in keeping this one command: 'Love your neighbour as yourself.' If you bite and devour each other, watch out or you will be destroyed by each other.

So I say, live by the Spirit, and you will not gratify the desires of the flesh. For the flesh desires what is contrary to the Spirit, and the Spirit what is contrary to the flesh. They are in conflict with each other, so that you are not to do whatever you want. But if you are led by the Spirit, you are not under the law.

The acts of the flesh are obvious: sexual immorality, impurity and debauchery; idolatry and witchcraft; hatred, discord, jealousy, fits of rage, selfish ambition, dissensions, factions and envy; drunkenness, orgies, and the like. I warn you, as I did before, that those who live like this will not inherit the kingdom of God.

But the fruit of the Spirit is love, joy, peace, forbearance, kindness, goodness, faithfulness, gentleness and self-control. Against such things there is no law. Those who belong to Christ Jesus have crucified the flesh with its passions and desires. Since we live by the Spirit, let us keep in step with the Spirit.

5:1–25, NIV

Because I am set free from the law, I am not free to do as I like. In other words, for example, I can be a total abstainer because I am free to be one, because I choose freely to be one, because I want to love my neighbour. I think in my circumstances I can most help those who can't control their drinking by being a total abstainer myself, but it is a free choice. It is not a rule of the Christian life. It is not something that I am told to do. It is not something that I must do to be a Christian. It is a complete act of freedom. You are free not to be such if that is how the Spirit leads you. You are not free to be other than this if it is just the flesh that has told you to be free.

Now it is this understanding of freedom which makes a person really know liberty. We begin then with the simple fact that in every Christian there is a conflict, which only they have. If you become a Christian you will have more conflict then you ever had before. You will lose the peace that you had before because this conflict was not present. What is the conflict? It is that between flesh and Spirit. Every Christian is torn two ways. Do get it absolutely clear in your mind that by "flesh" I do not mean "body", and by "spirit" I do not mean "mind". It is extraordinary how many people think that way. By the word "flesh" the Bible doesn't just mean this body, it means everything I am by birth, everything I am by my nature, whether it is my physical habits and desires or my mental habits and desires, or my affections, or my ambitions – anything at all that is of *me* that I was born with and everything I would be if God had not touched my life.

The word "spirit" here refers to everything I am by being born again. When I became a Christian, the Holy Spirit took up residence in my heart and everything *he* has created within me is spirit. Now then the conflict between these two really is terrible. At times it is a warfare and a person becomes a civil war. His old nature pulls one way; his new nature pulls another, and he feels torn in two. One thing is absolutely certain in the conflict, and Paul makes it clear: it is absolutely impossible to do both.

It is this that Paul is writing about in vv. 16–18 which very simply tell us that if you are letting the flesh pull you then the Spirit can't; if you are letting the Spirit pull you the flesh can't. The Christian is the only kind of person in the world who has the choice of letting one or the other take over the leadership. That is why Paul says: walk after the Spirit; walk by the Spirit.

What he means is that every Christian, every moment of every day, is confronted with two paths leading in opposite directions. His old nature is walking down one path; his new nature, filled with the Spirit, is walking up another path. Every moment of every day we are either following this path or that, but you certainly can't mix them up. If you are walking in the Spirit today it will be impossible for you to walk after the flesh. If you are walking after the flesh it will be quite impossible for you to respond to the Holy Spirit.

Paul puts it more strongly in the original language: "I say walk by the Spirit and you will not gratify the desires of the flesh. You won't need to bother about that if you're walking by the Spirit."

How do you know which road you're on? How do you know whether a particular action is of the flesh or the Spirit? It is one of the most important questions that you could ever ask, because it is awfully difficult to sort out when the flesh is pulling and when the Spirit is. In your early Christian life you can make a lot of mistakes here. For example, you want a particular job or you want to marry a particular person and so you say, "Is it of the flesh or of the Spirit? Is it my old nature wanting to do this, or is it my new nature wanting to? Is this the old me reasserting itself or is this the new me wanting to do something that's right?"

How do you do it? One way is to see where the roads lead. So Paul now describes the consequences of going on one road or the other – the works of the flesh; the fruit of the Spirit. See where these ways lead us. First of all, take the works of the flesh. I think it is very interesting that he uses the word "works" and not the word "fruit". The word "works" speaks to me of a factory, of man-made products that don't need God at all. Man can produce works and so let us see what the factory of the flesh produces, turning out the same things with monotonous regularity. It is a plural word because you won't find all of these things in the same person. You might find one in one and one in another. But sooner or later this kind of thing appears, and this is not a complete list because it says at the end of it, "...and the like."

There are four areas of life in which things will go wrong when you walk after the flesh and follow your old nature: in the realm of sex, religion, society, drink. I think nowadays Paul would have added drugs. This is what you can expect to happen if you are following your old nature; these are the consequences. First, in relation to sex, Paul says that if you follow your old nature then sooner or later immorality, impurity and licentiousness will appear.

Now I give you the exact meaning: the first word means, "sex outside marriage," the second word means, "dirty mindedness", the third word means, "to shock public decency." Now inevitably if you walk down the road of your old nature one of those three things will appear in this area of life, and maybe more. You will either deliberately do something you know to be wrong, or you will keep it inside your mind, or you will let it right out and deliberately shock public decency, but that is what happens down that road.

The second thing he mentions is religion. What happens in religion when you follow your old nature? Two things: idolatry and sorcery. Let me explain those. First of all, your religion will become an outward thing in which you have to see something before you can feel religious. Therefore you will want images or a nice Gothic building, or something that will help you to be religious. Because when you are walking down the road of the flesh you have nothing inside to make you godly, so you want more and more outside help. So you want images, idols and things to make you feel religious. That is what happens when you are walking the road of your old nature.

The other thing is sorcery. What does that mean? It means superstition: touch wood, cross your heart, throw salt over your shoulder, walking under ladders (though there can be a sensible reason for that which is not superstitious). It means playing around with magic, dabbling in spiritism or getting interested in the occult. Paul is teaching that this is the kind of thing that happens down that road in religion.

What happens in your social life? He lists eight things: enmity, which means hatred of people, prejudice against them, which could include their class or race; then strife, violence. You will intrigue and scheme. There is jealousy, that burning destructive attitude towards other people which destroys them; anger, which literally means "boiling point", that is the word Paul uses – boiling over in temper. There is selfishness, which means to be filled with personal ambition; dissension, which means to love competition and rivalry, and party labels and strife against others; party spirit, which means to prefer sects and cliques instead of being loving to all. Envy means bitter resentment at others who have got more than you have. That is what happens when you walk the way of the flesh.

Paul says that drunkenness is the inevitable outcome of following your lower nature to its logical conclusion. That will lead to carousing, which is revelries, orgies, debauchery, in which you disgrace yourself as Noah disgraced himself when he got out of the ark. Here is a list, which Paul says is far from complete, which can appear in your life even as a Christian if you walk after the flesh—that is how you tell. Are you getting more bad-tempered? Are you getting divided from people? Are you getting jealous of others? Do you envy others? Then this is your nature leading you by the nose down that path. Paul says that sooner or later if you go down that path of doing what you like, you will find yourself under law again, because law is precisely to stop people damaging others by walking after the flesh.

The law of the land is (or should be) designed to prevent the flesh harming another person. Why are there laws restricting my driving speed? Because it is my flesh that wants to drive fast, and my flesh would hurt and injure another person if there is no law to stop me. So sooner or later, if you walk the way of the flesh, even if you don't get into trouble with human laws you will most certainly run smack into the law of God, because there is a law of God that says those who do such things shall not inherit the kingdom. It is a pretty terrible picture.

Let us now look at the lovely side. Suppose the Spirit leads somebody – they start following the Spirit. Do you know what will appear in their life? Fruit will appear. Now I love the word "fruit" and it is a very important word for this reason: man produces works but God produces fruit. No man has ever been able to manufacture fruit, nor ever will; only God can produce it.

The word "fruit" also tells me that you can't have it without the tree and Jesus said that unless you abide in the vine – unless you are in touch with him – you can't produce fruit. It tells me also that this fruit does not grow overnight. It grows gradually and steadily. But the most interesting thing about this word "fruit" is that the word is in the singular whereas the works of the flesh are plural. Fruit all appears together – one fruit with nine flavours, and all nine appear together in the life of someone who is walking after the Spirit. You don't need to try to have the fruit. They grow in the character of one who is walking this way. Three of them put us right with God, three of them put us right with others, and three of them put us right with ourselves. The three towards God are love, joy, and peace. Need I say any more? When you are walking after the Spirit you love God, you enjoy God, you have peace with God—it is as simple as that. What about other people who are so awkward and so irritating? When you are walking after the Spirit you are patient, kind, and good toward them. You don't have to try to be. The fruit will grow. You will be patient, you will be kind, you will be good. Toward yourself, you will be faithful. That means stick-ability—being reliable. It is tremendous to be a reliable person. You will be gentle and meek. Gentleness is what gives courtesy, and that is not a matter of social background. Something that strikes me about modern man is we can control everything but ourselves – but a person who is walking after the Spirit will find they have self-control.

Paul teaches that if you walk this road you will never come into trouble with man's laws or God's laws. Why? Because there never has been a law against any of these things, against such there is no law. There has never been a law that says, "Thou shalt not enjoy God and life." There has never been a law against peace, nor against patience, nor against kindness, goodness, reliability, gentleness or self-control. Doesn't this make sense? If you are a Christian, is not this your life? Flesh and Spirit are tugging you in different directions and you know you can't go both ways. You know perfectly well that when you give in to your old nature and follow that path this is the kind of thing that appears in your life: you get irritable, you fall out with people, you lose your temper with them, you envy what they have that you haven't.

I hope you know that when you walk after the Spirit and let him give you life then you are completely free. For I will tell you this: the biggest freedom in the world is to be free *from* yourself. Isn't that the biggest freedom there is? Isn't that the freedom nobody else has? Isn't that the freedom that nobody seems interested in having? I want to be free to do what I want. I want to be free *for* myself but the Bible says that is slavery. You can be free from yourself by being led by the Spirit. You will then be free from the law too, because the law won't be able to touch you. There is no law against being free from yourself — that is real freedom. Legalism and license, the two forms of slavery, are left behind. You are neither a slave to other people nor a slave to yourself. You are free. You are not free *from* God; you are free *for* God. You are not free from your neighbour you are now free for your neighbour. You are not free from love, you are free for love — that's real freedom. It is why a well-known prayer in the Book of Common Prayer has that lovely phrase "whose service is perfect freedom". You will never be free until you are led by the Spirit. You are free to have exactly the attitude that the Holy Spirit leads you to have. In summary, that is perfect freedom because at last you are free from yourself and free for God.

Is it an open option to a Christian to decide whether to walk according to the flesh or the Spirit? Am I free as a Christian to say, "Well now, what shall I do? Shall I walk according to the flesh or the Spirit today?" To those whom the Spirit is pulling one way and the flesh another, I say that when you became a Christian you already decided which way you were going to go. It is not an open option to go out and decide whether you will spend a day in the flesh or in the Spirit, because when you came to Christ and to the cross what did you do with your flesh? You crucified it. We learn from Paul that everyone who belongs to Christ made a decision when they came to Christ that their old nature was not going to lead them any more. Paul is saying that when you were converted, when you belonged to Christ, when you became a Christian, you said: I crucify my flesh with all its pull, its passions and its desires. What does he mean? He doesn't mean that it's dead, because crucifixion doesn't kill. A person can be on a cross for up to six or seven days. Jesus was there six hours. Crucifixion puts a person in a place where they will die if they are left there. That is what crucifixion means. When a man was crucified he was nailed to the cross, and he was left there until he died. Sometimes, maybe through a plea to the governor, he was taken down and allowed to live, but if he was left where he was put at the point of crucifixion he would ultimately die.

What you did when you were converted was to say, "Lord, here's my old nature, my flesh. I put it on the cross where Christ was nailed for me. I nail my old nature to that cross and I'm going to leave it there till it's dead. But your old nature, hanging there crucified, keeps pleading, "Take me off the cross for a little while. Just take me off again." Alas, whenever we walk after the flesh we are taking the flesh off the cross again and saying, "All right, you can have a respite. You can lead me again," and that is a dangerous thing to do.

Those who belong to Christ, when they came to Christ said, "I do not want to be a slave of self." You said that when you were converted, didn't you? You said to Christ, "I've made a mess of my life. I can't lead myself. You must lead me." You meant it. You crucified your flesh with its passions and desires. Then, I plead with you, leave it there. Leave your flesh on the cross. Leave your old nature there until it dies. Don't take it down again and play with it or, sooner or later, it will put you back under the law from which you were set free by Jesus Christ. Isn't it wonderful that you can be free, that you can crucify your old nature and leave it there to die, and be led by the Spirit and walk after the Spirit? Without the effort of *trying* to be patient, *trying* to be kind, you find that the fruit grows because you are walking in the right way – the fruit tree produces the character of Jesus Christ in you. Love, joy, peace, patience, kindness, goodness, faithfulness, meekness, self control – there can be no doubt who sat in the studio of Paul's thoughts when he painted that picture of perfect character. It is a portrait of Jesus. What he is saying is that if you are led by the Spirit the love of Jesus fills your heart and you become like him.

Since we live by the Spirit, let us keep in step with the Spirit. Let us not become conceited, provoking and envying each other.

Brothers and sisters, if someone is caught in a sin, you who live by the Spirit should restore that person gently. But watch yourselves, or you also may be tempted. Carry each other's burdens, and in this way you will fulfil the law of Christ. If anyone thinks they are something when they are not, they deceive themselves. Each one should test their own actions. Then they can take pride in themselves alone, without comparing themselves to someone else, for each one should carry their own load. Nevertheless, the one who receives instruction in the word should share all good things with their instructor.

Do not be deceived: God cannot be mocked. A man reaps what he sows. Whoever sows to please their flesh, from the flesh will reap destruction; whoever sows to please the Spirit, from the Spirit will reap eternal life. Let us not become weary in doing good, for at the proper time we will reap a harvest if we do not give up. Therefore, as we have opportunity, let us do good to all people, especially to those who belong to the family of believers.

5:25–6:10, NIV

250

Walking is now an abnormal activity. It is not something we do much. A couple of generations ago, most people would walk to church. You would have been pleasantly tired and could relax in the pews and restore yourself for the journey home. I heard of a man who regularly walked every Sunday twenty miles to church and twenty miles back again, but walking is out of fashion. Most drive nowadays. Fit young people regard walking as something only to do for money, as something so extraordinary, such an effort, that they really should be paid to do it for some charity. The very idea that walking should be paid for – as if you had done something marvellous, something great, something unusual!

Because of all this it is awfully difficult to understand the New Testament. It is always talking about the Christian life as walking: walking in love, walking in the light, walking in the Spirit, walking after Christ. If you study the life of Jesus Christ he was a great walker. He must have walked hundreds of miles, always teaching as he walked, as he was in the way—walking, walking. After his resurrection he was still walking on the road to Emmaus. Even now in heaven he is still the one who walks among the lampstands. The Christian life is to be a walk but it is awfully difficult to see that today. In our "riding" society in which we all expect to ride everywhere if we possibly can, whether by bus, car or something else, it is very easy to drop into the kind of thinking that you are looking for a church in which you can ride to heaven – looking for a religion in which you can ride, in which you have to do very little. Of course, if that is the kind of concept of religion which you have, and you are looking for a church to ride into glory, then your first concern will be the comfort of the seats.

In Galatians 5 Paul teaches us that to live the Christian life is to walk in the Spirit. That is not as spectacular as running. But far more frequently than being exhorted to run the race, we are told to walk. From experience I know that you get much further walking than you do running. One of the temptations of the young Christian life, is to want to run before you can walk, to want to get there quickly and in a spectacular way. But the Christians who get furthest in the Christian life are those who plough on, walked steadily, taking one step at a time in the right direction all their lives. Forty years walking with the Lord will take you far further then five years running. Indeed, you won't be able to run for forty years. There will be times when having done all you must stand, but as soon as possible you must get walking again.

So in Galatians 5 Paul is talking about how to walk in the Spirit. In vv. 16–24 the walking that is described is your private walk with God—how you walk when you are alone. Indeed, walking alone is something that every Christian will need to do – to walk after the Spirit rather than after the flesh when they are alone. But now in v. 25 we are told again, "Let us walk by the Spirit." Unfortunately, in English it is rendered using the same word, so it leads many of us to think Paul is just repeating himself, but he doesn't do much of that. He has got much to say, and the second time he uses a different Greek word for "walk". The first time in v. 16 it is the word for a person walking on their own, but the second word he uses here is a word that means to walk in step, in line with others. I suppose it would be better translated, "Let us march by the Spirit." In other words, there are two kinds of walking a Christian needs to do: the kind of walking that walks after the Spirit by yourself, and the kind of walking that walks by the Spirit in line and in step with others who are walking in the Spirit too.

This of course, knocks right on the head any idea that you can be a Christian on your own. Whenever somebody says to me, "I can be a Christian without going to church," one just doesn't know what to say. One wants to say, "How on earth can you? How can you fulfil the teaching of Christ and not walk with others?" It is an impossibility since he told us to do this. How can you say "I can be a Christian by myself," when the only new commandment that Jesus ever gave us was "Love one another." It is an absolute impossibility to walk by yourself to heaven. We are to walk after the Spirit not just as individuals but as a mighty army moves – the church of God, keeping in line, keeping in step.

We look now at walking in the Spirit together. Now he gives us three ways in which you can get out of step with other people, and three ways in which you can get out of step with yourself. In each case the Christian must watch his step very carefully to make sure he is in line, to make sure he is with the others—out of sheer love for them. Paul says love one another; don't envy one another; bear one another's burdens. Christianity is your attitude to your fellow Christians.

How can we get out of step with others on the negative side? I was never any good at marching. I remember when I joined the RAF as a chaplain. I hadn't been in the forces, I had been in agriculture, which was a reserved occupation when butter was more important than guns. So when I went into the RAF I suddenly stepped in as an officer without any square-bashing at all, if you know what that is. I had no training, the first week came and I had to appear before about two thousand people on a parade ground and march around in front of them while they were standing there. I didn't know my left from my right. It was such chaos, that first parade. I shall never forget it; I still have nightmares about it. I was helped by the Anglican chaplain arriving the following week. He forgot to salute somebody, did an about turn on his wrong foot and fell flat on his face, and

I felt greatly comforted. But I remember going and eating humble pie, going to a sergeant, and by giving him cigarettes persuaded him to come round to the chaplains' office after dark, and then drilling me around the office. He was yelling commands while I marched around the desk to learn how to do it! Just to learn to walk in step with others requires an effort when you have only been used to walking in your own style, at your own speed, all your life. You have got to learn, and the young Christian needs to learn how to keep in step with other Christians of all ages and temperaments.

How do you get out of step? Sometimes I found that I was getting out of step and I had three feet, and I didn't know which one to put forward first. How do you get out of step with your fellow Christians? Three ways: conceit, provoking them, and envying them. Take the first – conceit. A man who has too big an idea of himself will try and step out ahead of the others, and will get out of line. If you have a superiority complex you will not be able to keep in step with other people in the church. If you think you are better than them you will be striding out ahead and saying, "Look at me, I can take bigger steps than you," and therefore you will get out of line, and the line will be broken. Just remember there are spiritual equivalents of banana skins, and pride goes before a fall according to my Bible. A man who steps out ahead of others out of conceit is a man who will soon fall down.

The second way is to provoke people which means, literally, "needling" them. You are keeping in line but you have needles stuck on both armbands. You just cause it to be very difficult for the people who are walking next to you to keep near. So gradually they draw away sideways, the line is broken, and the enemy can break through because the line is weak. You are provoking them and that means: "To challenge to a contest." It is to regard them as rivals rather than colleagues. You might get a little touch of envy in your heart. "He's got more gifts than I have. He's got a better position in the church than I have. She was given that job and I've always had it up till now." If there is a touch of envy you tend to drop behind. It is like an inferiority complex.

So a Christian must not say, "I'm better than you and I'll prove it," nor must he say, "You're better than me and I resent it." A Christian says, "We're all colleagues." It doesn't matter who is better or worse than whom, I count others better than myself and I walk in line with them and count it a holy privilege to do so. Together, in line, you march in step forward into the kingdom.

If you do get out of step with your fellow Christians you will not be walking in the Spirit. The next thing that Paul mentions here is the three ways in which somebody else can drop out of line and how you can get them back into line, and this is the other side of it. Not only must we be careful to keep in step ourselves, we must also be careful to help others to be in step. Paul here is saying that there is a right way as well as a wrong way to get people back into step with each other when they get out of line. By the way, you notice he now says "Brethren". I am my brother's keeper if I am a Christian. It is my business if my brother is out of line and not in step with the others. You are not appealing to a bunch of people who are just members of a club. You are appealing to brothers. In any true family, if someone falls then the rest of the family pick them up. Isn't that natural? In a church, if someone falls you don't just gossip about that person and say, "Isn't it terrible," and let them stew in their own juice. You pick them up. Brothers, keep each other in line.

If a brother is overtaken in trespass – what does that mean? If one of your Christian brothers trips up, slips, stumbles, falls down. Now this can happen to every Christian and most of us have probably slipped or fallen since we became Christians and it has become known to other believers. What happens then? If it is a real family of Christian brothers and sisters, then as soon as someone has slipped, the others who know them do all they can to pick the person up again and get them walking again—that is the instinctive reaction. Not to hit them when they are down by talking about them, but by surrounding them with love, picking them up and saying, "Come on, back into line quickly." They have fallen, they have stumbled, they were taken by surprise and overtaken by temptation. I remember this happening within the confines of a Christian college when a student fell. For about three days no student could concentrate on work, I will never forget it. They were so concerned that they just surrounded this boy with their prayer and their love. They went on doing that until they had got him back on his feet and he was walking ahead with them again. It was a lovely example of Christian fellowship. "Brothers, if someone is overtaken in trespass, if they do fall, you who are spiritual..." which means don't try and pick them up unless you are spiritually strong, unless you are full of the Holy Spirit, but pick them up, and then help them to walk along with you, but do it in a spirit of meekness and gentleness because you could have been the person who fell.

Only a really spiritual person can do it gently because only he or she knows that they too could have been on the ground just like the person who has fallen. An unspiritual Christian will say, "Well, how on earth did you get into that kind of trouble? If you had only copied me and lived as I live you would not have got into this mess." Bang, bang, bang, the poor chap is knocked further down.

I was once talking to a man whose job it is to straighten out cars. He told me that if your car gets a dent in the wing or the body, the worst thing you can do is to take a hammer and hit that dent in the middle at the back, which is what most of us would do. He said, "What you've got to do is to tap gently, all around the bubble. Go on tapping very gently, working in towards the centre. You gradually get it straight. But a good bang in the middle and it will crack and you will get some nasty lumps."

That is what Paul is teaching us here. If somebody has fallen and an unspiritual Christian tries to pick them up and says, "Come on, get on your feet. What did you do that for?" they will crack that Christian. But a spiritual person is able gently to restore and to mend. The word used here is the word used for setting a bone so that it grows together again. You have got to feel it into place gently. So the first thing is that if somebody gets out of line through falling into a sin and doing wrong, then you who are spiritual pick them up gently.

The next point is that if anybody is carrying too big a burden they are likely to get out of step. The way for the fellowship to cure that is to bear one another's burdens. Once again the picture is utterly simple, I don't need to explain it. But if a lot of soldiers are walking in line and one poor soldier is carrying a heavy load on his back, then he is going to get out of line sooner or later, and this is what happens in a fellowship. Sometimes a Christian is carrying too big a burden, something that is overwhelming them, and they cannot keep up. Instead of just saying, "Oh, so and so is falling behind," Paul says, "Bear one another's burdens." If someone is carrying too much, the rest should say, "Come and give me a bit of that load. I must take that off your hands."

It may be an utterly practical load. It may be a woman whose husband is in hospital and who needs the children looked after for a time. It may be a deeply spiritual thing, that someone has too many jobs in the church and it is too much of a strain. Other people should rally round and say, "You shouldn't be doing all of this, we'll take that job."

Paul now adds a strange thing, a word about pride: "But

WHAT THE BIBLE SAYS ABOUT THE HOLY SPIRIT

if anyone thinks he is something when he is nothing he deceives himself." Why does he say that here? I will tell you why from my experience in pastoral work. The one thing that stops people bearing one another's burdens is pride. Either someone is too proud to take a burden off someone else, or that someone else is too proud to let the burden be taken from them. Either way somebody is thinking they are something when they are nothing. If you think you are nothing you can bear one another's burdens.

You may be too proud to tell anyone that you have a burden – to say, "Look, I'm under strain. I can't take what I've got to carry. Will you help me?" Because we think we are something, there is this streak of pride, that little cast iron muscle in the back of our necks.

Bear one another's burdens and so fulfil the law of Christ, and if anyone thinks he is something when he is nothing he is fooling himself, he doesn't fool other people.

Finally, in the Authorized Version the word "burden" comes again in v. 5. But a better translation uses a different word: "For each man will have to bear his own load." In the Authorized Version, "Each man will have to bear his own burden. Now this seems to contradict the earlier verse, "Bear each other's burden"/"Each man will have to bear his own". But when we look at the difference of word we understand what it means. Each soldier needs to carry his own kitbag. The word "load" here is the word used in the Roman armies and in the Greek armies for a soldier's kit bag. In other words, you will never walk in line unless everybody is carrying as much as they ought and no more. If they have got too much to carry, bear each other's burdens. But if they are not carrying their own load, the load will come on others.

Every church I have ever encountered imposes too much burden on some people because some members do not carry their own load, and this is not true Christian fellowship.

On some there is a greater burden than there should be. If God puts members into a church, he does so because in that church every member is needed to carry their load. There is no room for passengers on the gospel train, only crew. Every member who does not carry the full responsibility they ought under God does not do the job God wants them to do. Then what happens? The load is shifted down the line. Those who are willing get asked to do more and more. I have seen this happen so often. I ask members who are not carrying their load if they realise what they are doing to others. If you are a member of a church, then your responsibility is to ask, "What is my load? Is it to teach in the Sunday school? Is it to greet people at the door? Is it to help keep the buildings clean and comfortable? Is it to help with the outreach? Is it to help with the visiting? Is it to help with the fellowship groups? What is my load?" Every member who doesn't carry the load will be overburdening somebody else. So Paul says every one of you must carry his own load. Then and only then will you be able to bear one another's burdens because then and only then is the load properly spread.

Now forgive me for being direct but I am passing on to you what Paul said to the Galatians: it is very important that there should be no parasites in Christian fellowship. Indeed, Paul once said to the church at Thessalonica, "If there is a member of the church who won't work, neither shall he eat." In other words, don't give charity or food or money to those who won't work if they can. Doing so would not be Christian love but pure sentiment. Let each man carry his own load. I had an ambition to be pastor of a church where every member carries their own load, where if any member gets overloaded the others are therefore able straight away to help to bear one another's burdens. It is an army we are in, and in an army you cannot afford to have a single soldier not pulling his weight in some way.

In vv. 7–10 there is a proverb, a principle, a promise, and a precept. First of all the proverb: the law of cause and effect. What you put in is what you get out. That law of God applies right through life. It applies to your bank balance. It applies to your garden. If you sow cabbages you are not going to get roses. What you put in is what you get out. It applies to your social life. Isn't it funny, but sometimes on the same Sunday two people can say these things to me: one says, "What a friendly church this is," and the other says, "Oh, what an unfriendly church this is." Neither remark tells me anything about the church; each remark tells me something about the person who made it.

Quite frankly, what you get out of a church is what you put into it. If you are bearing other people's burdens and friendly towards them, you will find it is a wonderfully friendly church. If you keep aloof and keep to yourself in a church then don't blame the church if you feel that they keep aloof from you. Friendship is two-way: what you put in you get out. I will tell you this, those who get most out of house groups are those who are putting most in. Those who are reading the passage beforehand, who have prepared, come, make a contribution, and speak to the others, will get most out of the house groups. If somebody comes to me and says, "I'm getting nothing out of the house groups," my reply would be, "That's probably because you're putting nothing in."

What you put in you get out. It applies spiritually, it applies financially, it applies materially; it is God's law. Don't fool yourself because God is not fooled and you are going to meet him. Everything you do will have its consequence and you cannot escape from it. This is one of the laws written into the universe: that if you sow sparingly you reap sparingly. If you sow good seed you will reap good seed; if you sow bad you will reap bad. It's a written law of God. It comes all the way through the Bible, and indeed it is a proverb in ordinary language.

The worst kind of deception is to fool yourself because there is nobody to help you to undeceive yourself then. Paul is saying don't fool yourself. Don't think you can do a thing and get away with it. Don't think you can sow in one way and reap in another. Don't think that if you sow this kind of life you will reap another kind. You will have the same back. For what you put in you will get out again. Life is like this and God will not let anyone get away with a thing. It is his law that even if you fool yourself and think you can get away with it, you cannot. In Galatians he is talking to Christians. Christians, don't fool yourselves. Any Christian who walks after the flesh will ultimately destroy and break down his physical health, mental peace and spiritual effectiveness. It is a law of God. But if on the other hand you are sowing to the Spirit all the time, walking in the Spirit as an individual and as a fellowship, there is a lovely harvest of eternal life to be reaped.

In these days "instant" is the word that sells anything. The trouble is that in an "instant" life we want instant sainthood, as if there was some event or experience that could suddenly make you a saint. You will be tempted to be discouraged with the spiritual harvest that does not come quickly. Having worked on a farm, I know this to my cost. I was once in my early days on the farm given the job of sowing a field, and I remember sowing it badly. It was a field over the top of a hill. I did not realise then that the drill needed to be adjusted if it was going uphill and downhill. So what happened was it sowed uphill only. For months I was quite happy about my work until it began to come through. It was on a main road in Yorkshire. It was part of a mountain and everybody driving along that road could see a field with green and brown stripes over the whole field. I had a very painful

261

interview with the farmer at financial cost. I had sown it months earlier and it was too late by then to do anything about it, but it stood there the whole summer and I had to see it every time I came along the road. The farmer's leg was pulled unmercifully, so I had to learn. But when I learned how to sow seed properly I was content to wait three, four, five months until the harvest came. Every farmer has to be patient, and every Christian needs to realise that you don't always get the harvest of doing well straight away. So don't be weary in well doing, don't faint, don't give up. It may be years before you see the fruit of your labours.

A Sunday school teacher once gave up Sunday school teaching because she was seeing no results at all from her work. But during the war a soldier lay dying and he said to one of his pals, "Please write to so and so, and tell her that what she told me in Sunday school is now helping me to die." The letter came all the way back to England to the Sunday schoolteacher, and she had given up because she didn't see the harvest quickly and had stopped doing it. Don't be weary in well doing. Don't give up because you don't see instant fruit, instant harvest. Keep on sowing the seed, sowing what is good – well doing. Even if you don't get results quickly just keep on. The harvest is bound to come. Just as a man who plays the fool will one day pay the bill, the man who walks in the Spirit will one day see a wonderful harvest.

"Therefore, do good to all men but especially to those who are of the household of faith." Charity begins at home. A Christian who is so busy doing things outside his own church that he never helps fellow members is not fulfilling the law of Christ. On the other hand, a Christian who does so much in the church he never helps anybody else is not fulfilling the law of Christ. The law is, "Do good to all men as you get an opportunity, but let charity begin at home." The first call on the Christian is to help other Christians. The first responsibility you have is to help others to walk in step with you. So balance your doing good. Do it first to those who are of the household of faith. Let your charity begin in your spiritual home, but don't let it end there; let it stretch out to all people who are in need.

Chapter Twelve

THE HOLY SPIRIT IN EPHESIANS

We have now finished studying all the passages in the New Testament that are directly on the teaching of the Holy Spirit. In Paul's letters, we have looked at Romans 8, 1 Corinthians 2, 1 Corinthians 12, Galatians 5 – and that pretty well covers all his systematic teaching about the Holy Spirit. But the thing that strikes me tremendously about Paul is that whenever he writes a letter he keeps mentioning the Holy Spirit almost as an aside. There is one letter in which he does this more frequently than others: his letter to the Ephesians.

Once in each of the six chapters he mentions the Holy Spirit, and something different each time that the Holy Spirit does for you. Here is the first instance:

And you also were included in Christ when you heard the message of truth, the gospel of your salvation. When you believed, you were marked in him with a seal, the promised Holy Spirit, who is a deposit guaranteeing our inheritance until the redemption of those who are God's possession – to the praise of his glory.

1:13–14, NIV

From time to time every Christian ought to take a piece of paper and a pencil or pen, and write down all the blessings you enjoy. It is easy enough to be vague about your blessings and just say, "Thank you God for blessing me." It is much better to make a list of your blessings and to count them.

Name them one by one and it will surprise you what the Lord has done.

The list Paul is making here is not of physical, material blessings. He says, "Blessed be God, who has blessed us with every spiritual blessing...." It is your spiritual blessings that I am advocating you write out sometimes. Anybody can write out physical blessings, but only a Christian can write out spiritual blessings. If you were making a list of your material blessings, you would write: my health, my strength, roof over my head, enough clothes to wear, enough food to eat, enough money to buy what I need to buy, and so on. But a Christian can make a list that nobody else could make.

Paul makes it now: Blessed be God for choosing us in him before the foundation of the world. Only the Christian can write that down. Blessed be God, who destined us in love to be his sons. No non-Christian can write that down. Blessed be God for our redemption, why the very word you will hardly meet on anybody else's lips but the Christian's, because nobody else really knows what it means to be redeemed. Blessed be God for the forgiveness of our sins. That's a thing nobody knows but the Christian, the relief of having sins blotted out. And so he goes down the list.

Finally, he addresses the Ephesians and points to three things: first, that somebody preached to you; second, you believed; third, God sealed you.

Step number one: somebody took the trouble to tell you about Jesus. But that was not enough. You can sit and listen to all the preachers in the world and it doesn't take you right through to where you need to be. The second thing he says about the Ephesians: it was a blessing that somebody preached to you. In fact, it was Paul himself. The second blessing was that you believed it. That made it yours. But now he says that the third blessing that came to you at the beginning of your Christian life was that God sealed you with the promised Holy Spirit, and that is something to put in your list. Why does he use this word "sealed"? We could get a little misled by thinking of what a seal is today, and I began to toy with this. I have, in my little museum of things I have picked up over the years, John Wesley's very seal, the impress in the sealing wax. But why do we use seals and sealing wax? I suppose the simplest use of it is to make sure that a parcel gets somewhere without being tampered with. That is why God sealed you with the Holy Spirit – that you might be delivered to heaven without anybody tampering with you. If you are filled with the Spirit nobody can tamper with you, but that is not what Paul means here.

A second use of seals today is when you have completed a contract. You have signed the thing, having discussed it. You have decided what you are going to pay the other party and what they are going to pay you. Many legal documents are then still sealed, and it means settled once and for all, it cannot be altered now.

In a marriage service the marriage is sealed. That has settled it. They don't need to keep coming back every time they feel they are not quite as much in love as they thought they were yesterday. They don't need to keep coming and sealing it. It is settled once and for all; it is sealed and signed and it is safe. It is sealed but that is not what Paul meant.

In the olden days, here is what a seal was used for. If you went to market and you were going to buy some corn, and there were twenty bags of corn which you wanted, and you bid for them and you got them, you would then take out your seal and you would put your seal on the bag. That meant the bag now belonged to you even though you had not yet got it. You went home and, maybe some days later, a cart rolled up at the door and there were your sacks with seal on them. Sometimes in a furniture shop you will see on some items of furniture a little sticker which says "Sold", and maybe there is a name written on it. That is the exact equivalent of the seal and that piece of furniture, however much you would like to have it, belongs to someone else and it will go to their house one day. You can look at it, but it's not yours, it has been sealed. Paul is teaching this: when you believed the gospel, God sealed you and stamped you, and said you are mine; you must be delivered to my house one day.

Every believer who has the Holy Spirit is like that piece of furniture in the shop. You have been bought, you belong to God, and you will one day be delivered to the Father's house. You are sealed with the promised Holy Spirit, which is why Paul goes on to say that the seal of the Holy Spirit is the guarantee of our inheritance.

Sometimes a man who bought twenty sacks of corn would have one sack delivered to him straight away as what was called an "earnest" or a "pledge" of the rest. Just as today we use almost the same word when we put a deposit down on something, which is a guarantee, we will pay the rest later. Paul here uses the word translated "guarantee" but it means the deposit of our inheritance. The Holy Spirit is the first deposit of heaven, the first little bit of heaven that you get. All that you have in the Holy Spirit is the guarantee of all the rest that is to come. So this is a very rich concept.

He came and preached peace to you who were far away and peace to those who were near. For through him we both have access to the Father by one Spirit.

2:17–18, NIV

In the old days, before telephone exchanges became computer controlled, a phone operator would say "You're through." Then you hear the familiar voice, maybe a voice of someone you love, a voice of someone with whom you can share so much. But sometimes you couldn't get through.

Some people's religion is just like that. They can't get through. They have no access to God. They try so hard to get through. Some people do try really hard and very sincerely to get through to God. Some of them try to get through by being religious. Some try to get through by going through all the rites and ceremonies that the church can offer them. Some try to get through by getting worked up into frenzies. Some people try to get through by taking drugs. Some people try to get through by just doing good to their neighbours. You don't get through in any of these ways.

Now we have a magnificent statement: that in one Spirit we have access to God. In your worship, the Holy Spirit whispers in your heart: you are through. You know that your prayers have got higher than the church ceiling. Our praise and our prayers are "through".

Jesus wanted people to get in touch with God. He said, "No man comes to the Father but by me." In Ephesians 2, Paul is dealing with the basic reason why so many people can't get through to God. There is a blockage, a barrier between them and God and they can't break through that barrier. To use his own language: "We are by nature children of wrath, children of disobedience," and that is why we can't get through.

If I am not obedient to God, then he doesn't listen. He cannot listen *because* he is a good God. Just as I would sometimes say to my children who came and asked for something, "I'm sorry, I'm not going to give it until you've put so and so right or until you've said sorry for this." Until that relationship has been restored, then many an earthly parent can't listen to a child. In the early part of this chapter, Paul is saying that you will never get through to God until you realise that what you need is the grace of God to forgive your sin. By the grace of our Lord Jesus you will be saved, and that means you must stop trying to get through to God by works and by doing good deeds. The average person in Britain desperately hopes that they will get through to God by doing good deeds, but here is Paul teaching that you will have to drop that idea altogether. It is by grace that you get through, which means it is by the free forgiveness of God.

Then there is something more needed. That will deal with the barrier, but when you get through to God, will you know how to talk to him? People find it so difficult to know what to say in prayer, both in private and in public. Jesus Christ has "linked" them to God the Father, yet they still don't have that free access that comes from being relaxed in the Lord's presence and knowing how to talk to him freely and naturally.

This is where the Holy Spirit comes in. We do not know how to pray as we ought, but the Spirit himself helps us. He knows our weakness. He helps us to pray, to talk naturally to the Father. It is as natural and as easy to talk to him as to talk to people. You can soon tell when someone has the Spirit in their prayer. Prayer becomes natural, prayer becomes access, and prayer gets through. When you listen to someone praying in the Spirit, they are through straightaway, and you sense that. They are not struggling to tell God something. They are not trying to get through to him to get in touch. They are in touch; they are through and so they talk and this is the kind of prayer we are meant to have.

That doesn't mean that we won't use prayers that others have written from time to time, that we won't use hymns that others have written, but even when you use a hymn or a prayer that someone else wrote, you can tell when someone has got through to God, when they are singing from the depths of their hearts, because they are in touch, they are excited and the Holy Spirit has said, "You're through." Both Jew and Gentile have one access to God. There had been a time when the Jew got through to God, or tried to, in one part of the temple, the Gentile tried to get through in another part and there was a great wall between them. But, in fact, neither of them got through. Paul says that the middle wall of partition has now been broken down and you who were far off, the Gentiles, and the Jews, who were on the inside, now you have both got through in one Spirit. Now we come to Chapter 3.

> For this reason I kneel before the Father, from whom every family in heaven and on earth derives its name. I pray that out of his glorious riches he may strengthen you with power through his Spirit in your inner being, so that Christ may dwell in your hearts through faith. And I pray that you, being rooted and established in love, may have power, together with all the Lord's holy people, to grasp how wide and long and high and deep is the love of Christ, and to know this love that surpasses knowledge – that you may be filled to the measure of all the fullness of God.
>
> Now to him who is able to do immeasurably more than all we ask or imagine, according to his power that is at work within us, to him be glory in the church and in Christ Jesus throughout all generations, for ever and ever! Amen.
>
> *3:14–21, NIV*

Here is a glimpse into Paul's prayer life. It has been said that if you really want to know what a man believes, listen to his prayer rather than to his preaching and what he says about his belief. You may think you have problems with your quiet time—getting alone, getting quiet, getting concentrated, well what about Paul? When he wrote this he was permanently chained to a Roman centurion by three feet of chain, and he says: "I bow my knees." I want you to imagine the circumstances in which he had to pray. Paul, the prisoner, had to say to the soldier: "You'll have to sit down because I want to kneel down." There, with the centurion listening to him, Paul had to pray. If you think you have problems, just imagine that. Paul prays that his readers may have power in the inner man. The world loves power, but that is always outward power and may be military power, financial power, industrial power, scientific power. But Paul wants Christians to have power in the "inner man", a term that was used in the Greek language to cover three things within a person. First: his reason or thinking. He is praying that the believers may be strong in their thinking, which means that you may think for yourself, have your own convictions and not be tossed around by the world or by every wind of strange doctrine. This is something every Christian needs: to be strong in reason, able to think straight and to think God's thoughts after him. We need people who know what they believe, who don't just read a book or a newspaper and believe the latest thing they have read. That is to be very weak in the inner man.

Secondly, this is about having a strong conscience. Most of us have a pretty weak one. Paul prays that the believers may be strengthened with might in the inner man. You need a strong conscience that really does light up with a big red light as soon as you are heading for trouble, not a feeble glow five minutes after you did whatever it is.

The third thing that "inner man" means is "will". Paul wants them to have a strong will. Perhaps the sign of a strong will is the ability to say no. It is a very little word. Of course, most children begin life with a strong "won't". Psychologists tell us that children learn the word "no" before they learn the word "yes". They learn the word "no" for purposes of misbehaviour, doing what is selfish and wrong. A strong character who has been strengthened with might in the inner man has learned to say no to wrong and yes to what is right.

Why does Paul want all this for them? Why does he want them to be strong characters, strengthened with might inside, even if weak outside? He must have had a strong "inner man" to get down on his knees in front of that centurion. Paul wants believers to be strong in the inner man to explore the love of God, which is even bigger than space: the breadth, and the length, and the height and the depth – to have the power to get into the love of God and to explore it in all its wonderful dimensions. The apostle wants Christians to be strong in the inner man because only then can God put all his fullness in you and fill you up. Then Christ will be dwelling in you, which means he will be there all the time. That is the meaning of Paul's prayer.

Where is the blockage? Why are we weak in our reasoning, conscience and will? The answer is very simple: the fault is not on God's side; it is on my side. "God is able to do exceedingly, abundantly above all that we ask or think...." Then why doesn't he? Because I don't ask and I don't think. It doesn't say, "God is always doing more than we ask or think," as many people take this text. Why is he not doing more than we could imagine? Because we don't imagine it. In fact, it is the limit of our imagination and our intercession. If you ask for little things in your prayer life, you will get little things. Ask for big things. He is able to do exceedingly above all that we ask or think.

So Paul is asking for big things for his readers. He doesn't just want them to know a little of the love of God but all of it: the breadth, length, depth, and height; not just to have a little bit of what God gives but to be filled with all the fullness of God. He asks for big things, he thinks big. If you really want to know the power of God in the inner man, think big and ask big, and God will do big things to his glory.

All these incidental references to the Holy Spirit show that there is really no need you have as a Christian that cannot be met by the Holy Spirit. Is your need to be more sure that you are going to heaven? Then sealing with the Spirit is the answer to your need. Is your need to know that you can get through to God and that he is listening to your prayer? Then the Holy Spirit is the answer to that need. Is your need that your conscience is weak, that your mind is weak and easily affected by what you read and see? Is your will weak so that you can't say no? Then again the answer to your need is the Holy Spirit.

> As a prisoner for the Lord, then, I urge you to live a life worthy of the calling you have received. Be completely humble and gentle; be patient, bearing with one another in love. Make every effort to keep the unity of the Spirit through the bond of peace.
>
> *4:1–3, NIV*

Is your problem that you can't get on with your fellow Christians? Then the Holy Spirit is the answer to that need too. Paul makes two points, and in both these I want you to notice that he is addressing a local church at Ephesus. Unity, like charity, begins at home. The tragedy is that I know local churches that have been split over the question of unity with other churches. A more ludicrous thing you cannot imagine. Before you think about any denominational mergers, the first question to ask is whether I am at peace with my fellow Christians where I live and where I worship. Paul speaks, firstly, of the unity of the Spirit and secondly of the bond of peace. The first is something that neither you nor I can do anything about. It is either there or it is not. When you meet a person, you either have unity in the Spirit or you don't. If the Spirit is in them and in you, then already there is the unity of the Spirit. It can't be manufactured and it can't be lost.

In the Shetland Islands there are one hundred islands of different sizes and shape, about twenty of which are inhabited. I discovered that all those little islands appeared to be separate, but deep down they were part of one lump of granite sticking up from the seabed. In the same way, Christians may look separated, but if they have the Spirit they are already one in the Spirit because there is only one Holy Spirit.

But it is right that Christians should maintain and express the unity that already exists in the bond of peace. Paul says nothing about making this visible. He says nothing about getting into one organisation with mergers. He talks about four things: humility, meekness, long-suffering and forbearance. These are the ingredients of unity and peace that cement the church together. You can have all your organisation; you can have a big headquarters in London, you can have all the bureaucracy you like, but without humility, meekness, patience and forbearance, you will not have unity. That is what creates the bond of peace, linking Christians together.

Writing whilst chained to the Roman soldier, Paul is showing the links in the chain that will bind you to another Christian: patience, meekness, humility, and forbearance. So he is a prisoner of the Lord, chained to the Lord, and does not say he is a prisoner of Rome. He is bound to the Lord, cannot break that chain and does not want to. The believers are also bound to each other because there is one Spirit, one Lord, one God and Father of us all, one faith, one baptism, one hope, one body. They have not had to *create* one body – it is already there. The Holy Spirit is already there. To express that unity be humble, meek, patient, forbearing with one another.

When Christians draw closer together, they always find each other's weak points. I have had many people say this kind of thing to me, "I would rather go to a church where they don't speak to you and so I'm going to go to a church where nobody makes a fuss of you and people don't get close to you, and I don't want to get involved too closely with Christians. I like to go to church, but I just like to go to the service and come away again." That is not maintaining the unity of the Spirit and the bond of peace, keeping people at arm's length is doing the exact opposite. Somebody said to me, "I extend to everybody the hand of fellowship and keep them at arm's length." That is not Christian fellowship. You put your arms around each other if you love each other; you don't keep others at a distance. So Paul wants his readers to be closer to each other as well as to the Lord. But you will never do that without the Holy Spirit. If you try to do so, then frankly, you will irritate each other and fall out. So the answer to unity is the Holy Spirit.

Now we move to Ephesians chapter 5

Therefore do not be foolish, but understand what the Lord's will is. Do not get drunk on wine, which leads to debauchery. Instead, be filled with the Spirit, speaking to one another with psalms, hymns, and spiritual songs. Sing and make music from your heart to the Lord, always giving thanks to God the Father for everything, in the name of our Lord Jesus Christ.

5:17–20

"Be filled with the Spirit" is so often taken out of context that I am determined to put it back in its context. Every time I have heard it preached, the words before and after it have been ignored and I have heard a sermon on holiness. But in its context it is concerned with *happiness* rather than *holiness*. It is answering the question as to how a Christian can have a good time. How do Christians go out and celebrate?

We know how the world goes out and has a good time. The world goes out and gets drunk or at least gets merry. Indeed, one famous preacher who preached on this text once began his sermon by saying, "You've got to fill a man with something if he's going to have a good time," and that is perfectly true. What are the alternatives? There is what is here translated "debauchery" but which would be much better rendered "wastefulness". It is the word used in Luke 15 of the prodigal son, who went into a far country and had nothing to show for it the day after, except a thick head. You will have wasted your time.

Paul just says in the verse before: make the most of the time; redeem the time. If you go out and get drunk, you are wasting time because there will be a whole slice of your life you can't remember and which has done no good for you. It will waste your money certainly. It is an expensive game. It will waste your health sooner or later.

What is the alternative? We must find an alternative. There is nobody as miserable as the man who has stopped being filled with wasteful things but has not found anything positive to have a good time with. So Paul tells his readers how to have a good time. Do you want a good time and to be happy? Of course you do; everybody does. Then you be filled with the Holy Spirit. The Spirit will do more for you than alcohol does for you. He will release your emotions. He will loosen your tongue (and that is why people have cocktails: to get people loosening their tongues and talking). Your self-consciousness will be overcome and friendship will be created.

Some people make for the pub because, as they will tell you, they have a good time there and they find friendship and fellowship there. More people in this country drink for fellowship than for any other reason, I am quite sure. What is the positive alternative? Be filled with the Spirit and you will start singing too, and you will be happy. You will be at ease with other people and not on edge with them.

So Paul is not talking about holiness here, but about

Christian happiness, being filled with the Spirit and having a good sing. Do you notice that he says, "Be filled with the Spirit and address one another," which means, quite simply, that you are far more likely to be filled with the Spirit in Christian company, where there are people you can address. Then what you will find yourself doing is singing with them using Jewish songs, psalms, Christian songs, hymns, spiritual songs in which words and music are supplied by the Holy Spirit but you will want to sing. You will have a happy time singing the songs of Zion. After all, when you get to heaven you will be singing a new song. A little foretaste of heaven is to be filled with the Spirit down here and sing, and that is how Christians should enjoy themselves.

There was a time when Christians did far more of this, before they got rid of the piano and put the television set in its place and, instead of singing, then sat and watched, which is passive. Christians used to go straight from church to someone's home and get around the piano (or guitar) and sing. May I commend that practice to you? Let's revive it! Christians should have a good time and be happy in the Lord. So if your problem is how to enjoy yourself, again the Holy Spirit is the answer.

The result will be seen in grateful, life-giving thanks in everything. The person who gets drunk usually has such a bad head the following morning that it leads to grumbling and complaining. Someone who tries to get happiness that way will always be grumbling and complaining, but a person who gets happy in the Spirit is happy because they are thankful. In the Greek it says, "*In* everything give thanks," which is a great relief because there are some things you cannot give thanks *for*, but *in* everything you can. There is always something for which you can say thank you to God. This is the kind of thing that will happen when you have been singing and making melody to the Lord.

If I were to stop there, you might gain the impression that the Christian life is one big picnic and that we just go from one hymn singing session to another, we have a great time all the time, and you will always feel wonderful. Don't you believe it! We move on to the last mention of the Spirit in this letter.

Finally, be strong in the Lord and in his mighty power. Put on the full armour of God, so that you can take your stand against the devil's schemes. For our struggle is not against flesh and blood, but against the rulers, against the authorities, against the powers of this dark world and against the spiritual forces of evil in the heavenly realms. Therefore put on the full armour of God, so that when the day of evil comes, you may be able to stand your ground, and after you have done everything, to stand. Stand firm then, with the belt of truth buckled round your waist, with the breastplate of righteousness in place, and with your feet fitted with the readiness that comes from the gospel of peace. In addition to all this, take up the shield of faith, with which you can extinguish all the flaming arrows of the evil one. Take the helmet of salvation and the sword of the Spirit, which is the word of God.

6:10–17, NIV

The Christian life is a battle and a struggle. The Bible is absolutely honest. Once again Paul, chained to a soldier, starts thinking about his armour. He sees the Christian as a soldier and tells us to put on the whole armour of God. You have to put it on. It doesn't go on automatically. You must put on the whole armour, not just protect one part of you and leave another part open to the enemy. It must be the armour *of God*. He will supply it, and its purpose is that you should not yield an inch to your enemy; that you should stand. There will be times when you can do little else but just stay put.

Most of the armour mentioned is defensive: the shield, the breastplate, the helmet, the loins girded with truth, feet shod with the preparation of the gospel. But the best form of defence is attack. In a Christian's armour, he needs one thing to strike a blow at the enemy, not just cowering behind the shield of faith. The Christian is meant to get the victory, not just to stand; he is meant to take the initiative when the battle is right and he is meant to attack, and that attack will be made with the sword of the Spirit, which is the Word of God. If I could put it this way: throw the book at the enemy.

Christians again and again have found the way to deal with the devil is throw the book at him. Cromwell used to fight (literally) with a Bible in one hand and a sword in the other. The Bible is your sword. You fight the devil with that. It means a bit of stockpiling before you get into the battle. As the soldiers of old with swords used to spend hours sharpening their blades, a Christian will need to spend a lot of time studying his or her Bible.

The one thing that defeats the devil is the truth because he is a liar from the beginning. He loves telling lies. Therefore you attack the devil by throwing the truth at him and saying: "I don't care what you say. I don't care if you say, 'my feelings don't tell me I'm a Christian.' The word of God says I am. I throw the book at you. I don't care if you tell me the world is getting worse and worse. I know the kingdom of God is coming on earth."

But Paul calls it the sword "of the Spirit", not the "Word of God". Which may mean that the Spirit will bring a particular part of scripture to your mind and use, one which is appropriate for that occasion – as he did for Jesus himself when the Spirit led him into the wilderness to be tempted by Satan.

Chapter Thirteen

THE HOLY SPIRIT IN REVELATION

As we have gone right through the Bible looking at the work of the Holy Spirit, the thing that strikes me is that the Holy Spirit is the person who brings the miraculous into human life. The Holy Spirit makes miracles possible. It is he who brings supernatural power and supernatural purity into the lives of ordinary human beings. We have been thinking of the gifts and the fruit of the Spirit: the gifts representing his power, the fruit representing his purity. Neither of these things is within our reach until the Holy Spirit himself makes them possible.

Without the Holy Spirit we would not have the Bible. This is the supernatural book which nobody ever decided to write. Of the people who were involved in the actual writing down of the words, not one of them had any idea that he was writing the Bible.

Those who think highly of the Bible get criticised. We don't worship it. Nevertheless, we think very highly of it. Why? Because whenever we take up this book (and whenever you do so you should think of this) you are looking at something supernatural, for this book claims to be the Word of God. Every word in the Bible is a word that he wanted there. He so overruled men by his Holy Spirit that even though their personalities were used,what comes out and what we have is what he wanted to say to us. That involves just as big a miracle as raising the dead and healing the sick, just as big a miracle as anything that Jesus did with the storm on Galilee. Most of the men used to write scripture did not set out to try and discover what they came to know.

You find that time after time, instead of people looking for God, God was looking for them. What happened to Abraham and Moses was not because they were looking for God, but because God was looking for them: he chose Abraham and went looking for him; he chose Moses and appeared to him in a burning bush. This is not a book of human discovery but a book of what we call "divine revelation".

The word for the miracle of God giving his word through human lips or human writing is "prophecy". That word stands for the miracle whereby some human being can open his mouth and speak, and the words that come out are not his, but the words of God – and without the Holy Spirit such things could not happen. I can't get up and suddenly say, "I'm going to tell you what God thinks about you," but the Holy Spirit makes miracles possible.

This is why the Bible is a finished book and why in services we don't take readings from other books. Somebody once asked me, "Why don't you read Bunyan's *The Pilgrim's Progress* some Sunday morning as a kind of serial, a chapter a Sunday? It would be very helpful and interesting." But I don't do that and never would, much though I love Bunyan's book. Some people say, "Well why don't we add to the Bible all the thrilling stories of Christian history?" We don't do that. Why not? Because the Old Testament began with a prophet, Moses, and it finished with a prophet, Malachi. So the Old Testament is limited to those who had a gift of prophecy. As we have seen, prophecy began again when John the Baptist was born and the gift was given to the apostles.

Here is one of the strangest facts: some of the greatest brains in the world have failed to understand the Bible and cannot seem to get hold of its message. Yet some of the simplest people I have met, without much education, have taken the Bible and have become wise and educated through reading it. They have loved it and said, "Isn't it thrilling? Isn't it exciting?" The reason is as simple as this: since the Holy Spirit was needed to write it, he is needed to read and understand it. Whenever you pick it up, you should ask him to tell you what it means because only he can do so. All of which is an introduction to the book of Revelation, because it is the outstanding example of these facts. Some people cannot make head nor tail of the last book in the Bible. They are really baffled by it. I will tell you this: if you don't rely on the Holy Spirit when you read your Bible, this book will be a closed book to you. You will be utterly bewildered, confused and perplexed by it. You may read it through, but you will not read it through by choice or by desire, and you will not read it for your devotional life. But with the Holy Spirit you will come to love this book as much as any other.

There is a curse on those who add to this book or take away from it. There is a beatitude, a blessing, pronounced on those who read it. Those who read this book with understanding love it and become confident. It cures their fear, gives them courage, helps them to face the future without any qualms or worries, and it helps them to face the end of the world without being afraid of that happening.

So you cannot read this book without the Holy Spirit, and it could never have been written without him. Here we come to the references to the Holy Spirit in Revelation. How did it come to be written? It is the fullest prophecy in the Bible. By that I mean it has more predictions in it about the future than any other part of the Bible. If you want to know what is going to happen to the world in the future, how it is all going to end and how it is all going to begin again, this is the book to read, and this is why it is called "the Revelation" (Greek: *Apocalypse*) which means the unveiling, the showing of something that nobody else could see. So it is supernatural because only God knows the end from the beginning, and only God can tell you.

How did John come to write it? It happened completely unexpectedly. He had no idea that he was going to write the Revelation because he had no more clue than anyone else as to what the future was going to hold. But one morning he began to write this book. He was imprisoned on a little island in the Aegean Sea, and he was chained to the wall. He was separated from his church because he had been arrested for being a Christian. He had been put in the top security block on Patmos. His body was chained, but where was his mind? It was in the scriptures. In 400 verses there are over four hundred allusions to the Old Testament. He was a man whose mind was steeped in the Bible.

Where was his heart? The answer is his heart was over the little Aegean Sea and in what we now call "Turkey", Asia Minor, with the congregations where he used to go and preach.

Where was his spirit? If you had looked into that cell you would have seen a man seemingly unconscious, in a faint and not moving about. I don't know if he would have his eyes open, but he was in a trance. You would see a man who was just a body there because his spirit had left it. We know that at death the spirit leaves the body, but the spirit can leave the body before death. John's body was in prison, but where was *he*? The answer is that he was in the Spirit and out of his body. That is a strange thing to begin with, but he was travelling out, far away from that cell. He was travelling not only around earth, as is obvious from the first few chapters, he was in Spirit travelling around seven churches. But then we find in chapters four and five that he is travelling in heaven and he is up in heaven, seeing what it is like there, his body lying chained in the prison. So he is not there but in the Spirit looking through a door into heaven, and then he is going in and looking around. In the next few chapters he is even travelling into the future. He is no longer living in the present where his body is chained in that prison cell. He is travelling further into the future than we are now. He is in the Spirit. Then we find, finally, that he is even travelling beyond this universe into a new universe, and is looking around a new heaven and a new earth and looking at a New Jerusalem. Now then you may think either I have gone crackers or that he did. Yet this is the miracle that made possible the last book in the Bible. Only the Holy Spirit could enable a man's spirit to leave his body before death and enable him to leave the present and travel into the future, to leave the earth and travel around heaven, to leave time and explore eternity, and that is what he did.

Four times in the book of Revelation the phrase "in the Spirit" occurs. It comes in each of those four sections as if John is being taken on a journey four times by the Holy Spirit. That is why I say I ask you to look at this book and notice that you are looking at an absolute miracle, because it is not naturally possible for a man to leave his body and travel elsewhere.

Sometimes people say to me, "I'm sorry I can't be with you on Sunday, I've got something else to do. I'll be with you in spirit." But you can't be! What you mean is that wherever you are, you will be thinking and praying for us. You will be where your body is, unless the Holy Spirit does a similar miracle for you as happened to John, which is possible! But we use the phrase in a different sense from John's here. John could go travelling in the Spirit and the Holy Spirit enabled him to explore places that he could not get to because his body was bound. He could go into heaven and into the future, and even see the next world—a new universe.

After every one of these journeys, the command was to write what he had seen. John was the only man to have seen these things. We have an account of the journeys he made and what he saw. If we had not got his words we wouldn't know so much about the future and about the new universe that is coming. Don't you get excited to have this book in your hands? Aren't you kicking yourself for not having read it? Aren't you sorry now that you just failed to understand it so didn't ask the Holy Spirit to help you, and left it alone and went back to things you did understand? Here is the most amazing travel book that has ever been written about the most astonishing adventures. Here is a journey that leaves all others at the starting post, an exciting book that is true, and it tells you far more about the universe in which we live and where history is heading.

"I was in the Spirit on the Lord's Day," says John. What do you think that means? It was not a title for Sunday in scripture. The book of Revelation was written circa 96 AD under Domitian, the first Roman emperor to demand emperor worship. Once a year every Roman citizen had to appear in public, stand before a bust of Caesar, salute that bust, and say that Caesar is Lord. So the day was called by the emperor "the lord's day". It is actually an adjective so we might render it "the lord-y day". John was in prison for testimony for Jesus, and he was in the Spirit on that very day when the emperor demanded to be worshipped.

Persecution was under way and John could see there was going to be a choice: would Christians deny Christ, and therefore have him deny them? But if we die with him we shall reign with him. That is the setting, so he is really preparing them. Jesus is preparing the church through what the Spirit is saying to the church, for tougher times ahead. The Spirit is telling the church to get the church right first. The churches are not ready for this tough time. They have got idolatry in them and they have immorality in them. The appeal is to the individual believer to be an overcomer first within the church because if you can't overcome in the church you will never overcome in the world. The church is in a mess and confused. You read the seven letters to the seven churches. The appeal is in the words: "He who overcomes...."

The most serious message of the book of Revelation can be summed up in two verses. "Overcome" is the key word that opens up the whole book, and here are the two key verses: "He who overcomes, I will not blot out his name from the Book of Life." What does that say about those who don't overcome? Then, finally, at the end, when it says things are going to get better after they get worse, and there is a wonderful picture of a recycled universe with a new earth, we are told that he who overcomes will inherit all this. But the cowardly, the liar, the immoral, the idolaters, are in the lake of fire. It doesn't say, "He who *believes* will inherit all this," or, "He who *becomes a Christian* will inherit all this," but, "He who overcomes". There will only be overcomers in the new heaven and the new earth.

It is a simple message and the Spirit is speaking all the way through. The glorious finish is: "The Spirit and the Bride say, 'Come.'" Whenever there is a genuine move of the Holy Spirit in the church there is a renewed emphasis on the second coming of Christ. If he is not coming back to earth I have no hope for the future of this earth whatsoever. While I believe in social action and political prophetic protest, nevertheless I have no hope that *we* are going to bring the kingdom. The King has got to do that, but I have this certain hope that Jesus will one day take over the government of this world and share that government with us. That is a terrific motivation to get ready to share that government and to take responsibility, because the job you take when Jesus gets back depends on the job you have got now and how you do it – and I don't just mean "spiritual" jobs.

Of course the book of Revelation was written primarily to Christians who were suffering. It was written by a sufferer. It is a book of encouragement to those who are suffering for the faith and even dying and becoming martyrs. One of the most precious words of the Spirit in this book is wrongly used at funerals today. It is a word for Christian martyrs, "Blessed are the dead who die in the Lord, henceforth. 'Blessed indeed,' says the Spirit, 'For they rest from their labours, and their deeds do follow them.'" That is a lovely word to those who are suffering. People dying for their faith – don't be upset. It is a blessing because you are going to rest from your labours and your deeds will follow you.

If you are not living right, the thought that your deeds follow you after death would be the most frightening thought of all, wouldn't it? If somebody said to me, "Everything you have done is going to follow you after life ends" it would be frightening, but if you are living with the Lord and if you are dying in the faith, then remember: "Blessed are those who die in the Lord, for their deeds follow them." They died for the faith, and that will follow them and they will wear the crown of a martyr. What an encouraging book this is.

My last word must be the last mention of the Holy Spirit at the end of the Bible. We started in Genesis with the Spirit brooding over the chaos. We have seen the unfolding: the power of the Holy Spirit lifting people into things that are supernatural, bringing the miraculous to them, enabling them to do and say and be things they could never otherwise do and say and be. We saw how the Holy Spirit brought Jesus to earth, enabled him to do miracles, raised him from the dead. We saw how the Holy Spirit was poured out on the church and as soon as that happened they began to do supernatural things. We saw how they went everywhere in the power and by the guidance of the Spirit. We have looked at walking in the Spirit, living by the Spirit, the fruit of the Spirit, the gifts of the Spirit—all of that miraculous.

Now we come to the very last word the Holy Spirit says in the Bible. It is in v. 17, "The Spirit and the bride say, 'come.'" That is one of the loveliest words in the Bible. Jesus was always using it. "Come unto me, all ye that labour and are heavy laden...." "Him that comes to me, I will in no wise cast out." Now the Holy Spirit, at the end of this wonderful book which he created, without whom we could not have had it, says at the end: "Come". The Bible invites you to leave your sin and find the Saviour. This book invites you to come to heaven – to leave yourself and come to God. It invites you to leave your fears and come to peace, to leave this world and come to the next, to leave a universe that is full of sin and pain and death – and you are invited to come to a universe in which there is only righteousness and peace.

The invitation is: "The Spirit and the bride say, 'Come'." What do we mean by "the bride?" We mean the church. The church, when filled with the Spirit, will have one word on its lips more than any other: "Come". Because when the Spirit fills a fellowship, that fellowship will keep saying to people, "Come and hear about Jesus. Come and have faith with us. Come and share what we've found. Come and taste. Come and buy wine and milk without money and without price. Everyone who thirsts: come to the waters."

This word "come" is there all through the Bible but I am so glad that the Holy Spirit, after speaking of the judgment and of the end of history, finishes on this positive note. The last two pages of the Bible are not the end of the world, but the beginning. They are not the end of everything, but the beginning of everything. Thank God that everything we know is going to end and something much more wonderful is going to take its place. So the Holy Spirit, through the church, says to people: he that thirsts let him come and freely take of the water of life.

We saw how the Bible begins in Genesis 1 with chaos and the Holy Spirit brooding over the chaos. We gradually see the whole purpose of God unfold, until we see that there is going to be a new world altogether. The last word of the Holy Spirit is to everyone who desires life and forgiveness and peace and a future that is secure: "Come." If we won't come in response to such an invitation, then frankly we have no-one to blame, but ourselves.

Chapter Fourteen

THE HOLY SPIRIT IN HISTORY

A brief survey of two thousand years of church history means sweeping generalisations and simplistic treatment which risks giving a distorted picture, but we have to think about this because there are people who think that the Holy Spirit was not at work between the first and the twentieth centuries. The "latter rain" people in particular seem to think there was a huge gap in the Holy Spirit's activity. Well there has been an ebb and flow, times when the Holy Spirit's work has been very obvious and periods when that has not been the case.

That faces us with the biggest question of all that you have to settle before you study church history: who is responsible for the ebb and flow of the manifest effects of the work of the Holy Spirit through history? There are two answers. One viewpoint is what I would call the "deterministic" – that it is entirely within God's choice and decision whether there is revival or not. It is entirely his plan whether the Spirit is flowing in power or whether there is a dearth. That is a deterministic (I nearly wrote Calvinistic) view that over-emphasises divine sovereignty and says, "Well we just happen to live in a time and place when God has not chosen to move by his Spirit." If that is the case then we have nothing to learn from church history at all. There would be no point in studying the past because we could not learn from it. It's just a question of, "Will God choose to move by his Spirit in our day or not?" We are left with an arbitrary approach. The only point of studying church history then would be out of historical interest—if you are interested.

The other view is the dynamic view, in which the relationship between God and his church is a dynamic one and therefore mutually reciprocative. Let me tell you what I mean. There are those who believe in deterministic relationship with God – that, "He's God, he decides and that's all. I'm just the clay in the hand of the potter." But if you read the story of the potter and the clay in Jeremiah 18 it is not a deterministic relationship but a dynamic one. "Go to the potter and look at him," and Jeremiah went and this potter was trying to make a beautiful vase out of a lump of clay and the clay would not run in his hand so he pushed it into a lump, put it back on the wheel, and made a crude thick pot out of the clay. God said, "Jeremiah, have you learned the lesson of the potter?" The lesson is: if the clay doesn't run in his hands he makes another kind of vessel of it. So the message was, "If Israel will run in my hands," says the Lord, "I will make her a beautiful vessel of mercy. But if she won't respond to my hands I will make her a crude vessel of judgment." The clay has decided what kind of vessel the potter makes. Do you see the dynamic inter-relationship? It is still the potter who decides, but the clay has a very real part in what the potter does. God in his grace has chosen not to treat us as robots or as puppets, but to respond to our response. It is a dynamic relationship and I believe the basic reason why there are periods when the Holy Spirit does not move in great power or in obvious might is due largely to the failure of the church to respond, and not to God's arbitrary choice that it's not the right time.

We are living in the last days, we are living in the age of the Spirit. Everything that is in the Spirit is available to the church at any time and in any place—I really believe that. Now that makes me an Arminian; they call me that, I don't care about these labels. I do believe in a dynamic relationship. I do not believe in irresistible grace. I believe you can resist the Holy Spirit, and when you do resist he doesn't operate. Not because he can't but because he won't. Now that is a profound question that you have got to settle before you study church history. Otherwise you are just studying God's arbitrary timing rather than learning from the past.

So having given you my answer to that question I then approach the two thousand years. What can I learn from the periods when the Spirit was not so active? Why was he not? I look for the human reason rather than any arbitrary, divine choice. I realise that is a very big controversial area but nevertheless I feel there is no point in tackling this subject if I can't learn from it. I find that when you study church history it is a thrilling study. I gave lectures on church history to our church and I took hymns from every single century to teach them. I don't believe we have done right in throwing away all those devotional treasures. I made them sing hymns from every age because in every century the Holy Spirit has produced saints, and in every century the Holy Spirit has produced songs. Some of the greatest songs were written in those dry periods by saints who were open to the Spirit. The Spirit has never stopped operating, but there has been an ebb and flow, so why was there the ebb and flow?

Let us begin with the first five hundred years. There was a slow but steady decline in the obvious demonstrations of power in the Holy Spirit. The evidence is that the Holy Spirit's gifts were freely used up to about 250 AD. They did not altogether cease then. They have never altogether ceased but they have declined slowly but steadily until they were still there but certainly not evidenced in the majority of churches. Justin Martyr talks freely about the gifts of the Spirit, so does Irenaeus the Bishop of Lyon. Prophecy, tongues and healing were common, so they did not die out with the apostles. But there was a decline. A fine Catholic theologian wrote a book demonstrating that even as late as the fifth and sixth centuries they were still talking about being baptised in the Holy Spirit.

So why the decline? There were two reasons that I could find. You could just say, "Well, God didn't need them any longer." I think one of the most damaging ideas that is being freely preached is that once we had the Bible we didn't need the gifts – as if now we can just throw the book at people and they are "slain" in the scripture. I just don't believe that, I believe God wanted to equip his church for the entire church age, the last days in which we live.

So why the decline? First, the church became too institutional. Second, it became too intellectual. I necessarily simplify and summarise this. It became too institutional in two ways—whenever things become institutional the Spirit is not so free to move. The ways in which the church became institutional were: it became *clerical* and it became *political*. There was a total change in the concept from every member ministry to a professional ministry. The division of the church into clerical and lay was never of God. It split the people of God and put ministry on one side of the split.

It happened fairly early. Michael Harper shrewdly said, "There's a fog in the first century as far as church structure goes. Immediately after the New Testament we go into a fog. We don't quite know what happened. What we do know is that apostles went into the fog and bishops came out of it." Now it is still happening. There has been a lot of discussion about who are apostles today, but I call many of them "bishops" (overseers) because that is what they are.

There were bishops before the fog mentioned by Harper, but the difference was that there were many bishops to one church. After the fog there was one bishop to many churches. That is a huge difference because it laid the foundation for a hierarchy, and when you get a hierarchy you always get a lower-archy. That's my word but do you know what I mean? The "lower-archy" don't minister, they become passive spectators of the hierarchy who do. Ministry is to serve until the saints are equipped. It was a total change.

Since the clerical ministry was limited to males, that cut out much ministry by women. Then even within the male priesthood you had a hierarchy, so there was monopoly of ministry instead of multiplicity. You had to be at a certain level before you could minister in a certain way. See how it all happened? They didn't have the whole New Testament yet, but they did have the whole Old Testament and there was a ready made model in there for priesthood, for a hierarchy, a high priest. In fact, the church took over the Old Testament model of ministry—hook, line, and sinker. They took over altars, priests, incense, vestments, the lot.

I don't know if you know about vestments—the Pope was dead against clergy wearing special clothes as late as Pope Celestine I in 428. It was the bishop of Aix in Provence who first began to wear special dress for clerics. The Pope wrote him a letter asking what on earth he was doing, putting on special clothes. (The priesthood of all believers means that the Pope is sometimes right!) He said, "Let clergy be differentiated from common folk by our learning and not our garments, by our life, not what we wear, by purity of thought and not by peculiarities of dress." I want to send that to every cleric who loves dressing up!

So a professional priesthood came in and nothing so damages the ministries of the Spirit. There are still churches where people claim to be baptised in the Spirit but will not throw off clericalism. You can see from church history what happened. For the first time they were allowed to build churches. What did they model them on? Not on the synagogues but on the temple. Soon there was a holy end where God lived, which had a better carpet than where the people were. We even do it in our buildings if we are not careful. It implies a localised God at one end like the Holy of Holies. What we need is synagogues, not temples. So clericalism came in, sacerdotalism came in, which simply means a monopoly of handling sacraments or word.

The other form of institutionalism came in with Constantine's conversion. I don't know why that is regarded as a triumph. I regard it as an utter tragedy. Christian behaviour could be imposed on people with legal sanction. It was Constantine who brought in the Sunday observance laws. The church had done without Sunday observance and had never grown so fast. I am sorry but I have mixed feelings about the whole "Keep Sunday special" campaign.

Once again, the model for all this was the Old Testament theocracy which had no distinction between believers and state. The New Testament draws a very clear distinction between church and state. "Render to Caesar the things that are Caesar's, to God the things that are God's."

Alas, legalised anti-Semitism came in, and laws were passed forbidding people to be Jews or to worship publicly in a Jewish way. So by the year 400 the gifts were not in evidence. There had been protests about this decline of spiritual gifts, and we can learn from the protests as well. One of the big protests was from a man called Montanus, and the "Montanism" that gathered around him. He revived prophecy, for men and women. He revived the spiritual gifts, and this was one of the first Pentecostal movements. You might ask why Montanism become a heresy or a deviant group. It is very important to learn. One of the great Christians of the early church, and I have been studying his life more and more and learning so much from him, was Tertullian. He never actually became a Montanist but he had great sympathy with them because they were restoring the charismatic ministry. The problem was this: the Montanists did not test prophecies properly. They let anything go through and their prophecies became more and more radical, and more and more weird. People were just thrilled to be getting prophecies, they didn't weigh and judge them. Now I have been in so many charismatic fellowships where they never weigh and judge prophecy. They let anything through. If someone gives a prophecy we should stop and say, "Let's pray and let's find out if that's from the Lord or if it's from man, or if it's a mixture," which many are. I always notice the pause. Have you ever noticed it? Somebody gives a great word of prophecy, quite a brief word, and then it's a pause. You can almost hear their mind ticking. "That's not long enough for a prophecy. I must add a bit more." I often find what is before the gap is much better than what is after it. You have got to be discerning. Many prophecies are a mixture. We need to know what is of God. If God takes the trouble to speak to us, we should take the trouble to find out what he really means. It is very important to weigh and judge prophecy.

Untested prophecy is one thing that has brought down the charismata again and again through church history. Be warned because what happens is that those churches who don't have prophecy react against the whole idea and dismiss it. That is what happened in the early church. Because the Montanists got bad prophecies and didn't judge them, the whole church said, "We don't want any prophecy." When spiritual gifts are abused the church doesn't want them. They don't see that the answer to abuse is the proper use, not misuse, not no use at all.

The other protest was monasticism. I don't think everybody realises the charisma in monasticism. The monks originally were protesting against a worldly church, because when Constantine was converted you would have thought: "that will get the church into the world" – it didn't, it got the world into the church. When the lifeboat is in the sea that is good, but when the sea is in the lifeboat that's bad. The church became established, socially acceptable, and it became very worldly, and that is when infant baptism became the norm. It had come a bit earlier, but it became the norm because you baptise not those who were born again but those who were born. Because when you were born into the state you were born into the church. The two were one and the same and that is how it all happened. You cannot actually have a state church that baptises believers. It is an impossibility because the establishment must recognise that citizenship and membership is one and the same—that is the big issue. There has never been a state church that practised believer's baptism. You see why. You must recognise the baby as born into Christendom. The kingdom and the state are one: Christendom.

The monks protested against the worldliness. At first the protest was individual and they were largely hermit monks. We call them the "Desert Fathers". Some went and sat on top of a pole in the middle of the desert, or they went into a cave. They were making a protest. The interesting thing is that as they devoted themselves to holier living the charismata reappeared. Many of those desert fathers had a ministry of exorcism and healing. People would come from far and wide to the desert father to be delivered from a demon or to be healed.

Then, at a later stage, as the number of desert fathers increased they began to form communities of monks— separated from a worldly church. But they became obsessed, unfortunately, with their personal holiness rather than the edification of others – you became a monk to be holy. Because of that, and it is a strange development, one or two of the leaders of those monastic communities began to discourage the charismata because they saw it led to pride in the person who was healing or casting out demons. They began to teach that charismata led to pride and therefore shouldn't be exercised. I am afraid they probably had an element of truth in that. There is another thing we can learn. If God uses me to heal, that is not to make me a healer but to give health to a member of his Body. The gifts are not given to us to make us great but to help the Body. They are to give away and you are just a postman. But some monks who were known far and wide for the healing gift became rather proud of their reputation.

So they began to discourage it and that view got right into the whole church – that, in fact, spiritual gifts made you proud. There is enough truth in that to hurt. Because you are baptised in the Spirit and you have got gifts, does that make you better than anybody else? No, you may still be carnal. But it can have that effect: you can do it and the others can't. This is what happened to some monks. Then, because of their asceticism, they didn't eat. St. Anthony never washed his feet. They suffered because they were not looking after their bodies. They began to be sick and suffer pain. A teaching came in that illness somehow was a sign of holiness, and healing should therefore be left aside.

So we have noted the institutionalising of the church and protests against it. But now we come to the intellectualising of the church that confuses education with edification, and moves from experience to explanation, from dynamic to dogma. The doctrine of the Holy Spirit for the next fifteen hundred years became more of a dogma than a dynamic. Two men were largely responsible for this, and they both cut the Jewish roots of the church and turned it into a Greek-thinking church. One was Augustine and the other was Aquinas. Still today, generally in the Western world, evangelicals are influenced in their thinking about the Spirit by Augustine and Aquinas rather than by Paul.

If you say to an evangelical, "Would you preach on this text, 'I want you all to speak in tongues, and I thank God I speak in tongues more than you all'," many wouldn't even touch it. Why not? Because Augustine and Aquinas have really conditioned their thinking. They would like to think they are going back to the Bible for their views. In fact they have been more influenced than they know. It is a disaster that Greek thinking replaced Hebraic in the church. As I have mentioned, Augustine brought Plato into the church's thinking and Aquinas brought Aristotle.

The Greeks never got it together. They saw the spiritual and the physical as two different worlds and the eternal and the temporal as two different worlds. Therefore they divided a man up: whereas Hebrews thought of a whole person, the Greeks said a human being is a body with a soul in it. So they divided the world into sacred and secular. I hate Christians saying, "I'm in a secular job." I always reprove them. If you are a Christian you are in a sacred location. It was the Greeks who divided the world into natural and supernatural. That is a wrong division because if you divide reality into natural and supernatural, which side of the line do you put the devil? You tend to put him on the same side of the line as God. The Bible's division is between creatures and Creator. Where is the devil now? He's on our side of the line. Do you see what I mean?

"Democracy" is a Greek word and there is nothing about it in scripture. Our politics are based on Greek thinking. Sport is a Greek pastime. Yet sport is the religion of so many. Our educational system is based on Greek thinking. It is no wonder then that, even in the church, for Augustine, Aquinas and others, Greek thinking has had a devastating effect on our understanding of the ministry of the Spirit. It is only because we are getting back to Hebraic thinking that the Spirit is able to move again as freely as he is moving today.

That is a big thesis and I do no more than outline it briefly. Augustine was primarily influenced by two things: first of all, his promiscuity as a young man, his inability to control the flesh gave him a horror of the physical side of life. When he heard of the Greeks who divided the spiritual from the physical he went overboard on the spiritual—because of his background. Celibacy starts with Augustinian thinking. A celibate priesthood, it's holier to be celibate than married— that was his fear of the flesh. The other thing was that he was brought up with a classical Greek education. Put those two factors together, one emotional and the other intellectual, and it is no wonder that he "Platonised" the Christian faith. He brought this sharp division between spiritual and physical, so that no longer did people think of the Holy Spirit operating in physical spheres, or having anything to do with your body, that was purely activity in your soul. Many evangelicals still think that the Holy Spirit only operates on your soul.

Since tongues is a physical thing, and so is healing, that kind of spirituality can't handle these things. Plato had taught that there are two worlds. One is the "spiritual" world beyond time and space. In that world there is no change. God himself is changeless, timeless. But we are tied with our bodies into this changing world. So the activity of the Spirit is thought to be in that spiritual, timeless world, and things that happen to us in our bodies are part of the changing world of time in which our bodies tie us down. When we die, our souls are released into that spiritual sphere. It is going to be more effective for people in that spiritual sphere to pray for me than for me to pray for myself. So I am going to pray to those who are in that sphere. I will pray to the saints because they are up in that eternal realm where the Spirit really moves. I am caricaturing this to try to help you to understand.

There was a "spiritualising" of everything. It grew out of the theology of Alexandria, where Origen and others had already begun to spiritualise the scripture. We do this when we preach on the miracles – we spiritualise them. So, when we read that if you had faith to move a mountain, and tell it to jump in the sea it would go, we then talk about moving the mountains of difficulty and moving the mountains of depression—that is "spiritualising". I could take you to a place in Japan where a group of praying children caused a physical mountain to be thrown into the sea off Tokyo, and that is what Jesus is talking about.

You see how we transfer it from the physical to the spiritual. We spiritualise the Bible. I have to tell you that towards the end of his life Augustine got a shock because he was baptising someone and that baptised person came up out of the water and went and prayed for someone with cancer, and they were healed instantly. Augustine did a somersault, and toward the very end of his life he began to believe in healing. He collected records of seventy healing miracles in his church in North Africa but he never got it into his theology. It is his theology that became the abiding influence and it was what we call "cessationist", maintaining the idea that the gifts died out with the apostles. That has come right down to today. You hear it even in Brethren assemblies. Alas, Augustine was living in two worlds, and at the end of his life, because he didn't think it through theologically, he encouraged people to get healing any way they could. If they could get it out of a saint's relic, he encouraged them to do that. If they could get it by praying to a saint he encouraged them to do it. He didn't use his theological mind to discern and distinguish between superstition and genuine healing. The result is that through the Middle Ages you had this mixture of the credal and the credulous. The authorities of the church became totally credal. They argued about the Trinity. The biggest split in the church had been over one clause: "Who proceeds from the Father and the Son", the notorious

Filioque clause, which split all the Orthodox churches in the East from the Catholic Church in the West. In 1054 the churches of eastern Europe and western Europe split over a doctrinal dogmatic statement about the Holy Spirit because by then teaching about the Holy Spirit had become a dogma.

At the popular level you had all these superstitions of relics healing, saints healing, and all the rest of it. So in the Middle Ages you had this strange thing that the church officials are really working through dogma but the popular people are going to shrines and relics and getting healed.

Then came Aquinas and he introduced Aristotle. If for Plato the spiritual was the real world, for Aristotle the material was the real world and he is the founder of modern materialism. He believed the real world was the world of change. But he said that the real world being a material world, you can only find truth through your senses — through your physical senses – and that was what lay behind the development of modern scientism. This was brought right into the church from Aquinas. For the first time Jesuits and others began to question the healing miracles associated with relics. They began to have a scientific approach to them.

Luther, Calvin and Zwingli did many good things. They replaced the authority of tradition with the truth of the scripture. They rediscovered the second person of the Trinity in a wonderful way. Christ was pre-eminent again but they never broke the link between church and state. They used the power of the state to change people into Protestants. They produced state churches, and by law you had to be Protestant. Instead of allowing the Holy Spirit to convert people, they got the governor, the king, the prince or the council to change everybody by law — that is not the power of the Spirit. But funnily enough they had so imbibed Aquinas and Aristotelianism, that they became sceptical about all claims of healing in the Middle Ages and threw it all out, and they were just as "spiritual" as Augustine, in a sense.

All through the ages there had been beautiful exceptions. God had never left himself without witness. I visited a Catholic church in Pembrokeshire and went to their bookstore. It was all Catholic Truth Society booklets, and one was on St. David of Wales. I thought, "Well that's my namesake so I had better read that." So I did, and I was thrilled. St. David was chosen to be bishop of Wales in the sixth century. He wanted to be consecrated in Jerusalem so that he would get a special anointing in the Holy City for his ministry. He set off with two monks to walk to Jerusalem. No jumbo jets in those days! The monks kept a diary of the journey. They got as far as Lyon in Gaul and in the diary I read this, "In Lyon, ye Holy Father David was baptized in ye Holy Ghost and spake in other tongues as in ye days of ye apostles." I thought, "Pentecostalism didn't start in Wales in the twentieth century!" I love to tell the Welsh, "Forget your daffodils and leeks. Get back to St. David of Wales."

I was preaching in Liverpool in the Roman Catholic Cathedral. I walked down Hope Street to the Anglican Cathedral and saw there a glass case containing a handwritten life of St. David. Reading it, I was astonished. He raised the dead and healed a boy of blindness. He was using the gifts of the Spirit.

God has not left himself without witness but the Reformers did not bother to try and disentangle the true from the false. They threw it all out as Catholic superstition. Though they spoke of the Holy Spirit they limited his work to his inward spiritual work on the self and his work through the scripture. To this day evangelicals tend to limit the work of the Spirit to the soul (not the body), and to the scripture and not to other words. It has not come from the New Testament but from Augustine, Aristotle and the Protestant reformers.

What happened in the twentieth century? I have to say

with tears that Calvinism has been a barrier to the free movement of the Holy Spirit. It tended to put too much emphasis on the sovereignty of God and not enough on the responsibility of man. The Spirit wants to do everything he used to do. We are the blockage. Now what broke that was a man called Arminius, who never argued with Calvin. Calvin was not as Calvinist as everybody makes him out to be. Calvin believed you could lose your salvation. It is written in the *Institutes*. Calvin believed that Jesus died for all and not just for the elect. It was a man called Beza, a follower of Calvin, who produced what we now know as Calvinism – the five points and all the rest – and it was Beza that Arminius argued with. I believe Arminius was right to teach that our relationship with God is not deterministic but dynamic. God responds to us. I can trace a direct line from Arminius to modern Pentecostalism. It passes through Wesley and the Holiness Movement. But this new concept of a dynamic relationship between God and man was picked up by Wesley. An Anglican theologian, Dr Conyers Middleton, wrote a book against tongues in the eighteenth century, and Wesley wrote against Dr Conyers Middleton about prophecy, tongues, and healing. I was trained theologically as a Methodist minister, but they never told me that Wesley believed in prophecy, tongues, and healing. They told me about his conversion on May 24th 1738, in Aldersgate Street. They never told me about January 1st, 1739 when a whole group including Wesley said, "We demand, we want the Holy Spirit. We're going to pray until you give us the Holy Spirit," and in the early hours of the morning they were baptised in the Holy Spirit.

John Wesley records in his Journal, "I determined to say much more about the Holy Spirit in my preaching." In his letter to Conyers Middleton he defends the fact that there have been prophecy, tongues, and healing all through the church and he lists them in the Huguenots and so many groups. He says, "The only reason we don't see these widespread in the church is because the church doesn't believe in it any more." You can't have it both ways. Either God withdrew them or Wesley is right. They weren't preached and believed in.

From Wesley there came the Holiness Movement, which began again to use the phrase "baptised in the Holy Spirit". Unfortunately they linked it with a second blessing of sanctification rather than seeing it as the very beginning of the Christian life. Yet out of the Holiness Movement came the Pentecostals of the twentieth century.

The door was opened again to a dynamic relationship with God, and ultimately to a return to the Hebrew view of man as a whole person. The Spirit can touch your spirit, he can touch the whole of you, and he can do physical things. The gap between the spiritual and the physical began to be closed.

Where are we now? The good news is that never have the gifts of the Spirit been so widely accepted in the church as today. The charismatic Pentecostal stream is going to be the biggest stream of all in the worldwide church. But here is the bad news: whereas the *gifts* of the Spirit have been widely accepted, the *baptism* of the Spirit has been widely rejected. I firmly believe that the gifts of the Spirit will not survive the loss of the baptism in the Spirit—the one leads to the other.

Very few still argue about the charismata. Those who say that tongues are of the devil are getting dangerously near the unforgiveable sin. I have rarely encountered it in unbelievers, I have found it much more in believers. It is serious to call the work of the Spirit the work of the devil.

The gifts are widely accepted but baptism in the Holy Spirit is being widely rejected, and I believe they belong together. Jesus came to take away the sins of the world and to baptise us in the Holy Spirit. I believe that is going to be one of the big issues. The other big issue is this: those of us who are experiencing spiritual gifts, if we let go of scripture we let go the very basis on which we can discern, and then we are vulnerable to the latest fashion, the latest craze, and we will bring charismatic renewal into disrepute in the eyes of the rest of the church by not testing and judging prophecies, by not being disciplined, by not bringing scripture and the Spirit to bear. I believe totally in theology because everybody has one. It is what you believe about God.

The philosopher Descartes wrote: "I think therefore I am," but he got it wrong. The Bible got it right: "As a man thinks in his heart, so is he" – not "so is his opinion." I believe the theology that we plant in our hearts, if it is biblical theology, will be the spring of everything else. I believe in a dynamic theology that is expressed and experienced, but I don't believe in an experience that can't be theologically based.

Word and Spirit must go together. They need each other.

THE NORMAL CHRISTIAN BIRTH

Classic study of initiation in the New Testament: repentance, faith, baptism in water and baptism in the Holy Spirit. The second section provides an exegetical study of two dozen crucial or controversial passages, questioning many traditional interpretations. The final section demonstrates the inadequacy of much modern evangelistic counselling.

JESUS BAPTISES IN ONE HOLY SPIRIT

Clear, detailed exposition on the topic of baptism in the Holy Spirit, asking how, when and why the Holy Spirit is received. This popular book has been translated into many languages.

WORD AND SPIRIT TOGETHER

Charismatic and Evangelical Christians should be united in witness and proclamation. This book helps us to see how this is possible, as the author goes behind and beyond the controversies and considers the content and application of Scripture.

A COMMENTARY ON ACTS

Acts is a book of 'firsts': the first outpouring of the Holy Spirit, the first converts, the first healing, the first arrest and trial, the first deacons, the first martyr, the first persecution, the first Gentile mission and many more. Nothing can stop the spread of the gospel when the church is on fire! The founding fathers were beset by troubles which, under God's direction, were all turned into triumphs. Study of their exploits will leave you with some disturbing questions. Should our church be like this? Could it be? Above all, do I want it to be?

A COMMENTARY ON THE GOSPEL OF JOHN

Eyewitnesses, Jesus' own words and astonishing works all point to one who was truly God come in the flesh, the living Word, the very glory of God among humanity. John's collected evidence and proof all make the most compelling testimony to Jesus' right to demand our ongoing trust and obedience.

A COMMENTARY ON GALATIANS

Attacks by the enemy against the church are much more successful when they come from the inside, and one of the quickest ways to do that is to pervert or corrupt or erode the gospel. Legalism and licence are still with us. But so is true liberty. We are free not to sin – and free to be bold, if we will only walk in the Spirit.

A COMMENTARY ON THE BOOK OF REVELATION

The book of Revelation focuses on the future and is the only book in the whole Bible to which God has attached a special blessing and an awful curse. Written for ordinary people under extraordinary pressure, suffering is the key to its understanding. It is a manual for martyrdom. As history draws to a close, all Christians need its message of warning and encouragement.